SPIDER-MAN

THE LIFELINE TABLET SAGA

STAN LEE & FABIAN NICIEZA
WRITERS

JOHN ROMITA SR., JIM MOONEY & STEVE RUDE WITH JOHN BUSCEMA
PENCILERS

JIM MOONEY & BOB WIACEK
INKERS

GREGORY WRIGHT
COLORIST

SAM ROSEN, ARTIE SIMEK & JOHN COSTANZA
LETTERERS

BRIAN SMITH
ASSISTANT EDITOR

STAN LEE & RALPH MACCHIO
EDITORS

STEVE RUDE
FRONT COVER ARTIST

JOHN ROMITA SR.
BACK COVER ARTIST

COLLECTION EDITOR **MARK D. BEAZLEY**
ASSISTANT EDITOR **CAITLIN O'CONNELL**
ASSOCIATE MANAGING EDITOR **KATERI WOODY**
ASSOCIATE MANAGER, DIGITAL ASSETS **JOE HOCHSTEIN**
MASTERWORKS EDITOR **CORY SEDLMEIER**
SENIOR EDITOR, SPECIAL PROJECTS **JENNIFER GRÜNWA**
VP PRODUCTION & SPECIAL PROJECTS **JEFF YOUNGQUIS**
RESEARCH **MIKE HANSEN**
LAYOUT **JEPH YORK**
PRODUCTION **RYAN DEVALL**
BOOK DESIGNER **JAY BOWEN**
SVP PRINT, SALES & MARKETING **DAVID GABRIEL**

EDITOR IN CHIEF **AXEL ALONSO**
CHIEF CREATIVE OFFICER **JOE QUESADA**
PRESIDENT **DAN BUCKLEY**
EXECUTIVE PRODUCER **ALAN FINE**

SPIDER-MAN CREATED BY
STAN LEE & STEVE DITKO

SPIDER-MAN: THE LIFELINE TABLET SAGA. Contains material originally published in magazine form as AMAZING SPIDER-MAN #68-75 and SPIDER-MAN: LIFELINE #1-3. First printing 2017. ISBN# 978-1-302-90710-5. Published by MARVEL WORLDWIDE, INC., a subsidiary of MARVEL ENTERTAINMENT, LLC. OFFICE OF PUBLICATION: 135 West 50th Street, New York, NY 10020. **Printed in the U.S.A.** DAN BUCKLEY, President, Marvel Entertainment; JOE QUESADA, Chief Creative Officer; TOM BREVOORT, SVP of Publishing; DAVID BOGART, SVP of Business Affairs & Operations, Publishing & Partnership; C.B. CEBULSKI, VP of Brand Management & Development, Asia; DAVID GABRIEL, SVP of Sales & Marketing, Publishing; JEFF YOUNGQUIST, VP of Production & Special Projects; DAN CARR, Executive Director of Publishing Technology; ALEX MORALES, Director of Publishing Operations; SUSAN CRESPI, Production Manager; STAN LEE, Chairman Emeritus. For information regarding advertising in Marvel Comics or on Marvel.com, please contact Vit DeBellis, Integrated Sales Manager, at vdebellis@marvel.com. For Marvel subscription inquiries, please call 888-511-5480. **Manufactured between 3/17/2017 and 4/18/2017 by LSC COMMUNICATIONS INC., SALEM, VA, USA.**

10 9 8 7 6 5 4 3 2 1

The ancient clay tablet saga, so nicely collected herein, really hits all the sweet spots for any Spiderophile worth his webs. You have the mysterious tablet from antiquity as the MacGuffin of our piece. Then, there're the villains searching for said object, including the Kingpin, the Shocker and Man Mountain Marko of the Maggia, among others. You toss in one angst-ridden, web-spinning wonder who just can't catch a break and you have the makings of a classic. The tightly knit plot interweaves perfectly with all the soap-operatic elements that Stan Lee made famous throughout the Marvel line, though nowhere more poignantly than in *Amazing Spider-Man.*

Sometimes I think we forget just how innovative those elements were. In a traditional super-hero story, the hero would inevitably take down the super villain, sometimes aided by the police and the public, who were unfailingly on his side. It all ends nice and tidy with the status quo restored and the public cheering on our protagonist. Well, that ain't what happens here. The Kingpin is able to convince the authorities that Spider-Man was his accomplice in the crime of stealing the tablet, so they're out to nail him. Publisher J. Jonah Jameson continues his crusade through the *Daily Bugle* to malign the poor web-slinger and turn the public against him through slanted editorials. And to top it off, the Kingpin escapes jail and is never caught again. Is it any wonder Peter Parker is continually at odds with himself as to the value of maintaining a separate identity that only seems to bring him untold grief? Like Sisyphus endlessly pushing that rock up the hill because the gods cursed him to, Peter fights crime in the city relentlessly with no reward and constant harassment. Then, he must convince himself that his efforts as Spider-Man have meaning and worth. In the pages to follow, you'll see the poor lad almost reach a breaking point that has terrible consequences for all concerned. It's all part of the larger story of this young man's life.

Of course, the Kingpin of Crime isn't bothered by such primal doubts. He wants what he wants and nothing will stop him. I recall hearing John Romita Sr. say that his inspiration for the Kingpin's appearance came from Sydney Greenstreet's unforgettable portrayal of "the fat man" Gutman, in the classic Bogart film *The Maltese Falcon.* The twist John and Stan put on it is that Marvel's version of the Gutman character is not only highly intelligent, but an awesome physical powerhouse able to go toe-to-toe with Spidey himself in a fight. I remember toiling on the *Daredevil* title during Frank Miller's much-admired run and loving the way Wilson Fisk was able to transition from being obsessed with destroying Spider-Man to reducing the Man Without Fear to a man without hope. It's a real tribute to Fisk's potential and Frank's enormous talent that his malignant nature could so effectively permeate two titles. Actually, once the Kingpin found a home grinding down Daredevil, he became far more associated with that character than with his Spider-Man roots. Perhaps they seemed even more natural antagonists. I don't know.

Other criminals came to the fore as the Kingpin disappeared from the clay tablet saga by issue #71. And I relished the arrival of these Maggia menaces. Silvermane, Man Mountain Marko and Caesar Cicero are part of a long tradition in *Amazing Spider-Man* of non-costumed, though no less lethal, foes who rear their ugly heads and provide the requisite *Godfather*-style mischief. Anyone here who recalls "The Man in the Crime-Master's Mask" from *Amazing Spider-Man #26,* go to the head of the class.

In the midst of the hot pursuit of the tablet, there were some exceptional scenes of characterization, particularly those between *Bugle* City Editor Robbie Robertson, his son Randy and *Bugle* Publisher J. Jonah Jameson. Robertson, as written by Stan, is an employee of the *Bugle* who refuses to join Jameson in his misguided mission to use his newspaper to destroy the hated Spider-Man. Robbie is a man of guts and integrity, who risks his very job to keep the *Bugle* on the straight and narrow. Yet he is also the father of a college-aged son, rebelling against the Establishment in true 1960s tradition. And he and his son are both African American, adding an additional layer of complexity. As you'll read, Stan handles the campus protests and the interaction between Robbie and his son in a deft, sophisticated manner. No easy answers or pat solutions are provided. Meanwhile, Peter's relationship with his main squeeze, the gorgeous Gwen Stacy, was entering a very rocky patch. And his friendship with both Harry Osborn and his former high school tormentor, Flash Thompson, was on shaky ground. There is just so much story packed into this volume that you'll be relieved you can read it all without having to wait a month between issues as Marvelites such as myself had to do way back when. What a thrill for you to be able to peruse this Lee/Romita masterpiece in one sitting if you like.

And speaking of the redoubtable Mr. Romita, his work on the clay tablet story upheld the high artistic standards we had come to expect in the *Amazing* title. Although the extent of John's penciling chores varied from issue to issue, as you'll note when you read the credits, the singular Romita style was always in evidence. The way Spidey swung through the concrete canyons; the visual take on the villains and the to-die-for females; the utterly effortless way the story flowed. All this was the product of John's potent presence here. Naturally, having longtime pros such as John Buscema and Jim Mooney lending their own considerable talents to the visuals kept it all so satisfyingly consistent. The art is always in service to the story, never just drawing attention to itself.

We're not quite at the end yet. Almost 35 years after the original storyline appeared, yours truly wound up editing a three-issue sequel called *Spider-Man: Lifeline* in 2001 that truly added to the original myth. I don't recall the details, but my friend and former Marvel editor Fabian Nicieza approached me about doing a follow-up series with none other than Steve Rude of *Nexus* fame as our illustrator. This was too good to pass up. Fabian was one of the primary architects of the X-Men explosion that rocked the comics industry during the nineties, as well as doing terrific work on many other titles. And I'd always wanted Steve Rude to take a crack at a Marvel book. His superb storytelling skills and wonderful feel for the visuals, with a tip of the artistic hat to Jack Kirby, were hard to beat. Of course, we also lucked out by getting my old buddy Bob Wiacek on the inks, who seemed born to embellish Rude.

We decided to more fully explore the infamous clay tablet (which we referred to as "stone" for some reason) and plumb its many mysteries. We asked ourselves where the tablet originated; was there more to the hieroglyphics than Dr. Curt Connors had initially discovered; what happened to the tablet after *Amazing Spider-Man* #75's fast-paced finale; who would want the blasted thing now? From those questions arose a trio of issues that I am immensely proud to have my name on as editor. Doubly so, because I had so much enthusiasm and respect for the original Lee/Romita issues.

This was one of those happy circumstances where all the bases were touched. Fabian found a logical way to continue the tale by specifying that the tablet was not complete; fragments were missing. This led to a stunning reinterpretation of the symbols. Well done. Lots of the old players came back for an encore, including Caesar Cicero, Man Mountain Marko and Dr. Curt Connors, plus his reptilian alter ego, the Lizard. Some new cast members entered, including Hammerhead, Doctor Strange and the Sub-Mariner himself. The quest to unearth the tablet's myriad secrets had lost none of its luster. Who ultimately winds up with the tablet, and why he/she wanted it, will rock you to your core, I guarantee it. It's nothing you might suspect, and we planned it that way over many a long plotting session. Fabian, Steve Rude and myself were determined that if we were going to revisit one of the real classics in Spider-Man lore, we had to find some way to equal the power and intensity of the original, whose ending is also utterly shocking. As you have the entire epic collected for you right here in one handy trade paperback, you get to be the judge. We gave it our best and I have only the fondest memories of the entire project.

Now it's your turn to dip into this truly charmed collection of the web-spinner's finest fables. If some nonbeliever ever asks you why *Amazing Spider-Man* is so revered, just smile and toss this little tome into their lap and they'll be hooked by about page two.

Okay, let's all be quiet and listen in to the Kingpin of Crime as he begins a mad quest for this ancient artifact that mirror's Gutman's own obsession with the fabled *Maltese Falcon*. Although he only had to contend with gumshoe Sam Spade, let alone Spider-Man.

Enjoy.

Ralph Macchio

RALPH MACCHIO SPENT OVER 35 YEARS AT MARVEL, STARTING AS AN ASSISTANT EDITOR AND LATER WRITING *AVENGERS*, *THOR* AND MANY OTHERS. AS EDITOR, HE OVERSAW BOOKS ACROSS THE MARVEL LINE, INCLUDING SHEPHERDING THE ULTIMATE LINE INTO EXISTENCE, AND EDITING ALL OF STEPHEN KING'S MARVEL ADAPTATIONS.

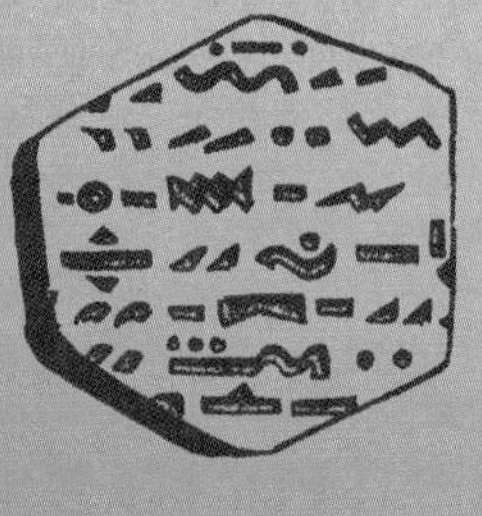

SPIDER-MAN
12¢
68
IND.
JAN
the AMAZING SPIDER-MAN
APPROVED BY THE COMICS CODE AUTHORITY
MARVEL COMICS GROUP
CRISIS ON CAMPUS!
A LOW
MUST
DON'T STALL MORE
WON'T
ROMITA

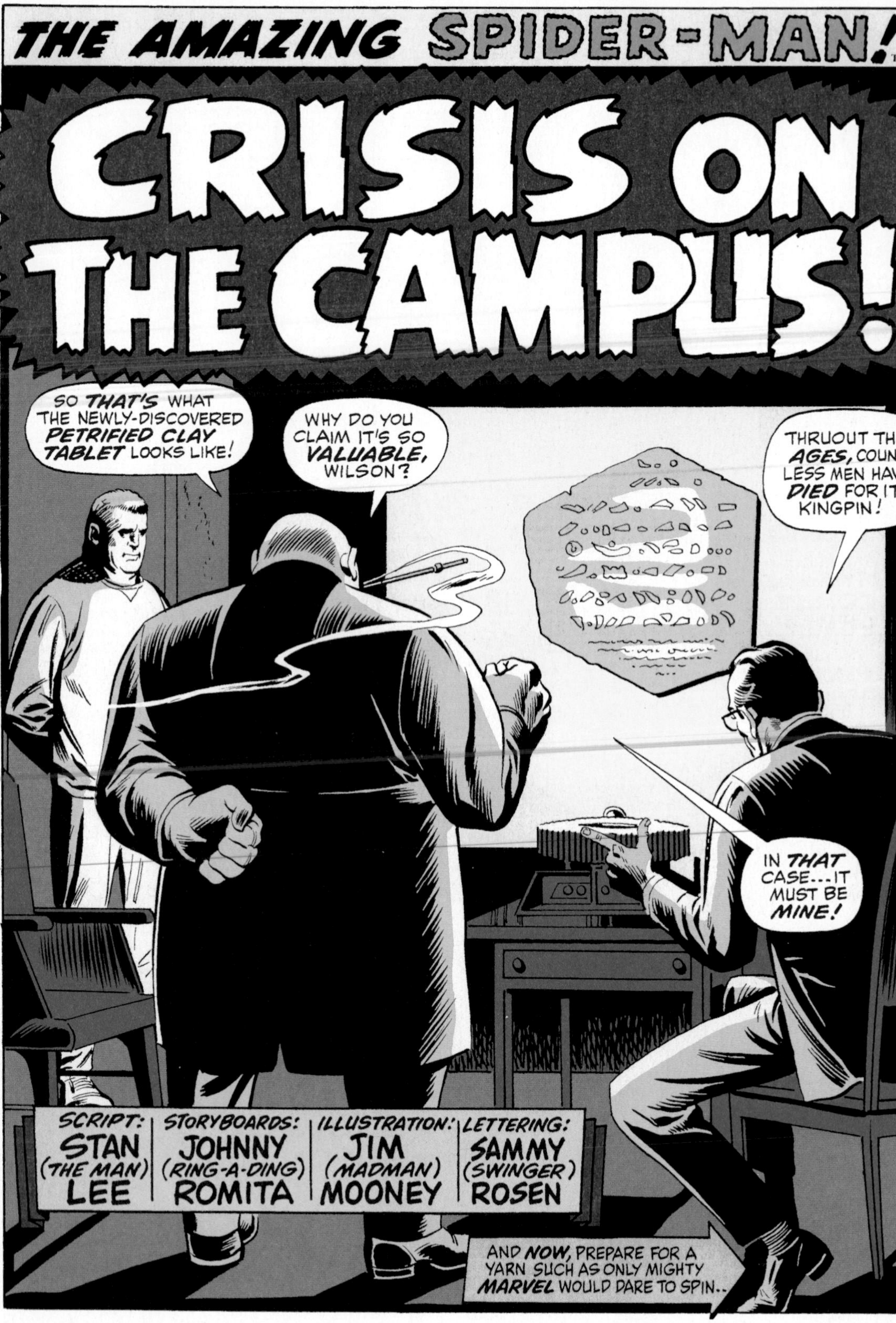
THE AMAZING SPIDER-MAN!
CRISIS ON THE CAMPUS!
SO THAT'S WHAT THE NEWLY-DISCOVERED PETRIFIED CLAY TABLET LOOKS LIKE!
WHY DO YOU CLAIM IT'S SO VALUABLE, WILSON?
THRUOUT THE AGES, COUNT-LESS MEN HAVE DIED FOR IT, KINGPIN!
IN THAT CASE... IT MUST BE MINE!
SCRIPT: STAN (THE MAN) LEE
STORYBOARDS: JOHNNY (RING-A-DING) ROMITA
ILLUSTRATION: JIM (MADMAN) MOONEY
LETTERING: SAMMY (SWINGER) ROSEN
AND NOW, PREPARE FOR A YARN SUCH AS ONLY MIGHTY MARVEL WOULD DARE TO SPIN..

IT'S EVEN OLDER THAN THE PRICELESS DEAD SEA SCROLLS!
THE MAN WHO CAN DECIPHER IT MAY LEARN THE GREATEST SECRETS OF ALL TIME!
I'VE HEARD ENOUGH!
WHERE IS IT NOW? HOW CAN I FIND IT?
FINDING IT IS SIMPLE!
THE SCIENCE FOUNDATION HAS BEEN SENDING IT TO DIFFERENT UNIVERSITIES...
HOPING THAT ONE OF THEM WILL BE ABLE TO READ ITS MESSAGE!
PRESENTLY, IT'S ON EXHIBIT AT THE CAMPUS OF E.S.U., HERE IN THE CITY!
GOOD! IT'LL BE CHILD'S PLAY FOR ME TO SEIZE IT FROM THERE!
BUT, IT'S UNDER HEAVY GUARD!
AND WHAT OF SPIDER-MAN?
YOU CAN'T EVEN SNEEZE IN THAT PART OF TOWN WITHOUT HIM CRAWLING OUT OF THE WOODWORK!
SPIDER-MAN?!!
DO YOU THINK I'D CHANGE MY PLANS FOR HIM?
THOK!
IT WAS ONLY THRU THE SHEEREST LUCK THAT HE MANAGED TO ESCAPE ME IN THE PAST!
I'VE BEEN HOPING OUR PATHS WOULD CROSS AGAIN!
FOR, I'LL NEVER LET MYSELF FORGET... WHAT I OWE HIM!
BUT, LEST YOU THINK I'M MERELY WHISTLING IN THE DARK...
I'LL SHOW YOU HOW EASILY THE KINGPIN CAN CRUSH A DOZEN SPIDER-MEN...!
2.

LOOK ALIVE, YOU WORTHLESS, INEFFEC-TUAL STUMBLEBUMS!
IT'S TIME FOR MY DAILY WORKOUT!
AND IF YOU DON'T PUT SOME MUSCLE INTO IT---
I'LL MAKE YOU WISH YOU'D NEVER HEARD OF ME!
BUT---IT'LL BE SIX AGAINST ONE TODAY, BOSS!
YA WON'T HAVE A CHANCE!
THAT'S WHAT THEY ALL THINK!
THE KINGPIN'S SUCH A NICE, OLD, JOLLY FAT MAN...
---HE PROBABLY CAN'T EVEN CLIMB A FLIGHT OF STAIRS!
TEAR INTO 'IM THIS TIME, YOU GUYS!
THE LONGER WE CAN KEEP 'IM FIGHT-ING, THE MORE HE PAYS US!
---AND THIS TIME WE OUGHTTA MAKE A BUNDLE!
YOU NEVER LEARN, DO YOU?
JUST AS SPIDER-MAN HAS NEVER LEARNED!
NO ONE SUSPECTS HOW POWERFUL I REALLY AM! NO ONE BELIEVES HOW FAST I CAN MOVE!
AND BY THE TIME THEY GRASP THE TRUTH... IT'S TOO LATE TO SAVE THEM!
THWUP!!
BOK!
3.

MY GREATEST ASSET HAS ALWAYS BEEN THE FACT THAT THE WORLD MISTAKES MY MASSIVE MUSCLES...
...FOR MERE, BLUBBERY FAT!
YOU! A BLACK BELT KARATE FIGHTER...!
NOT EVEN YOU CAN DOWN THE KINGPIN WITH A SINGLE CHOP!
THAK!
AND ONE IS ALL YOU'LL HAVE A CHANCE FOR!
CRUSHER!! GET 'IM... WHILE HIS BACK IS TURN...
UNHHH!
ZAP!
NO ONE "GETS" THE KINGPIN!
NOT WHILE MY SPEED IS FAR GREATER THAN ANYONE WOULD BELIEVE!
FUMP!
YOU'RE FIRED... ALL OF YOU!
I TOLD YOU I WANTED A WORKOUT...
YOU DIDN'T EVEN GIVE ME A CHANCE TO WORK UP A SWEAT!
GET DRESSED AND GET OUT! I CAN'T STOMACH LOSERS!
WE'LL GO... WE'LL GO!
NOTHIN' WOULD MAKE US TANGLE... WITH YOU... AGAIN!
4

ROUND UP A NEW CREW FOR MY NEXT WORKOUT!
AND NEXT TIME GET TWICE AS MANY... TO GIVE ME SOME COMPETITION!
I'VE NEVER SEEN YOU THIS WAY BEFORE!
YOU WERE LIKE A HUMAN BULLDOZER IN THERE!
DID MY MERE MENTION OF SPIDER-MAN'S NAME AFFECT YOU LIKE THAT?
SPIDER-MAN!! EVERY TIME I THINK OF HIM, MY BLOOD BEGINS TO BOIL!
ONLY HE HAS EVER THWARTED ME!
BUT, AFTER I STEAL THE PRICELESS CLAY TABLET FROM ITS RESTING PLACE AT E.S.U...
THEN, HE AND I WILL HAVE... OUR FINAL RECKONING!
AND, SPEAKING OF OUR WOEBEGONE WEB-SPINNER WHO, ONLY LAST ISSUE, DEFEATED THE MANIACAL MYSTERIO---
I OUGHTTA HAVE MY HEAD EXAMINED!
I DIDN'T TAKE A SINGLE PICTURE OF MY LAST BATTLE!
WHICH MEANS I'VE NOTHING TO SELL TO JONAH'S RAG!
YEP, THAT'S ME! I RISKED MY FOOL NECK LIKE A GRINNING IDIOT...
AND ENDED UP WITH A BIG, FAT ZERO!
SO HERE I AM... BROKE, AS USUAL!
WELL, AT LEAST I'LL GET SOME SHUT-EYE AND ---OH NO!
HARRY MUST HAVE LOCKED THE WINDOW!
5

NO WAY TO GET IN WITHOUT BREAKING IT!
AND HARRY'S SURE TO HEAR... UNLESS...
WELL, WHAT D'YA KNOW?
I'M IN LUCK... FOR ONCE!
HARRY'S WINDOW IS OPEN...AND HE'S NOT IN YET!
HE'S A BROAD-MINDED JOE AND ALL THAT...
BUT I WONDER HOW HE'D FEEL IF HE EVER LEARNED...
THAT HE'S BEEN SHARING HIS PAD WITH SPIDER-MAN ALL THESE MONTHS?
IT WOULD BE ALMOST AS BAD AS LEARNING HIS FATHER IS REALLY THE GREEN GOBLIN!
BUT LUCKILY, I'VE MANAGED TO KEEP THAT FROM THE POOR GUY, TOO!
BOY! THIS SECRET IDENTITY JAZZ CAN SURE BE A STRAIN!
THE NEXT MORNING, PETER PARKER REACHES THE CAMPUS AT GOOD OL' E.S.U., CHEERY AND UNWORRIED AS EVER...
THAT RUSH-HOUR SUBWAY IS FOR THE BIRDS!
IF ONLY I COULD HAVE AFFORDED TO KEEP MY BIKE!
THERE OUGHTTA BE A SUPERHERO UNION---TO DEMAND A LIVING WAGE!
RATS! IF I FELT ANY LOWER, I'D BE UNDERGROUND!
SAY, MAN... AREN'T YOU PETER PARKER?
IF YOU'RE NOT A BILL COLLECTOR, THE ANSWER'S YES!
MY DAD TOLD ME TO LOOK YOU UP!
YOUR DAD?
HE'S JOE ROBERTSON, CITY EDITOR OF THE BUGLE!
HE TOLD ME ONE OF HIS HOT-SHOT FREE-LANCE SHUTTERBUGS WAS A B.M.O.C. HERE!
B.M.O.C.!
I CAN'T EVEN GET MYSELF ARRESTED!
ANYWAY, ANY SON OF ROBBIE ROBERTSON CAN'T BE ALL BAD! --- EVEN IF YOU ARE NAMELESS!
SORRY, PARKER! MY DRAFT CARD SAYS RANDOLPH!
PUT 'ER THERE, RANDY!
WHEN I CAN FIND THEM, MY FRIENDS CALL ME PETE!
AMONG OTHER THINGS!
6

LIKE HI, JOSH!
SAY HELLO TO PETE PARKER!
WE ALREADY DID THE BIT, RANDY! I WANNA ASK YOU SOME-THING, PARKER!
WHERE DO YOU STAND ON THE EXHIBITION HALL ISSUE?
YOU'RE NOT REACH-ING ME, JOSH! WHAT ISSUE?
MAN! WE'RE TALKING TO A SPHINX!
GUESS I'VE BEEN, EH, OUT OF TOUCH, LATELY!
SINCE YOU'RE JUST BACK FROM THE MOON, I'LL CLUE YOU IN...
AFTER EXHIBITING THAT CLAY TABLET, THE "EX HALL" IS BEING TURNED INTO A PRIVATE DORM, FOR VISITING ALUMNI!
BUT, IT'S SUPPOSED TO BE FOR THE STUDENTS!
NOW YOU'RE GETTING WITH IT, MAN!
WE'VE BEEN PETITIONING THE DEAN TO TURN THE HALL INTO A LOW-RENT DORM FOR NEEDY STUDENTS!
THE OLD GRADS ARE LOADED... THEY CAN BED DOWN IN HOTELS!
SO WHAT'S THE VERDICT?
WHAT D'YOU EXPECT? THE ANSWER WAS NO!
BUT NOT FOR LONG!
SOUNDS LIKE TROUBLE BREWING!
JOSH IS SPOKESMAN FOR A LOT OF ANGRY CATS... AND I GUESS THEY'VE GOT A RIGHT TO BE!
I MIGHT HAVE KNOWN ROBBIE'S SON WOULD BE A RIGHT GUY!
WISH I HAD TIME TO GET MORE INVOLVED IN THIS THING!
GUESS WHO, GURU!
HEY... MARY JANE! WHERE'D YOU COME FROM?
MARY JANE! IS SHE THE FIRST GIRL YOU THOUGHT OF??
WELL, SHE'S MORE THE GUESS-WHO-ING TYPE!
SPIDEY-SENSE... WHERE WERE YOU WHEN I NEEDED YOU?
DON'T TELL ME I FINALLY FOUND THE MAGIC WORDS TO MAKE GORGEOUS GWENDOLYN JEALOUS!
NEGATIVE!! I DON'T HAVE A JEALOUS BONE IN MY BODY!
BUT MENTION HER AGAIN, AND WATCH THE ROOF FALL IN!
AND, SPEAKING OF FALLING ROOFS, LET'S SEE WHAT JOLLY JONAH JAMESON IS UP TO NOW...
THAT BLASTED SPIDER-MAN CAME OUT ON TOP AGAIN!
THE POLICE JUST REPORTED THAT HE BEAT MYSTERIO!
ROBBIE! I'M NOT BORING YOU, AM I?
CITY EDITOR
HUH? OH... NO, J.J....
I WAS JUST THINK-ING!
7.

THINKING? DO THAT ON YOUR OWN TIME!
I EXPECT MY CITY EDITOR TO COME UP WITH NEWS!!
YOU'VE ALREADY MADE THAT ABUNDANTLY CLEAR!
WHY DIDN'T WE GET THE STORY ABOUT SPIDER-MAN'S BATTLE WITH MYSTERIO UNTIL IT WAS ALL OVER?
BE REASONABLE, JJ! NO OTHER PAPER GOT IT, EITHER!
AND WHERE WAS PARKER, EH? ANSWER ME THAT! HOW COME HE DIDN'T BRING ME ANY PIX?
CONSIDERING THE WAY YOU TREAT THAT KID...
...IT'S A WONDER YOU EVER SEE HIM AT ALL!
I KNEW IT! THAT'S WHAT HAPPENS... WHEN YOU'RE TOO GENEROUS... TOO EASY-GOING!
PEOPLE START CRITICIZING YOU!
WHEN WILL I LEARN..??
IT DOESN'T PAY TO BE A LIVING DOLL!!
MY OWN CITY EDITOR ...TAKING PARKER'S SIDE AGAINST THE SWEETEST PUBLISHER IN TOWN!
WHY, OH WHY WAS I BORN TO BE A MARTYR?
POOR JAMESON! HE'S NEVER HAPPY... UNLESS HE'S MISERABLE!
BUT, HE'LL GET OVER IT SOON ENOUGH!
I WISH THAT I COULD GET OVER THIS FEELING OF APPREHENSION...
IF ONLY I KNEW WHAT WAS BUGGING RANDY!
HE MEANS SO MUCH... TO HIS MOTHER... AND TO ME!
FOR HER SAKE... AND HIS...
I MUST NOT FAIL!
SOMETIME LATER, AT THE MODEST HOME WHICH OUR HERO'S AUNT SHARES WITH ANNA WATSON...
PETER! AND GWEN!
COME IN! THIS WILL BE THE BEST POSSIBLE MEDICINE FOR ANNA!
HOW IS SHE FEELING, MRS. WATSON?
COME IN AND SEE FOR YOURSELF!
MUSTN'T SHOUT LIKE THAT, AUNT MAY! MUSTN'T SAP YOUR STRENGTH!
I FEEL STRONG AS A LION WHEN I SEE YOU, DEAR!
HE HAS THE OPPOSITE EFFECT ON ME!
HE MAKES ME FEEL WEAK AS A KITTEN!
8

YOU TWO HAVE BEEN ...SEEING QUITE A BIT OF EACH OTHER!
NOT NEARLY ENOUGH TO SUIT ME!
OH DEAR! I DIDN'T MEAN TO EMBARRASS YOU, GWENDOLYNE!
NEVER MIND ME, MRS. PARKER!
THE IMPORTANT THING IS... I HOPE YOU DON'T DISAPPROVE!
DISAPPROVE OF ME LATCHING ONTO THE BRIGHTEST, BOUNCIEST, MOST BEAUTIFUL BLONDE IN CREATION?
THAT'LL BE THE DAY!
YOU TWO SOUND AS THOUGH... IT MIGHT BE EVEN MORE SERIOUS... THAN I THOUGHT!
ALL I CAN SAY IS... YOU'VE MADE A SILLY, SENTIMENTAL OLD LADY... VERY, VERY HAPPY!
NO WONDER YOU'RE SO SLIGHTLY SPECIAL, MR. PARKER!
ANYONE LUCKY ENOUGH TO HAVE AN AUNT LIKE THAT!!
FUNNY... I USED TO THINK OF MYSELF AS THE ORIGINAL HARD-LUCK CHARLIE!
BUT NOW... I'M NOT SO SURE!
THAT WAS A LOVELY BOX OF CANDY THEY BROUGHT YOU, MAY!
MAY?!! WHAT IS IT, DEAR? WHAT'S WRONG?
YOU LOOK SO PALE! YOU SHOULD HAVE TOLD THEM... TO CALL THE DOCTOR!
NO... I COULDN'T!
I DIDN'T WANT... TO SPOIL... THEIR HAPPINESS!
BUT, ALAS... THE HAPPINESS OF PETER PARKER IS DESTINED TO SUFFER A RUDE INTRUSION IN ANY EVENT!
LET'S ACCOMPANY HIM TO CAMPUS, THE VERY NEXT MORNING...
LOOKS LIKE ANOTHER DEMONSTRATION! THE BIGGEST ONE YET!
MUST BE WHAT RANDY WAS TALKING ABOUT!
MATTER OF FACT, THERE HE IS NOW!
HI, PETE! COME ON OVER, MAN!
STUDENT COMMITTEE FOR A LOW RENT DORM
MUST BE SAVED
IF YOU CAN SPARE THE TIME, PARKER!
9.

WE'RE GONNA CLOSE THIS PLACE DOWN TIGHTER THAN A DRUM TILL WE GET WHAT WE WANT!
NOW HERE'S WHAT YOU CAN DO--- LINE UP ALL THE CATS YOU KNOW AND GET THEM TO CONTACT ALL OF THEIR FRIENDS!
HEY, WHOA! SLOW DOWN FOR A SEC, RANDY!
I FEEL LIKE I JUST ARRIVED SMACK-DAB IN THE MIDDLE OF A HITCH-COCK WHO-DONE-IT!
THEN, AS SOON AS WE HAVE ENOUGH PROTESTERS TO REALLY ROCK THE JOINT, WE MARCH ON THE EX HALL!
I'M STILL IN THE DARK ABOUT ALL THIS!
WE DEMAND LO
LOOK, WHITEY... HOW MUCH DO YOU HAVETA KNOW?
THE SCHOOL'S TURNING THE EX HALL OVER TO THE ESTABLISHMENT--- BUT IT BELONGS TO US--- AND WE WANT IT!
AND YOU JUST KNOW WE'RE GONNA GET IT!
OKAY, THAT'S YOUR SIDE OF THE STORY! WHAT DOES THE DEAN SAY?
WE AIN'T BUYIN' WHAT HE SAYS!
FROM NOW ON, WE DO THE TALKING!
HEY! WHAT'S THE BIT? WHERE ARE YOU GOING? WE'VE GOT SIGNS ENOUGH FOR EVERYBODY!
ANYONE CAN PAINT A SIGN, MISTER! THAT DOESN'T MAKE YOU RIGHT!
THEN GO ON... CUT OUT!
YOU'RE TOO CHICKEN TO GET INVOLVED!
DO OR DIE THE DORM
ESU PHEW!
WELL, BROTHER PARKER, YOU DID IT AGAIN!
MY SYMPATHIES ARE ALL WITH THE KIDS DOWN THERE... BUT JUST BECAUSE I DON'T LIKE ANYONE TO PUSH ME, I FLEW OFF THE HANDLE AGAIN!
I CAN LIVE WITH IT IF JOSH THINKS I'M NOWHERE---
BUT THAT LOOK ON RANDY'S FACE REALLY SHOOK ME UP!
I GUESS THAT'S THE TABLET THEY'RE EXHIBITING HERE!
IF ANYONE EVER DECIPHERS THAT INSCRIPTION, HE'LL HAVE IT MADE FOR LIFE!
BUT IT SURE IS A SHAME THEY'RE TURN-ING THIS PLACE OVER TO THE ALUMNI AFTER THE EXHIBIT!
WE REALLY NEED A LOW-RENT DORM ON CAMPUS...
...AND THIS WOULD BE THE PERFECT PLACE!
I WONDER WHY THE DEAN'S SO OBSTINATE?
A SHORT TIME LATER...
NO SENSE WAITING ANY LONGER!
WE'VE GOT EVERYONE WE NEED!
EVERY-BODY GRAB A SIGN!
THIS IS IT!
DO OR DIE FOR THE DORM
ESU.. PHEW!
10

HEY! DOESN'T ROBERTSON'S FATHER WORK FOR THE DAILY BUGLE?
YOU SAY THAT AGAIN, AND I'LL...!
LOOK... COOL IT, Y'HEAR?
WE GOT A JOB TO DO!
WHO WANTS THE SON OF AN UNCLE TOM MARCHIN' HERE WITH US?
LET'S GO!
ON TO THE HALL!
ESU PHEW!
WE DEMAN LOW REN DOR
RANDY'S A SOUL-BROTHER ...AND DON'T FOR-GET IT!
EVERYONE LISTEN! THE ONLY WAY TO GET THAT DORM IS TO MAKE IT BIG!
WE NEED THE PAPERS --TV..RADIO --TO COVER THIS THING!
WE GOTTA SHAKE UP THE WHOLE ESTABLISH-MENT!
THAT MEANS WE GOTTA TAKE OVER THE HALL!
DO OR DIE
C'MON! EVERYBODY IN! IF WE MOVE FAST ENOUGH---IT'LL ALL BE OVER BEFORE THEY KNOW WHAT HAPPENED!
ESU PHEW
NOBODY LEAVES TILL WE'VE GOT OURSELVES A DORM!
AT THAT MOMENT, BACK AT THE BUGLE...
SIMMER DOWN, J.J.! YOU WANTED A STORY, DIDN'T YOU?
IS THAT ALL YOU'VE GOT TO DO---WATCH TELEVISION ON MY TIME?!!
TAKE A LOOK AT WHAT'S GOING ON!
IT'S A RIOT ---AT E.S.U.!
I'VE ALREADY DONE IT, MISTER!
WHY DIDN'T SOMEBODY TELL ME? WE'VE GOTTA COVER IT--- FAST!
AND NOW... IF YOU'LL STAND ASIDE---THIS IS ONE STORY I'M COVERING MYSELF!
QUICK! ALERT OUR MOBILE NEWS CARS ---SEND OUR BEST MEN---
MY BOY'S A STUDENT ON THAT CAMPUS!
BUT, OTHER EYES ARE ALSO WITNESSING THE PROCEEDINGS... WITH MORE THAN CASUAL INTEREST...
HMMMM... A MOST FORTUNATE DEVELOPMENT!
11.

WILSON! COME HERE!
I BELIEVE I HAVE FOUND THE MOMENT WE WERE SEEKING!
ASSEMBLE OUR BEST MEN!
AS SOON AS IT GETS DARK... WE MOVE!
WHILE, BACK AT E.S.U., THINGS GROW TENSER BY THE MINUTE...
LOOK, WHAT-EVER YOU'RE DEMONSTRATIN' ABOUT AIN'T NO CONCERN OF OURS!
ALL I KNOW IS WE'RE PAID TO GUARD THIS TABLET... AND NOBODY GETS NEAR IT!
HEY, GO EASY, MISTER! THEY'RE NOT PUBLIC ENEMIES!
KEEP OUTTA THIS, KID! WE'VE GOT A JOB TO DO!
SAY! THOSE PRIVATE GUARDS GAVE ME AN IDEA!
IF WE COULD GET OUR HANDS ON THAT TABLET, THEN THEY'D HAVE TO LISTEN TO US!
I DON'T BUY IT, JOSH! THAT'S PLAIN STEALING!
LOOK, MAN-- ...YOU HEARD WHAT THEY CALLED YOUR FATHER!
DON'T DO IT, JOSH!
RANDY'S RIGHT... AND YOU KNOW IT!
NOW MOVE ON, ALL OF YOU!
HEY... WHAT'RE YOU DOING? PUT THAT GUN AWAY!
YOU'RE NOT SCARIN' US, BIG MAN!
FIRE THAT CANNON AND THEY'LL TEAR THIS PLACE APART!
RELAX! IT'S THE ONLY WAY TO HANDLE 'EM!
NOBODY'S FIRING ANY-THING... JUST BREAK IT UP!
EVERYONE'S TOO UP-TIGHT! IN A SPOT LIKE THIS, ANYTHING CAN HAPPEN!
IT'LL BE A MIRACLE IF NOBODY GETS HURT BEFORE IT'S OVER!
BUT, WHAT CAN I... WHAT CAN ANYBODY ...DO ABOUT IT NOW?
AT A TIME LIKE THIS... EVEN SPIDEY WOULD BE HELPLESS!
12.

BUT, AS LONG AS I'M HERE... THERE'S NO SENSE WASTING TIME...
...NOT WHEN I CAN BE GETTING SOME EXCLUSIVE PIX... TO SELL TO JOLLY JONAH!
AND BOY...CAN MRS. PARKER'S NEPHEW USE THE BREAD!
BUT, ON THE OTHER SIDE OF THE BUILDING...
STOP RIGHT HERE!
THEY'RE ALL TOO BUSY TO NOTICE US!
SO THIS IS WHAT A COLLEGE LOOKS LIKE!
BIG DEAL!
TAKE YOUR PLACES, ALL OF YOU!
IT'S ALMOST TIME FOR OUR LITTLE DIVERSION TO BEGIN!
AND, WHEN IT DOES, YOU'LL GO INTO ACTION LIKE A WELL-OILED MACHINE...
...OR ELSE YOU'LL ANSWER TO ME!
THAT'S IT! EVERYONE WILL THINK THE DEMONSTRATORS WERE RESPONSIBLE!
FTOOM!
NOW!
WHILE EVERYONE RUSHES TO CHECK THE EXPLOSION, WE'LL HAVE A CLEAR FIELD FOR OURSELVES!
THE TABLET WILL BE SAFELY IN MY HANDS BEFORE THE FLAMES DIE DOWN!
THUMP! THOOM!
13

KRAKK!
STAY OUT OF MY WAY, AND NO ONE WILL BE HARMED!
WH--WHO'S THAT?
I DON'T KNOW... ...BUT HE TORE THE DOOR OFF ITS HINGES... BARE-HANDED!!
I RECOGNIZE HIM--!
GET BACK... ALL OF YOU!
HE'S THE KING-PIN!
BUT... WHAT'S HE DOING HERE??
STAND ASIDE, SONNY!
YOU CAN HAVE YER KINDERGARDEN BACK LATER ON... WHEN WE'RE DONE WITH IT!
TO THE EXHIBITION CHAMBER...QUICKLY!
WHEN I GIVE THE WORD... PREPARE TO USE YOUR GAS MASKS!
THUMP! THPOOM!
THE KINGPIN!!
WITH HIM ON THE SCENE... NOBODY'S SAFE!
BUT, WHERE DOES HE FIGURE IN??
AND WHY DID HE MENTION GAS MASKS?
HE'S COMING TOWARDS ME!
I'VE GOT TO ACT LIKE I'M NOBODY SPECIAL!
HEY! WATCH IT, MISTER! WHERE DO YOU THINK--??
SHUT UP! I'VE NO TIME TO WASTE ON JUVENILES!
THUD!
STRANGE! FOR A MOMENT THERE... I GOT A FEELING OF POWER... OF RAW STRENGTH...
FAR MORE THAN I'D EXPECT FROM A CALLOW, COWERING STUDENT!
I'M TOO KEYED-UP! I'M STARTING TO IMAGINE THINGS!
THAT LOOK HE GAVE ME... WHAT DID IT MEAN?
HOW CAN ANY SCRAWNY, SIMPERING YOUTH BE WORTHY OF THE KINGPIN'S ATTENTION!
THE TABLET! IT CAN'T BE MUCH FURTHER!
14

HOLD IT! KEEP THAT GUY AWAY FROM HERE!
HE'LL FOUL UP THE WHOLE DEMONSTRATION!
RANDY... NO!!
HE DOESN'T REALIZE THE DANGER!
NOW I'VE GOT TO CHANGE TO SPIDER-MAN!
YOU YOUNG FOOLS HAVE ALREADY SERVED MY PURPOSE!
NOW STAND ASIDE... IF YOU VALUE YOUR LIVES!
WE'VE GOTTA DO IT, RANDY!
THEY'RE ARMED!
I SHOULD HAVE GUESSED IT SOONER..!
IT MUST BE THE TABLET HE'S AFTER!
AND, IF I KNOW THE KINGPIN...
HE'LL STOP AT NOTHING TO GET IT!
THE KIDS SEE ME! THEY THINK I'M AIMING TO PUT THEM DOWN!
LOOK! FIRST THE KINGPIN... NOW SPIDER-MAN!
BUT THEY WON'T STOP US NOW!
STUDENT POWER!
ESU PHEW!
HAVEN'T TIME TO ARGUE WITH THEM...
NOT WITH THAT OVER-STUFFED KILLER ON THE LOOSE JUST AHEAD!
STAY OUT OF THIS, GANG!
FROM HERE ON IN, IT'S BETWEEN THE KINGPIN AND ME!
WE DEMAND
15

BUT DON'T JUST STAND THERE!
WARN THE POLICE THAT THE TABLET'S IN DANGER!
GO ON... MOVE! CLEAR THE HALL!
I SHOULDN'T HAVE LISTENED TO ANYONE!
I SHOULD HAVE TRIED TO STOP THE KINGPIN!
YEAH... AND WE'D HAVE BEEN PICKIN' UP YOUR PIECES!
WHILE OUTSIDE THE BUILDING---
DON'T WORRY, MR. ROBERTSON! WE'LL SOON HAVE EVERY-THING UNDER CONTROL!
DON'T WORRY? WHILE MY SON IS IN THERE?
AND, AT THE TABLET DISPLAY ROOM...
IT'S THE KINGPIN--- LEADING HIS HOODS!
THEY'RE AFTER THE TABLET!
AND THEY'RE ALL WEARING ...GAS MASKS!
DON'T MOVE! I'LL GIVE THE ORDERS NOW!
JUST GOT MY CAMERA SET UP IN TIME!
HE'S STARTING TO FIRE GAS PELLETS!
BUT, IT'S A BIG ROOM---IT'LL TAKE A LOT OF GAS TO DO THE TRICK!
AND I'LL MAKE SURE HE DOESN'T FIRE ANOTHER BURST!
THWIK!
WHA..?!
SORRY, CHUBBS!
IF YOU WANT THAT TABLET, YOU'LL HAVE TO GET IT THE HARD WAY!
SPIDER-MAN!
16

WHAT'S WITH YOU, MISTER?
WHEN I HIT A FELLA, I EXPECT HIM TO STAY DOWN!
EVERY TIME I FACE HIM, IT'S A NEW SHOCK ---REALIZING HOW POWERFUL HE REALLY IS!
SURELY YOU DIDN'T THINK A MAN LIKE ME IS DEPENDENT ONLY UPON DEVICES LIKE GAS?
THANKS TO YOUR INTERFERENCE, I'LL SIMPLY RESORT TO... BRUTE FORCE!
THE BRUTE PART OF IT IS OKAY---
BUT WHEN IT COMES TO FORCE, THAT'S MY DEPARTMENT, TUBBY!
WOK!
GUESS AGAIN, YOU ARROGANT CLOD!
UUMPHHH!
THE MAN DOESN'T LIVE WHO CAN ENDURE MY BEAR HUG WITHOUT BLACKING OUT!
NO PUNY SPIDER-POWER WILL SERVE TO SAVE YOU FROM ME NOW!
ANY-ONE ELSE WOULD BE A GONER BY NOW..!
BUT I'M STILL STRONGER THAN HE SUSPECTS!
THERE! I'VE OWED YOU THIS FOR MANY MONTHS!
AND THE KING-PIN ALWAYS PAYS HIS DEBTS!
SPIDER-MAN TRIED TO HELP!
CAN'T STAND BY WHILE HE'S TAKING HIS LUMPS!
WHOMP!
17.

WHAT'S THIS? ANOTHER PUNY FLEA--- TRYING TO STOP THE KINGPIN!
YOU CAN CALL ME WHAT YOU WANT...
BUT SOME-BODY'S GOTTA TACKLE YOU--- AND IT MIGHT AS WELL BE ME!
WHOP!
ONE FUMBLING STUDENT IS VIRTUALLY BENEATH MY NOTICE!
HAVE TO ATTACK NOW... BEFORE HE HURTS RANDY!
MMMPPHHH!
HERE, FATSO---CHEW ON THIS AWHILE!
THEN, WITH BLISTERING, MACHINE-GUN SPEED, THE AMAZING WEB-SPINNER UNLEASHES A DEVASTATING BARRAGE OF BLUDGEONING BLOWS...
...UNTIL...
THAT'LL HOLD HIM FOR A WHILE!
NOW WHAT ABOUT YOU, FELLA! ARE YOU HURT?
I...I GUESS ..I'LL LIVE!
WHICH IS MORE THAN SPIDER-MAN WILL BE ABLE TO SAY!
18

THIS TIME I'LL SHOW HIM NO MERCY!
LOOK OUT! HE'S GOING FOR HIS CANE BLASTER!
ZAT!
THE MARBLE WALL--- GONNA FALL ON RANDY!
CAN'T GET HIM AWAY IN TIME...
BUT AT LEAST I CAN SHIELD HIM---WITH MY BODY!
HERE IT COMES!
KRRAK!
ITS WEIGHT WILL BURY US BOTH!
SECONDS LATER...
EVEN IF HE STILL LIVES... BENEATH THAT RUBBLE...
NEVER AGAIN WILL SPIDER-MAN THINK HIMSELF A MATCH FOR THE INDEFATIGABLE KINGPIN!
THE VICTORY IS MINE!
MY WORST ENEMY HAS FALLEN AT LAST...
AND THE PRIZE I SOUGHT ---THE PRICELESS CLAY TABLET...IS MINE!
NEVER HAVE I KNOWN SUCH TOTAL TRIUMPH!
TRIUMPH, PERHAPS! BUT TOTAL? LET'S NOT BET ON IT...!
I FEEL LIKE I'VE BEEN WRESTLING A STEAM-ROLLER ---AND THE ROLLER WON!
BUT ANYWAY, RANDY'S OKAY!
THAT GUY HAS GUTS ENOUGH FOR A REGIMENT!
WAKE UP, FELLA! THE PARTY'S OVER!
WHAT HAPPENED? WHERE'S THE KINGPIN? HE.. HE MUST HAVE... GOTTEN AWAY!
AND THAT'S JUST WHAT I BETTER DO... BEFORE THE BOYS IN BLUE TRY TO GRAB ME!
THERE'S SPIDER-MAN ---AND ONE OF THE KIDS!
19

I GOT OUT JUST IN TIME!
WELL, WELL ...LOOK WHO'S TRYING TO MAKE A GET-AWAY!
BUT, BEFORE SPIDEY CAN POUNCE, HE NOTICES...
THE POLICE... ROUNDING UP THE PROTEST LEADERS!
THEY THINK THEY WERE IN LEAGUE WITH THE KING-PIN!
STAND BACK... ALL OF YOU!
THESE KIDS HAD NOTHING TO DO WITH THE THEFT OF THAT TABLET!
THAT GOES FOR YOU, TOO, MR. ROBERTSON!
OKAY! OKAY! THEY'LL HAVE THEIR DAY IN COURT!
DON'T WORRY, BOYS! I'LL SEE THAT YOU HAVE THE BEST LEGAL AID AVAILABLE!
THAT DAD OF YOURS IS A LOT OF MAN, RANDY!
I KNOW YOU DID WHAT YOU THOUGHT WAS RIGHT, SON!
TELL ME SOMETHIN' I DON'T KNOW JOSH!
I'LL BE BEHIND YOU ALL THE WAY!
UNTIL THIS IS CLEARED UP, WE'LL HOLD THEM FOR ILLEGAL POSSESSION AND PROPERTY DAMAGE!
OKAY--- INTO THE VAN WITH THEM!
RANDY'LL BE ALL RIGHT NOW!
AND THEY'LL ALL HAVE A CHANCE TO COOL OFF!
WHICH JUST LEAVES ME WITH SOME UNFINISHED BUSINESS!
BUT IT WON'T STAY UNFINISHED FOR LONG!
BOSS! IT'S THE WEB-SLINGER! HE'S TAILIN' US!
I'LL LEAD HIM INTO A TRAP FROM WHICH NO ONE CAN ESCAPE!
NEXT:
IN THE KING-PIN'S CLUTCHES!
20:

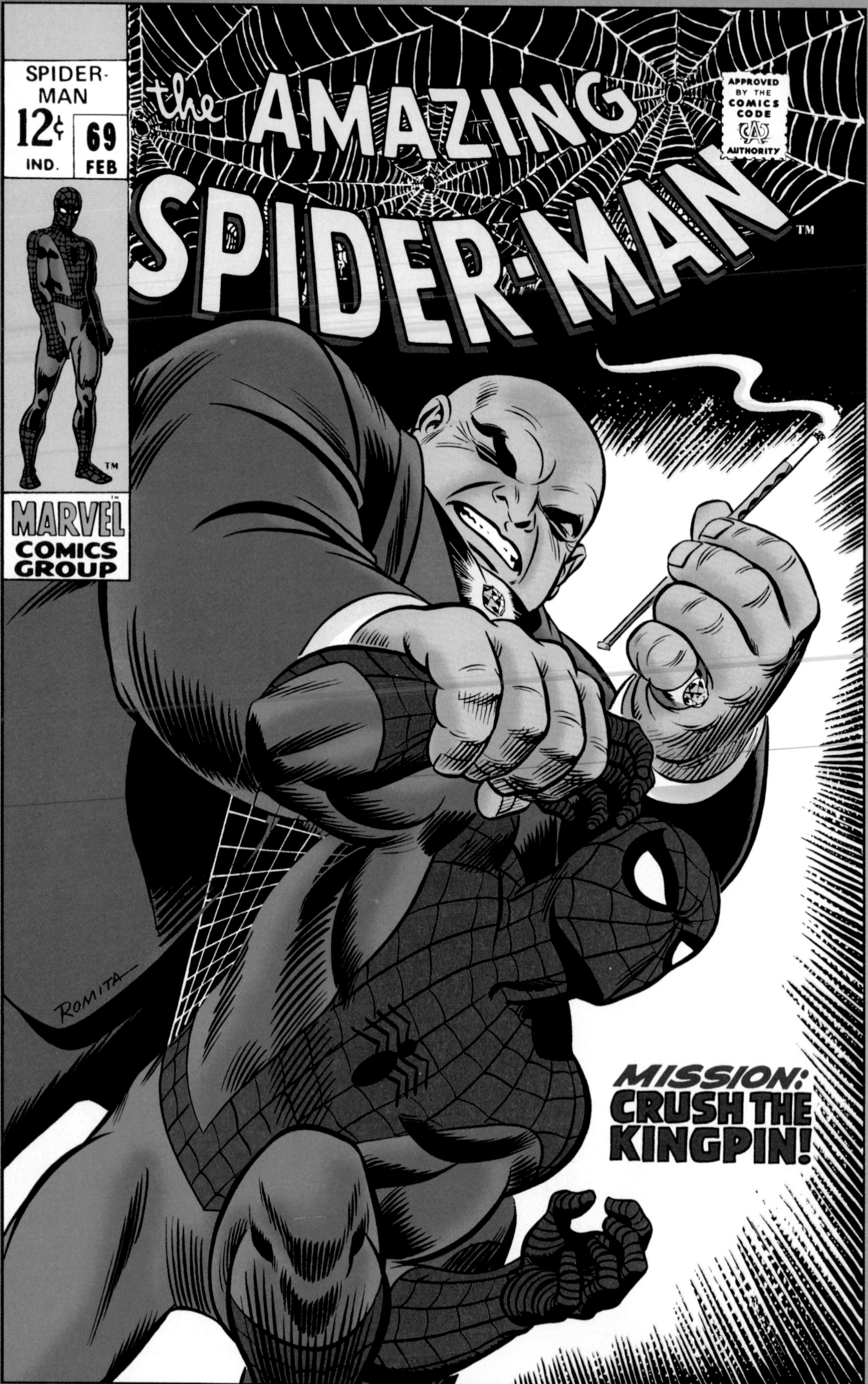
SPIDER-MAN
12¢
69
IND.
FEB
the AMAZING SPIDER-MAN™
APPROVED BY THE COMICS CODE AUTHORITY
MARVEL COMICS GROUP
ROMITA
MISSION: CRUSH THE KINGPIN!

THE AMAZING SPIDER-MAN!™
MISSION: CRUSH THE KINGPIN!
PRODUCED BY:
STAN (THE MAN) LEE, SCRIPT! JOHN (RING-A-DING) ROMITA, STORYBOARDS! JIM (MADMAN) MOONEY, ILLUSTRATION! SAM (SLEEPY) ROSEN, LETTERER!
THE KINGPIN'S HIDING SOMEWHERE IN THIS AREA!
AND, WITH MY SPIDER SENSE, IT WON'T TAKE LONG TO FIND HIM!

I CAN'T LET HIM GET AWAY WITH STEALING THAT PRICELESS TABLET FROM THE CAMPUS' EXHIBITION HALL!
...ESPECIALLY SINCE MR. ROBERTSON'S SON, RANDY, AND THE OTHER PROTEST LEADERS...
...ARE BEING BOOKED ON CHARGES OF AIDING THE KINGPIN IN HIS THEFT!
NOT TO MENTION THE FACT THAT THE TABLET IS SO PRICELESS, THAT FATSO CAN SELL IT TO ANY NATION HE CHOOSES!*
UH-OH! SPIDEY SENSE IS STARTING TO TINGLE!
I'M GETTING CLOSE!
*HOW'S THAT FOR A SNEAKY WAY TO SUMMARIZE OUR LAST ISH? ...SUBTLE STAN.
AND, JUST A FEW FATEFUL YARDS AWAY, WE FIND...
YOU DID IT, KINGPIN!
IT WAS A STROKE OF GENIUS FOR YOU TO USE THE STUDENT PROTEST DEMONSTRATION AS A COVER FOR STEALING THE TABLET!
BUT WHAT ABOUT SPIDER-MAN, BOSS?
COULD YOU EXPECT ANY LESS...FROM ME?
YEAH! THE BLASTED WEB-SPINNER IS STILL ON OUR TRAIL!
FORGET SPIDER-MAN! LOOK AT THE PRIZE I'VE WON!
THIS ANCIENT CLAY TABLET IS OLDER THAN THE DEAD SEA SCROLLS!
WHOEVER DECIPHERS IT WILL LEARN THE GREATEST SECRETS OF ALL TIME!
AND IT'S MINE! MINE!
2.

BUT I STILL DON'T UNDERSTAND!
WHY DID YOU ALLOW SPIDER-MAN TO FOLLOW US??
BECAUSE I WANT HIM TO FIND ME!
HOW ELSE CAN I DESTROY HIM?
IT WILL SAVE ME THE TROUBLE OF HUNTING HIM!
THE FOOL IS AS YET UNAWARE... THAT I AM HIS MASTER!
BUT THE WEB-SLINGER IS TRICKY...
WHAT DOES IT MATTER? AM I NOT MORE POWERFUL?
SPIDER-MAN WOULDN'T HAVE A CHANCE AGAINST THE BOSS!
RIGHT! HE'LL MAKE MINCE-MEAT OUTTA HIM!
THE KINGPIN AIN'T SCARED'A NOBODY!
...EXCEPT HIS MISSUS!
I HEARD THAT!
WHA... WHAT'D I SAY, BOSS??!
YOU MENTIONED MY WIFE!
ZAP!
NOBODY MENTIONS HER... EVER... DO YOU HEAR??
NOBODY!
GET RID OF HIM! HE'S WASHED UP HERE!
HE'S LUCKY... I LET HIM LIVE!
3.

WAIT THERE, WILSON! I'M GOING TO TO STORE THE TABLET!
BUT, WHAT ABOUT... SPIDER-MAN?
STOP CRINGING, YOU SPINELESS WORM!
I'LL BE BACK BEFORE HE ARRIVES!
TO THINK THAT WORTHLESS GUTTER RAT WOULD DARE TO MENTION MY WIFE!!
BUT, I HAD BEST NOT DWELL UPON IT!
THIS IS NO TIME FOR ME TO FLY INTO A RAGE!
NOW, MORE THAN EVER, I MUST HAVE MY WITS ABOUT ME!
THE DOOR TO MY VAULT REQUIRES NO LOCK WHICH SOME PETTY THIEF CAN ONE DAY OPEN!
ONLY THE KINGPIN'S NAKED STRENGTH CAN ACCOMPLISH SUCH A FEAT!
BUT, WHY SPEND ANY MORE TIME LISTENING TO OL' K.P. TALK TO HIMSELF WHEN WE COULD BE LISTENING TO J. JONAH JAMESON INSTEAD..?
THE BUGLE WANTS TO KNOW IF THOSE YOUNG ANARCHISTS WILL BE PUNISHED, STACY!
THAT'S A STRONG WORD FOR A GROUP OF YOUTH-FUL DEMONSTRATORS, JAMESON!
THEY HELPED THE KINGPIN STEAL THAT TABLET---AND YOU KNOW IT!
I'M AFRAID I HAVEN'T YOUR INSIGHT---OR PERCEPTION!
MEANWHILE, INSIDE THE PRECINCT INTERROGATION ROOM, WE FIND---
IF YOU BOYS WEREN'T PART OF THE KINGPIN'S PLAN ---
THEN WHY DID YOU BOTH PICK THAT SAME MOMENT TO BE AT THE EXHIBITION HALL?
EASY, SON! THE LIEUTENANT IS JUST TRYING TO DO HIS JOB!
WE WERE FIGHTING FOR STUDENTS' RIGHTS--- AND THAT'S ALL!!
DON'T MAKE US YOUR FALL GUYS!
4.

WHAT ABOUT SPIDER-MAN, RANDY? WHERE DOES HE FIT INTO ALL OF THIS?
I TOLD YOU, DAD! HE FOUGHT THE KINGPIN! HE SAVED MY LIFE!
OKAY, THEN! LET'S GET BACK TO YOU..!
HOW'D YOU GET MIXED-UP IN THIS WHOLE THING?
I DID WHAT I THOUGHT WAS RIGHT, DAD... LIKE YOU ALWAYS SAID I SHOULD!
WE WANT THE HALL CONVERTED TO A LOW-RENT DORM... FOR NEEDY STUDENTS!
BUT THE DEAN WOULDN'T LISTEN TO US!
A PROTEST IS ONE THING!
BUT, THE DAMAGE YOU CAUSED..!
BUT DON'T WORRY, SON! YOUR MOM AND I WILL STAND BEHIND YOU!
WE WON'T LET YOU DOWN... WHEN YOU NEED US!
I JUST HAVE TO FIGURE OUT ...HOW TO BREAK IT TO HER!
YOU'RE TALKING...AS THOUGH I DID ...SOMETHING AWFUL!
DON'T YOU SEE? CAN'T YOU EVEN UNDERSTAND? I HAVE TO BE TOUGHER... I HAVE TO BE MORE MILITANT ...BECAUSE OF YOU!
YOU'VE BECOME PART OF THE ESTABLISHMENT... THE WHITE MAN'S ESTABLISHMENT!
I'VE GOTTA LIVE THAT DOWN!
BUT ISN'T THIS WHAT WE ALL WANT... WHAT WE'RE ALL FIGHTING FOR, BOY?
TO MAKE IT ON OUR OWN? TO PROVE WE'RE AS GOOD... OR BETTER... THAN ANYONE??
I DUNNO! I DUNNO WHAT TO THINK!
LOOK, MAN... MAYBE YOU'RE AN OKAY CAT... BUT WE GOTTA DO THINGS OUR WAY!
WE AIN'T NEVER GONNA GET NOWHERE... UNTIL WE KINDA SHAKE WHITEY UP A LITTLE!
HOW'S A MAN TO KNOW... WHAT'S RIGHT?
I WISH... I COULD ANSWER THAT, SON!
LISTEN! SOMETHING'S GOING ON... OUTSIDE!
COOK AN EGG... COOK YOUR GOOSE! TURN THE DEMONSTRATORS LOOSE!
C'MON, BREAK IT UP... BREAK IT UP!
GOWAN HOME, KIDS! THE PARTY'S OVER!
5

THIS WON'T HELP! YOU'RE ALL MAKING THINGS WORSE!
GETTING OURSELVES ARRESTED WON'T GIVE US THE LOW-RENT DORM WE NEED!
OKAY, BEAUTIFUL! GOT ANY BETTER IDEAS?
HEY! IT'S GWEN STACY!
WHERE'S YOUR CHICKEN BOY FRIEND, LADY?
LET OUR LEADERS GO
HE HASN'T THE GUTS TO TAKE A STAND WITH US!
YOU SAID PETER PARKER DOESN'T HAVE GUTS?!!
YEAH... IT'S PARKER I'M TALKIN' ABOUT!
...AND YOU BETTER BELIEVE IT!
YOU CRUMMY, DIM-WITTED LOUDMOUTH!
HE COULD BE HALF THE MAN HE IS...
AND STILL MAKE TEN OF YOU!
POLICE
SAY, TAKE IT EASY, LITTLE GIRL!
YOU DON'T WANNA BE ACCUSED OF CIVILIAN BRUTALITY!
OH, GWEN STACY! I DIDN'T RECOGNIZE YOU!
I'M GOING IN...TO SEE MY FATHER!
GWEN! I DIDN'T THINK YOU'D BE HERE!
WHY NOT? I MAY BE YOUR DAUGHTER... BUT I'M STILL A CO-ED AT E.S.U.!
WHOA THERE, YOUNG LADY!
WHAT'S GOT YOU ALL STEAMED UP?
JUST SOME FEATHER-BRAINED LUNKHEAD OUTSIDE!
DID HE GET FRESH WITH YOU?
HIM? HE WOULDN'T DARE!
NO... HE SAID SOME ROTTEN THINGS... ABOUT PETER!
ARE YOU UPSET... BECAUSE YOU THINK THEY MAY BE TRUE?
I... WISH I KNEW!
6

BUT NOW, IT'S WEB-SLINGING TIME AGAIN...
THIS IS IT!
THE WAY I'M TINGLING...
HE HAS TO BE IN THERE!
IT'LL TAKE MORE THAN STEEL SHUTTERS TO...
NO! WAIT..!!
MY SPIDEY SENSE IS TINGLING TOO VIOLENTLY!
SOMETHING'S WRONG!
WHY DID HE LEAVE SUCH AN EASY TRAIL TO FOLLOW?
THE KINGPIN'S TOO SMART FOR THAT!
UNLESS ...IT'S A TRAP!
WHILE, IN THE DARKENED ROOM INSIDE...
BOSS, DO YOU THINK...?
QUIET, YOU FOOL!
HE'LL BE HERE ANY MINUTE!
JUST STAND THERE... AND WAIT!
I PROMISE YOU WON'T BE... DISAPPOINTED!
7.

THE SHUTTERS... THEY'RE OPENIN'!!
LOOK! THERE HE IS!
IT'S HIM! IT'S THE WALL-CRAWLER! WE GOT 'IM AT LAST!
YOU WERE RIGHT, KINGPIN!
IT WORKED OUT... JUST LIKE YOU SAID!
WAIT... YOU TRIGGER-HAPPY FOOLS!
HOLD YOUR FIRE!
TOO LATE!
WE ALREADY GOT 'IM!
I TOLD YOU I WANTED TO DOWN HIM MYSELF!
YOUR PURPOSE WAS MERELY TO PREVENT HIS ESCAPE!
I SHOULD HAVE KNOWN YOU'D PANIC AND...
WAIT! WHAT'S THAT?!!
IT... IT AIN'T HIM!
IT'S JUST... A WEBBED-UP DUMMY!
8

THWIP!
JUST WHOM ARE YOU CALLING A DUMMY?
LOOK OUT!
IF THAT WAS MEANT AS A WARNING TO ME, I'M ALL SHOOK-UP!
BUT YOU DIDN'T HAVETA DO IT!
SINCE IT'S TIME FOR FUN 'N GAMES,
LET'S ALL DROP OUR POP-GUNS!
THEY'RE LIABLE TO GIVE YOU CALLOUSED TRIGGER-FINGERS!
NOT TO MENTION DISHPAN HANDS!
DON'T BE IMPATIENT, K.P.! I'LL GET TO YOU IN A MINUTE!
...SOON AS YOUR LITTLE CHEERING SECTION GOES SLEEPY-BYE!
DON'T WORRY, SPIDER-MAN!... I'VE WAITED TOO LONG FOR THIS MOMENT TO RUSH IT NOW!
9.

UNHHH! HOW...DID HE MANAGE ...TO MOVE SO FAST??
HIS GRIP... LIKE BEING CAUGHT...IN TWO GIANT, LIVING VISES!
DURING ALL OUR PREVIOUS ENCOUNTERS!..
YOU ALWAYS MANAGED TO ESCAPE THRU SOME LUCKY ACCIDENT!
BUT THIS TIME I SHALL EXERCISE FAR MORE CAUTION...
THIS TIME WE BATTLE... TO THE END!
HE'S TOSSING ME TOWARDS THE WEB DUMMY!
THE GOOEY SUBSTANCE... IS STICKING... TO MY BARE SKIN!
IT'S WHAT HE WANTED!
HE'S GETTING SET... TO CHARGE!!
LOOK AT YOU...YOU PUNY PARODY OF A PRESENT-DAY SUPER-HERO!
10.

AND NOW... WHILE YOU'RE HOPELESSLY CAUGHT IN A WEB OF YOUR OWN MAKING...
I'LL SET YOU FREE... IN MY OWN... WHA..?!!
YOU SNIVELLING, SCRAWNY SCARECROW!! YOU'RE ONLY PROLONGING YOUR ULTIMATE ANNIHILATION!
HOW LONG DO YOU THINK YOU CAN KEEP DODGING ME?
THOOOM!
FACE IT, FATS... I'VE GOT TO KEEP DODGING YOU...
...AT LEAST TILL YOU CHANGE YOUR MOUTHWASH!
A JESTER TILL THE END, EH?
WELL, THAT'S FITTING, INDEED...
FOR THIS WILL BE YOUR END!!
I ALWAYS THOUGHT FAT FELLAS WERE SUPPOSED TO BE JOLLY!
THEY OUGHTTA TOSS YOU OUT OF THE UNION!
FAK!
UMMFFF!
11.

JUST WHAT I NEEDED..!
A FEW-SECOND BREATHER SO I CAN PUT ON MY SHIRT!
ANYWAY, I'M ALMOST FREE OF THE WEBBING BY NOW!
COSTUMING YOURSELF AGAIN, I SEE!
WELL, IT IS ONLY FITTING THAT YOU LOSE YOUR FINAL BATTLE ---SUITABLY ATTIRED!
PTAMM
MUCH OBLIGED, SKINHEAD!
NICE OF YOU TO JAR ME LOOSE AGAIN!
MY NEXT BLOW WILL JAR YOU---OUT OF EXISTENCE!
SEE HOW EASILY I CAN SWAT YOU OFF THE WALL...
---LIKE THE PUNY INSECT YOU ARE!
ZPAK
BIG DEAL! I WAS CUTTING OUT ANYWAY!
12

BUT HOW ABOUT I TAKE YOU WITH ME, DAD?
SHUCKS! I'LL BET YOU DIDN'T EVEN FEEL THAT!
...YOU ONLY LANDED ON YOUR HEAD!
FEELS LIKE HE WEIGHS A TON!
BUT IT'S NOT FAT... IT'S ALL MUSCLE!!
BTAM!
AND NOW... IT'S MY TURN!
YOU JUST MADE YOUR FIRST FATAL MISTAKE!
BY GETTING CLOSE ENOUGH FOR ME TO GRAB YOU!
...AND THIS TIME I SHALL NOT LET GO...
...TILL SPIDER-MAN IS A THREAT NO LONGER!
EVEN WITH... MY SPIDEY STRENGTH... I CAN'T... TAKE MUCH MORE... OF THIS!!
HAVE TO DO SOME-THING... ANY-THING... FAST!!
13

THE PRESSURE... IS... TOO MUCH!
NEVER... BEEN SO... HELPLESS... BEFORE!!
THIS IS HOW IT HAD TO END!
UHHHH
NO ONE CAN MATCH THE KINGPIN'S STRENGTH!
AT LAST... THERE CAN BE NO DOUBT THAT I'M THE VICTOR!
SPIDER-MAN HAS FINALLY MET HIS MASTER!
14

KINGPIN... LOOK OUT!
HE WAS ONLY PLAYING POSSUM!
TOO LATE! HE FELL FOR IT LIKE A TON OF BRICKS!
WHUUPPFFF!
OR, SHOULD I SAY... A BAG OF BLUBBER?
HE'S DOWN! BUT, FOR HOW LONG?
MY HAND IS ALMOST COMPLETELY NUMB!
HAVE TO KEEP RUBBING IT... MAKE THE BLOOD CIRCULATE!
GOT YOU, YOU BLUNDERING FOOL!
TWO CAN PLAY YOUR LITTLE GAME!
BTOK!
15

NOW I'LL FINISH WHERE WE LEFT OFF!
BUT THIS TIME I'LL BE LESS MERCIFUL!
COME OFF IT! A FLORENCE NIGHTINGALE YOU NEVER WERE!
HAVE TO PLAY FOR TIME...TILL THE NUMBNESS PASSES!
THWAP!
RUNNING WON'T HELP!
MY CANE WILL PICK YOU OFF THE WALL...
...LIKE THE HUMAN INSECT YOU TRULY ARE!
THANKS FOR THE WARNING, SKINHEAD!
I'LL DO AS MUCH FOR YOU SOME TIME!
PATHUPPPPP
PERFECT TIMING!
WHA..?!!
CLICK!
ARGHHH!
BTOOOM!
HIS CANE-GUN BACK-FIRED, AND...
UH OH! ONE OF HIS STOOGES...MAKING A BEE-LINE OUT OF HERE!
BUT, WHERE'S HE HEADING?
16

IF HE WAS TRYING TO ESCAPE... HE'D BE GOING THE OTHER WAY!
BUT, HE'S NOT...WHICH JUST MIGHT MEAN ONE THING...
HE COULD BE AFTER THE STOLEN TABLET!
THE KINGPIN'LL HAVE TO KEEP!
RIGHT NOW, THE TABLET IS MORE IMPORTANT!
WHILE OUTSIDE, AT THAT MOMENT...
THAT'S RIGHT, SARGE! I SPOTTED THE KINGPIN'S CAR OVER THERE...
AND THEN I HEARD A SHOT---FROM INSIDE THE BUILDING!
ALL RIGHT, MEN! WHAT ARE WE WAITING FOR?
THERE HE IS! WE FOUND 'IM!
QUICK! GET THE CUFFS ON HIM WHILE HE'S STILL GROGGY!
THE POLICE! ...THEY'LL NEVER BE ABLE TO HOLD ME!
BUT I WON'T YET RESIST! I'VE SOMETHING THAT MUST BE DONE FIRST...!
WHERE'S THE TABLET, KING-PIN? WE KNOW YOU'VE GOT IT!
DO YOU THINK I'D KEEP IT HERE---WHERE IT COULD INCRIMINATE ME?
UNTIL YOU FIND IT, YOU'LL NEVER BE ABLE TO PROVE MY GUILT!
AND, BY NOW, MY WEB-SWINGING ALLY HAS TAKEN IT SAFELY AWAY FROM HERE!
...JUST AS HE WILL FREE ME FROM CAPTIVITY--- WHEN THE TIME IS RIPE!
THEN JAMESON WAS RIGHT! SPIDER-MAN'S IN THIS AS DEEP AS YOU!
WITH A FEW CHOICE WORDS, I'VE SEALED THE WALL-CRAWLER'S DOOM!
17.

MEANWHILE, UNAWARE OF HOW DEEPLY HE'S BEEN IMPLICATED, SPIDEY CONTINUES TO DO HIS THING...
NO ONE CAN OPEN IT THE WAY THE KINGPIN COULD---
BUT, IF I CAN FIND MYSELF ENOUGH EX-PLOSIVES..!!
DON'T BOTHER, BRIGHT BOY!
WHO..??!
THERE! THAT'LL KEEP YOU ALL COMFY-COZY!
NO WONDER NO ONE CAN OPEN THIS THING---
THERE'S NO LOCK TO JIMMY! NO COMBINATION! NOTHING!
WHICH MEANS THAT TUBBY MUST HAVE USED RAW STRENGTH!
JUST EXACTLY LIKE...
THIS!!
18

AND NOW... IF MY HUNCH WAS RIGHT...
YEP! THERE IT IS!
IT'S HARD TO BELIEVE THAT THIS PETRIFIED STONE IS ONE OF THE MOST VALUABLE OBJECTS ON EARTH!
I WONDER IF THEY'LL EVER LEARN WHAT THESE HIERO-GLYPHICS MEAN?
WAIT! YOU CAN'T LEAVE ME HERE!
DON'T BET ON IT, MISTER!
THE COPS'LL PICK HIM UP BEFORE HE GETS TOO LONELY!
THEN, SECONDS LATER, AFTER FINDING THE KINGPIN GONE...
WOW! THE BLUECOATS HAVE LANDED ALREADY!
DIDN'T TAKE THEM LONG TO MAKE THE SCENE!
NOW I WON'T HAVE TO CARRY THE TABLET ALL OVER TOWN!
HOLD IT, GANG! I'VE GOT SOME-THING FOR YOU!
IT'S SPIDER-MAN!
HE'S OUT TO FREE THE KINGPIN!
WATCH IT! HE'S GONNA TOSS SOME-THING AT US!
SPAKK
THEY'RE FIRING AT ME!!
GIVE YOURSELF UP...OR OUR NEXT SHOT WON'T MISS!
19.

WHERE'D HE GO?
HE SWUNG AROUND... OUT OF THE LINE OF FIRE...
SO! NO MATTER WHAT I DO...
NOTHING EVER CHANGES!
THE MORE I TRY TO HELP THE LAW...
THE MORE THEY HUNT ME... THE MORE THEY HATE ME!
OKAY, THEN---IF THAT'S HOW THEY WANT IT...
I'M THRU BEING A PUBLIC FALL GUY!
FROM NOW ON... IT'S SPIDEY AGAINST THE WORLD!
IF THEY CALL ME A MENACE... AND TREAT ME LIKE A MENACE...
I MIGHT AS WELL BE A MENACE!
NEXT:
POINT OF NO RETURN!

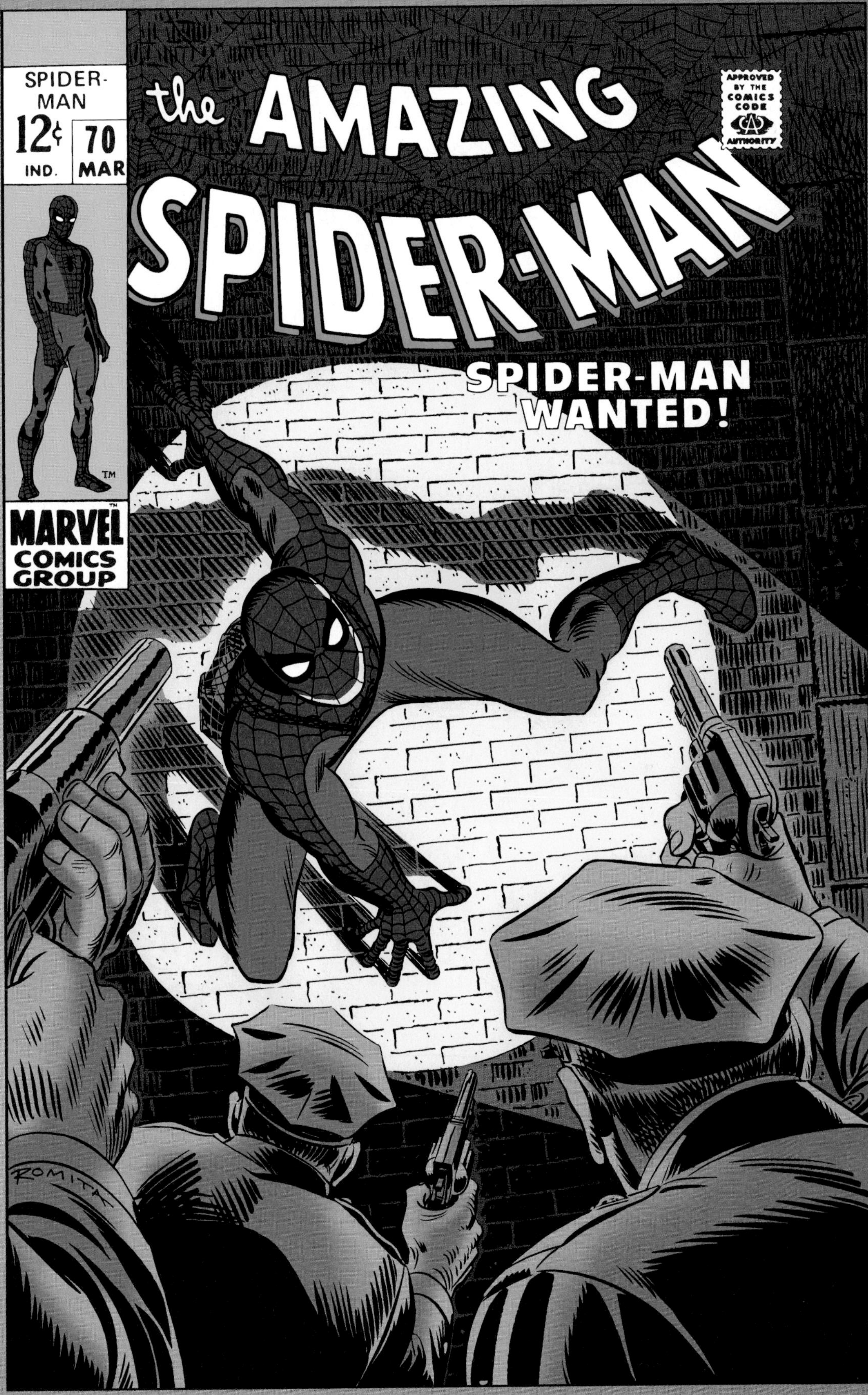
SPIDER-MAN
12¢
70
IND.
MAR
MARVEL COMICS GROUP
the AMAZING SPIDER-MAN
APPROVED BY THE COMICS CODE AUTHORITY
SPIDER-MAN WANTED!
ROMITA

THE AMAZING SPIDER-MAN!™
BUGLE
SPIDER-MAN WANTED!
THE WEATHER
MAKES OFF WITH PRICELESS CLAY TABLET AS POLICE APPREHEND HIS PARTNER, THE KINGPIN!
I'VE GOT TO GET OUT OF HERE! I'VE GOT TO CATCH THE WEB-SLINGER!
THE TABLET IS MINE! NO ONE ELSE CAN HAVE IT!
NO MATTER WHERE HE HOLES UP... I'LL FIND HIM... AND DESTROY HIM!
FANTASTICALLY FABRICATED BY: STAN (THE MAN) LEE, AUTHOR! JOHN (RING-A-DING) ROMITA, INNOVATOR! JIM (MAD-MAN) MOONEY, ILLUSTRATOR! SAM (ROSY) ROSEN, LETTERER!

SAVE YOUR BREATH, KINGPIN! YOUR DES-TROYING DAYS ARE OVER!
SOON AS WE CAN GET A PRISON SUIT BIG ENOUGH TO FIT YOU, YOU'LL JUST BE A NUMBER AROUND HERE!
ANYWAY, SPIDER-MAN'S YOUR PARTNER, ISN'T HE? SO WHY THE GRIPE?
HE RAN OFF AND LEFT ME... THAT'S THE GRIPE!
WAIT'LL I GET MY HANDS ON HIM!!
I FORGOT! I'VE CONVINCED EVERYONE THAT THE WALL-CRAWLER HELPED ME STEAL THE TABLET!
MUSTN'T GIVE THEM CAUSE FOR DOUBT!
HAH! LOOK AT 'IM--- THE GREAT, BIG KINGPIN!
THOUGHT YA WERE A BIG MAN, HUH...PUTTIN' ME DOWN JUST 'CAUSE I MENTIONED YER WIFE!*
YOU INSIGNIFICANT WORM! I COULD HAVE GROUND YOU INTO THE DUST HAD I WANTED TO!
HEY! SHUDDUP, YA FOOL! IF HE EVER ESCAPES...!
*IT HAPPENED LAST ISH, FORGETFUL ONE!...STAN.
ESCAPE? OF COURSE I'LL ESCAPE!
AND THEN, JUST IMAGINE YOURSELVES... HELPLESS IN THE KING-PIN'S GRIP!
HOW COME YOU'RE NO LONGER LAUGHING!
HE WUZ ONLY KIDDIN', KINGPIN---HONEST! YOU KNOW HOW SOME GUYS ARE ALWAYS SHOOTIN' OFF THEIR MOUTHS!
SPARE ME YOUR COWARDLY WHIMPER-ING! I HAVE THINK-ING TO DO!
I HAVE TO WORK THE BARS LOOSE...WITHOUT ANYONE NOTICING!
I'LL ACT AS THOUGH I'M GRIPPING THEM IN FRUSTRATED RAGE!
AND, ALL THE WHILE, I'LL BE SLOWLY TWISTING---AND TURNING THEM!
2.

MEANWHILE, WHAT OF OUR WONDROUS, THOUGH WOE-BEGONE WEB-SPINNER--?
FOR ONCE I THOUGHT EVERY-THING HAD TURNED OUT A-OKAY!
I HAD HELPED CATCH THE KING-PIN... AND SAVED THE TABLET, WHICH I WANTED TO RETURN TO THE EXHIBITION HALL!
BUT THAT FAT FOUL-UP CONVINCED THE POLICE THAT I'M IN LEAGUE WITH HIM...
AND, SINCE THEY KNOW MY POWER, THEY HAVE ORDERS TO SHOOT ME ON SIGHT!
SO NOTHING'S WORKED OUT RIGHT! POOR RANDY, AND THE OTHER KIDS WHO LED THE CAMPUS PROTEST, ENDED UP GETTING BOOKED...
AND EVEN THEY WERE SUSPECTED OF HAVING SOME ULTERIOR MOTIVES!
NOW, FROM THE LOOKS OF THINGS, I'LL NEVER HAVE A CHANCE TO RETURN THIS CRUMMY TABLET!
THWIP!
BUT FROM NOW ON, THINGS'LL BE PLENTY DIFFERENT!
I'M SICK'N TIRED OF BEING A FRIENDLY, NEIGHBOR-HOOD FALL GUY!
3.

IF EVER ANYONE HAD AN EXCUSE TO REALLY TURN BAD...
SPIDEY'S THE GUY!
OR, AM I JUST TRYING TO JUSTIFY MY CRIME...?
LIKE ANY OTHER CRIMINAL!
WATCH IT, SPIDEY! ...ALMOST SLIPPED JUST THEN!
AN INCH FURTHER ---AND I WOULDN'T HAVE MADE IT!
WHY DO I KEEP RISKING IT?
WHY??
EVERY TIME I SQUEEZE INTO THIS CORNY SPIDEY SUIT, I'M TAKING MY LIFE IN MY HANDS!
AND FOR WHAT?? THAT'S WHAT BUGS ME... FOR WHAT??
C'MON NOW, WEB-HEAD...GET HOLD OF YOURSELF!
IF I KEEP UP THIS NUTTY SOUL-SEARCHING, I'LL BE A CANDIDATE FOR THE FUNNY FARM!
THE FIRST THING FOR ME TO DO IS FIND A PLACE FOR THIS..!
I'M NOT ABOUT TO CARRY IT FOREVER!
4

BUT I'M NOT LEAVING IT ON ANY ROOFTOP, EITHER!
IT'S DARK ENOUGH NOW FOR ME TO HIT THE STREET AND... UH OH!!
SOMETHING'S WRONG! MY SPIDEY SENSE IS TINGLING LIKE MAD!
GUNFIRE! SOMEONE'S SHOOTING AT ME!
KRAK!
FZAK!
HE'S SHOOTING WIDE--- JUST TRYING TO GET ME DOWN!
KRAK!
GIVE YOURSELF UP, MISTER!
I'D RATHER TAKE YOU ALIVE!
FUNNY... THAT'S JUST THE WAY I FEEL ABOUT IT!
I NEVER COULD STAND THE SIGHT OF BLOOD!
...SPECIALLY MINE!
BLAP!
5.

YOU CAN'T ESCAPE US FOREVER!
BUT THERE'S NO HARM IN TRYING!
LOOKS LIKE IT'S BACK TO THE ROOF-TOPS FOR ME---
...WHETHER I LIKE IT OR NOT!
BOY! WHAT A PRIZE CHUMP I AM!
WHY AM I KNOCKING MYSELF OUT THIS WAY?
THERE'S ONLY ONE PERFECT PLACE TO HIDE THE TABLET...
AND I SHOULD HAVE THOUGHT OF IT RIGHT AWAY!
NOBODY'S EVER GONNA BOTHER TO LOOK IN THE PRIVATE CLOSET OF PETER PARKER, BOY SOPHO-MORE!
IT'S LUCKY FOR ME THAT HE'S DATING M.J. TONIGHT!
EVEN HARRY THINKS I JUST KEEP IT STUFFED WITH WORTHLESS OLD CHEM LAB EQUIPMENT!
EVEN TO HIM, A PETRIFIED TABLET MIGHT HAVE SEEMED A LITTLE BIT MUCH!
CLICK!
NOW I HAVEN'T A WORRY IN THE WORLD!
...EXCEPT WHAT I'D DO IF SOMEONE DOES FIND THE STOLEN TABLET HIDDEN IN MY CLOSET!
OR, IF ANYONE FIGURES OUT THAT SPIDEY IS REALLY MRS. PARKER'S FAIR-HAIRED NEPHEW!
OR, IF I HAVE TO FACE THE KINGPIN AGAIN---AND HE SQUASHES ME!!
YEP! LIFE SURE IS A MILLION LAUGHS!
...FOR THE OTHER GUY!
6

AND, LONG INTO THE NIGHT, AS SLEEP ELUDES THE TROUBLED YOUTH...
I HAVEN'T EVEN HAD A CHANCE TO LOOK IN ON AUNT MAY...
TO SEE HOW SHE'S FEELING NOW!
AS FOR JOLLY JONAH, HIS PAPER IS MORE ANTI-SPIDEY THAN EVER BEFORE!
AND HOW DO I EXPLAIN MY DISAPPEARANCE TO GWEN?
...OR TO HER DAD...WHO'S SHARPER THAN ANYONE KNOWS!
AND WHAT ABOUT JOE ROBERTSON... RANDY... JOSH... AND THE OTHERS?
NOT TO MENTION THE KINGPIN... WHOM I CAN'T FORGET!
OH, BROTHER! AM I IN GREAT SHAPE!
FINALLY, AS THE FIRST, FAINT, FLICKERING FINGERS OF DAWN BEGIN TO STEAL ACROSS THE AWAKENING CITY...
THE MORE I RISK MY LIFE... THE MORE DEADLY CHANCES I TAKE...
THE LESS GOOD IT SEEMS TO DO!
WITH ALL MY STRENGTH ...WITH ALL MY POWERS...
WHY CAN'T I EVER MAKE THINGS RIGHT?
AND, A FEW HOURS LATER...
WELL, AT LEAST I ACCOMPLISHED ONE THING...
I STOPPED THE KINGPIN FROM COPPING THE TABLET!
BUT NOW THAT I HAVE IT--
WHAT DO I DO WITH IT?
PETER!!
I'VE BEEN LOOKING ALL OVER FOR YOU!
SAY! DID YOU TAKE ZOMBIE PILLS THIS A.M.?
I'M OKAY, GWENDY!
JUST A LITTLE TIRED, I GUESS!
TOO TIRED TO PICK UP A PHONE, MR. PARKER?
7.

ACCORDING TO THE OTHER KIDS, YOU SHOULD BE EXHAUSTED...
FROM CHICKENING OUT WHENEVER IT'S TIME TO TAKE A STAND FOR SOMETHING!
SOMETIMES I WONDER IF THEY AREN'T RIGHT!
HOW CAN I TELL HER? WHENEVER THERE'S TROUBLE, PETER PARKER HAS TO LOOK LIKE A COP-OUT...
IN ORDER FOR SPIDER-MAN TO MAKE THE SCENE!
THE LEAST YOU COULD DO IS TRY TO FUMBLE FOR AN EXCUSE, MAN!
I WAS A FOOL TO THINK THAT ANYONE COULD LOVE ME ENOUGH--- TO TRUST ME BLINDLY!
OKAY THEN... STAND THERE CHEWING YOUR CUD!
THERE MUST BE A REASON FOR THAT DISAPPEARING ACT OF YOURS... AND I'LL WAIT TILL YOU LEVEL WITH ME!
LIKE I SHOULD HAVE MY HEAD EXAMINED --- BUT MAYBE I'M JUST TOO DUMB TO WRITE YOU OFF!
SHE DOES LOVE ME! SHE DOES TRUST ME!
HEY! YOU'RE CRYING! WHAT BROUGHT THAT ON?
SKIP IT, MR. PARKER! IT'S JUST NO FUN... LOSING YOUR STUPID HEART... TO SOMEONE WHO'S ALWAYS MAKING LIKE... A COWARD!
A COWARD!! YOU THINK I'M A COWARD??!
DON'T... MAKE ME ANSWER THAT... PETER!
BUT, HERE'S A GENT WHO WANTS AN ANSWER...
A FINE THING WHEN I HAVE TO COMB THE TOWN, LOOKING FOR MY OWN CITY EDITOR!
WHAT IN BLAZES ARE YOU DOING HERE, ROBERTSON?
I'VE BEEN WAITING FOR NEWS OF THE CAMPUS PROTESTERS, JJ!
THEY'RE INSIDE NOW... HAVING A MEETING WITH THE DEAN!
HAVE YOU LOST YOUR MARBLES, MISTER?
THAT BLASTED WALL-CRAWLER IS STILL AT LARGE ...WITH HALF THE POLICE FORCE OUT TO GET HIM!
SO LONG AS MY SON IS INVOLVED, NOBODY COVERS THIS STORY BUT ME!
IF YOU WANT SPIDER-MAN ...GO FIND HIM YOURSELF!
THAT'S WHERE THE NEWS IS, ROBBIE! ANYONE CAN COVER THIS KID STUFF!
YOU.. YOU CAN'T TALK TO ME THAT WAY!
DON'T BET ON IT!
8

WHILE, INSIDE THE WALNUT-PANELLED CONFERENCE ROOM...
DEAN CORLISS HAS A STATEMENT TO MAKE!
I'M PLEASED TO ANNOUNCE THAT THE TRUSTEES HAVE JUST VOTED TO CONVERT THE EXHIBITION HALL INTO A LOW-RENT DORM FOR NEEDY STUDENTS!
IT'S WHAT WE WERE FIGHTING FOR! THAT MEANS... WE WON!
IT'S A HOLLOW VICTORY, SON! ALL THIS TURMOIL WASN'T NECESSARY!
DEAN CORLISS WAS ON YOUR SIDE ALL THE TIME!
THEN WHY DIDN'T HE TELL US?
WHY DID HE REFUSE TO MEET US?
I'M NOT BLAMELESS IN THIS MATTER!
I THOUGHT STUDENTS SHOULD BE SEEN, AND NOT HEARD!
I REALIZE NOW... HOW MISTAKEN I WAS!
THEN, MAYBE EVERYBODY WON... A LITTLE!
SINCE NO DAMAGE WAS DONE... AND THEY HAD NOTHING TO DO WITH THE THEFT OF THE TABLET...
THE DEAN RECOMMENDED AMNESTY FOR ALL THE PROTESTORS!
BUT WHAT ABOUT THE MAIN ISSUE ...THE LOW RENT DORM?
WE GOT IT, DAD! JUST LIKE YOU SAID WE WOULD!
I KNEW DEAN CORLISS WAS IN FAVOR OF IT ALL THE TIME!
BUT HE HAD AN UP-HILL FIGHT TO CONVINCE THE TRUSTEES!
SOMETIMES IT ISN'T EASY TO TELL... WHO YOUR REAL FRIENDS ARE!
I SURE HAD YOU PEGGED WRONG, MR. ROBERTSON!
EVEN IF YOU WORK FOR WHITEY... YOU'RE A RIGHT CAT IN MY BOOK!
MAYBE... THERE'S A LOTTA THINGS ...I GOTTA THINK ABOUT SOME MORE!
AND HERE'S SOMETHING FOR US TO THINK ABOUT... ALL 300 POUNDS OF HIM...
I'VE DONE IT! THE BARS ARE LOOSE ENOUGH TO PULL OUT NOW!
I'VE ONLY TO WAIT FOR THE RIGHT MOMENT!
9.

AND, SINCE STAN AND JOHNNY ARE AS IMPATIENT AS THE KINGPIN, THE RIGHT MOMENT ISN'T VERY LONG IN COMING---
NOW!
HE DID IT! HE'S OUT!
WAIT! YOU... YOU CAN'T GO WITHOUT US!
THINK SO? JUST WATCH AND SEE!
THOOM!
THUMP!
LISTEN! WHAT'S THAT NOISE IN THERE?
SOUNDS LIKE A RUNAWAY HIPPO THUNDERING DOWN THE CORRIDOR!
WE'D BETTER CHECK IT OUT!
THOOM!
THOOM!
IT'S THE KINGP- OOF!!
I THANK YOU FOR THE LODGINGS...
BUT I NEVER OVERSTAY MY WELCOME!
10.

NOW, NOTHING MUST STOP ME FROM RETRIEVING THAT TABLET FROM THE MASKED WEB-SPINNER!
AND ONCE I MAKE IT PAST THE NEXT GATE... NOTHING SHALL!!
SECONDS LATER...
NOTIFY THE GOVERNOR! SEND OUT AN ALL-POINTS!
THE KING-PIN'S ESCAPED!
MEANWHILE, WHAT OF SPIDEY? (WE'RE SURE GLAD YOU ASKED!)
I SHOULD HAVE THOUGHT OF THIS LONG AGO!
THE TABLET CAN'T DO ME ANY GOOD GETTING DUSTY IN MY CLOSET!
BUT, IF I CAN LEARN WHAT THE INSCRIPTION SAYS..!
THERE'S A FORTUNE WAITING FOR THE MAN WHO DECIPHERS IT!
AND IT MIGHT AS WELL BE ME!
OF COURSE, I'LL NEED SOME HELP...
SO I LOOKED UP THE BIGGEST AUTHORITY ON HIEROGLYPHICS IN TOWN!
HIS STUDIO IS RIGHT BELOW ME...!
ARCH
IF I CAN JUST GET HIM TO---
WAIT!! WHAT'S THIS?!!
A SPOTLIGHT!! IT'S THE POLICE!
11.

I SHOULD HAVE GUESSED THEY'D HAVE A STAKE-OUT FOR ME HERE!
THE KINGPIN! HE MUST HAVE ESCAPED AGAIN!
SURROUND THE BUILDING!
IF SPIDER-MAN'S HERE...THE KING-PIN MAY BE HOLED UP INSIDE!
WHICH MEANS I'M IN GREATER DANGER THAN EVER!
THEY PROBABLY THINK I HELPED HIM ESCAPE!
ZAK!
WELL, I'M THRU WAITING FOR TROUBLE TO COME TO ME..!
THIS TIME I DON'T REST TILL I FIND THE KINGPIN!
AND I KNOW JUST THE WAY TO DO IT!
12

I'VE GOT TO TACKLE EVERY CHEAP HOOD I FIND DOWN BELOW!
IT WON'T TAKE LONG FOR THE KINGPIN TO HEAR THAT I'M ON A ONE-MAN WEB-SWINGING BINGE!
AND IF THAT DOESN'T SMOKE HIM OUT... NOTHING WILL!
WELL, WELL! JUST WHAT I'M LOOKING FOR!
A FEW OF KINGY'S EX-TORPEDOES!
LOOK OUT! IT'S SPIDER-MAN!
HOLD IT, GROUP! LET'S HAVE A HAPPEN-ING!
THAT'LL DO THE TRICK!
--SPECIALLY SINCE I MADE SURE THEY'D SEE THE TABLET ON MY BACK!
BUT, WHETHER IT'S BECAUSE HE WANTS TO LEAVE NO STONE UNTURNED, OR BECAUSE OF THE NAKED RAGE SEETHING IN HIS BREAST...
...THE WONDROUS WEB-SPINNER CONTINUES HIS "POUNCE-ON-THE-PUNKS" CAMPAIGN WITH EVER-MOUNTING FURY...!
WHOP!
13.

...UNTIL, AT LAST, HIGH ABOVE THE VERY HEART OF THE SLUMBERING METROPOLIS...
THE KINGPIN SHOULD HAVE SHOWN HIS HAND BY NOW!
HE MUST HAVE BEEN TOLD THAT I'M CARRYING THE TABLET!
AND I'M BETTING HE'LL DO ANYTHING TO GET IT BACK!
WELL, HOW ABOUT THAT?!!
A REAL, LIVE HI-JACKING DOWN THERE!
IS THIS A PRIVATE PARTY, GANG... OR CAN ANYONE JOIN IN?
IT'S SPIDER-MAN... JUST LIKE WE PLANNED IT!
CLAM UP, YA FOOL! HE'LL HEAR YA!
C'MON! WE GOTTA MAKE THIS LOOK GOOD!
DROP THE HARDWARE, YOU CREEPS!
YOU KNOW WHAT POWDER BURNS CAN DO TO DISHPAN HANDS!
OKAY, PAL... YOU CAN BURN RUBBER NOW!
THESE SLEEPING BEAUTIES HAVE SUDDENLY LOST INTEREST IN GRAB-BING OTHER PEOPLE'S DINKY TOYS!
BUT IT WAS NEVER THE VEHICLE THEY WERE AFTER...
HUH? WHO SAID THAT?
14

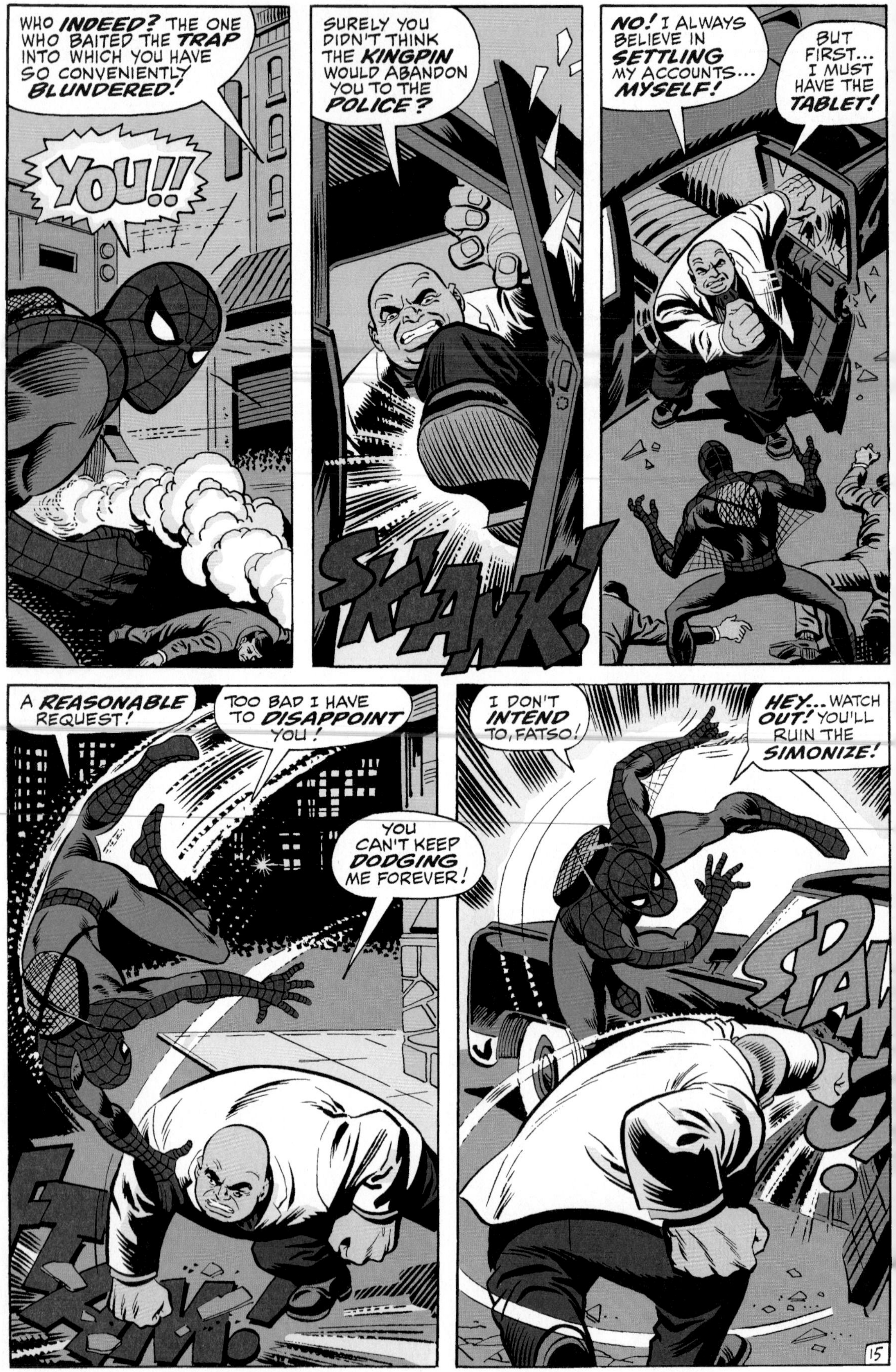
WHO INDEED? THE ONE WHO BAITED THE TRAP INTO WHICH YOU HAVE SO CONVENIENTLY BLUNDERED!
YOU!!
SURELY YOU DIDN'T THINK THE KINGPIN WOULD ABANDON YOU TO THE POLICE?
SKLANK!
NO! I ALWAYS BELIEVE IN SETTLING MY ACCOUNTS... MYSELF!
BUT FIRST... I MUST HAVE THE TABLET!
A REASONABLE REQUEST!
TOO BAD I HAVE TO DISAPPOINT YOU!
YOU CAN'T KEEP DODGING ME FOREVER!
I DON'T INTEND TO, FATSO!
HEY... WATCH OUT! YOU'LL RUIN THE SIMONIZE!
15

YOU PATHETIC PILE OF SKIN AND BONES...
YOU'LL NEVER ESCAPE ME!
I WON'T?
THEN WHY AM I KNOCKING MYSELF OUT?
I MIGHT AS WELL COME BACK FOR MORE FUN 'N GAMES!
IF THAT DIDN'T ROCK HIM TO DREAM-LAND, HE MUST HAVE ARMOR-PLATED SKIN!
OH NO! IT... CAN'T BE...!
HE'S ACTUALLY ... GETTING UP!
HEY! WHY'S THAT CAR RACING TOWARDS US LIKE THERE'S NO TOMORROW?!!
16

OH NO!
IT'S A DAILY BUGLE RADIO PATROL CAR!
JONAH JAMESON'S INSIDE--- WITH NED LEEDS DRIVING!
GET OUT OF HERE--- BOTH OF YOU! YOU'LL SPOIL EVERY-THING!
LEAVE THE KING-PIN TO ME!
HE STILL HAS THE TABLET STRAPPED TO HIM!
BUT HIS ATTACK WEAKENED ME--- AND I MUSTN'T FACE ---THE POLICE!
USE YOUR RADIO, LEEDS! CALL THE POLICE--- FAST!
WE'VE GOT 'IM FOR SURE!
LET THE TWO OF YOU ESCAPE AGAIN? NOT A CHANCE!

BUT SUDDENLY, ANOTHER SEDAN SKIDS TO A TIRE-GRINDING HALT!
SKREEEEEEEEEEEEEE
SSSSS
IT'S HARD TO SEE, WITH THE KINGPIN BLOCKING THE DOOR---
BUT THAT LOOKS LIKE A WOMAN AT THE WHEEL!
I DON'T LIKE IT, MR. JAMESON!
WE'RE SANDWICHED BETWEEN THE TWO OF THEM!
INTO THE CAR--- QUICKLY! ---WHILE THERE STILL IS TIME!
SAY! WHOSE CAR JUST PULLED UP NEXT TO THE KINGPIN?
HURRY! IF YOU WAIT ANY LONGER IT'LL BE TOO LATE!
EVEN IF I LEAVE NOW ---WITHOUT THE TABLET ---SPIDER-MAN LOSES!
HE'S STILL A FUGITIVE--- AND NOT EVEN THE TABLET CAN HELP HIM!
17.

THE WISE MAN KNOWS WHEN TO MAKE HIS EXIT!
THERE'LL BE ANOTHER TIME... ANOTHER PLACE... FOR SPIDER-MAN AND ME TO SETTLE OUR ACCOUNT!
IF ONLY ONE OF OUR PHOTOGRAPHERS WAS HERE!
YOU ARRIVED JUST IN TIME, MY DEAR!
NOW DRIVE ON!
LOOK! SPIDER-MAN'S MAKING A BREAK, ALSO!
QUICK, LEEDS! WE CAN BLOCK HIM WITH OUR CAR!!
YOU HYSTERICAL NUT! I WAS TRYING TO GRAB THE KINGPIN!
NOW, THANKS TO YOU... HE GOT AWAY!
YOU CAN'T FOOL ME, WALL-CRAWLER!
SHOOOM!
I KNOW YOU TWO PLANNED THE WHOLE THING!
YOU TRIED TO MAKE IT LOOK LIKE YOU'RE ENEMIES... BUT I'M WISE TO YOU!
YOU'VE MANAGED TO ESCAPE BEFORE... BUT THIS TIME... YOU'RE FINISHED!
I'LL KEEP THE PUBLIC CLAMORING FOR YOUR HIDE!!
I'LL ATTACK THE POLICE IN EVERY EDITORIAL ...UNTIL THEY'VE CAUGHT YOU!
I'LL USE MY PAPER TO... LEEDS!
STOP HIM! HE'S ABOUT TO ATTACK ME!
FOR ONCE YOU'RE RIGHT, JAMESON!
EVEN A WALL-CRAWLER CAN HAVE HIS BREAKING POINT!!
18

BEAT IT, LEEDS!
THIS IS BETWEEN ME AND THAT HUMAN HATE MACHINE!
NO! NO!
YOU'VE BEEN ON MY BACK EVER SINCE I CAN REMEMBER...
AND FOR NO REASON AT ALL!
SO MAYBE IT'S TIME I GIVE YOU A REASON!
SPIDER-MAN... DON'T!
LET'S GET TO THE NITTY GRITTY, FLAT-HEAD!..
EYEBALL TO EYEBALL--
NO! NO! NO!
NNNO... UHHHH!
THIS IS TOUGHER ON ME THAN YOU!
I HAVE TO LOOK AT... HEY!!
SOMETHING... HAPPENED TO HIM!!
HE...HE'S OUT LIKE A LIGHT!
JAMESON!! WHAT IS IT??
WHAT DID YOU DO TO HIM??
19.

THE POLICE! HAVE TO CUT OUT!
LOOK! I ONLY WANTED...TO GIVE HIM A SCARE!
YOU GAVE HIM MORE THAN THAT..
I...DON'T FEEL...A PULSE!
HE MUST HAVE HAD A HEART ATTACK!
BUT...IF HE DIES ...THEY'LL CALL ME A MURDERER!
DON'T SHOOT! TOO MANY WINDOWS ...WITH PEOPLE INSIDE!
NOW WHAT DO I DO? WHERE DO I GO? TO WHOM DO I TURN?
IN ONE BRIEF MOMENT-- I'VE LOST EVERY-THING!
...ALL BECAUSE OF THE KINGPIN ...AND THIS BLASTED TABLET!
IF JAMESON DIES, I...NO! I WON'T EVEN THINK OF IT!!
20
BUT, HAVE I ACTUALLY GIVEN HIM... HIS FINAL VICTORY?
BY LOSING MY TEMPER... BY LOSING CONTROL...
I'VE PROVEN MYSELF AS DANGEROUS ...AS HE ALWAYS SAID I WAS!!
NEXT:
THE MOST SHOCKINGLY UNEXPECTED SUPER-FOE OF THEM ALL!

SPIDER-MAN
12¢
IND.
71
APR
the AMAZING SPIDER-MAN
APPROVED BY THE COMICS CODE AUTHORITY
MARVEL COMICS GROUP
ROMITA
AND NOW...
QUICKSILVER!

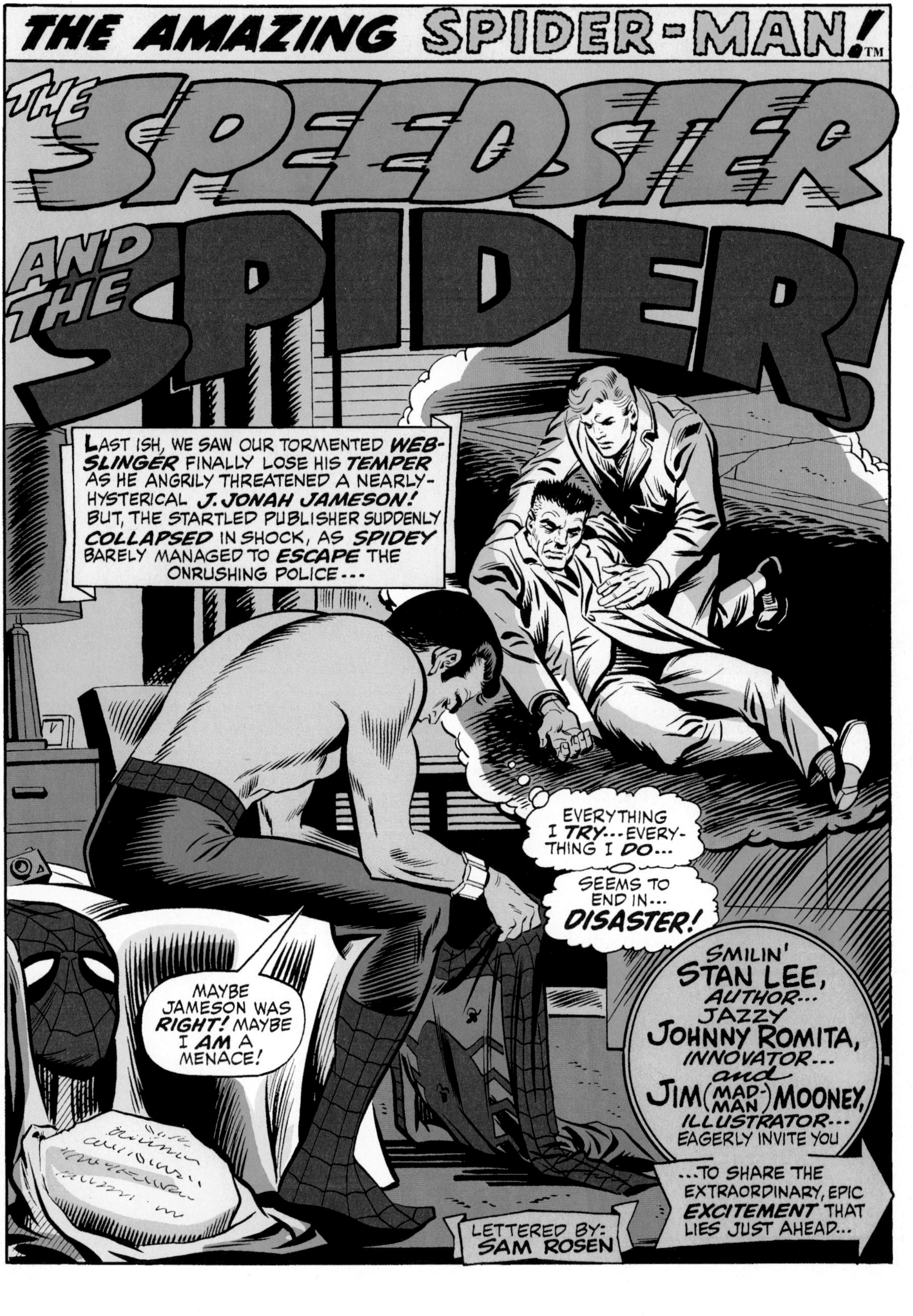
THE AMAZING SPIDER-MAN!™
THE SPEEDSTER AND THE SPIDER!
LAST ISH, WE SAW OUR TORMENTED WEB-SLINGER FINALLY LOSE HIS TEMPER AS HE ANGRILY THREATENED A NEARLY-HYSTERICAL J. JONAH JAMESON! BUT, THE STARTLED PUBLISHER SUDDENLY COLLAPSED IN SHOCK, AS SPIDEY BARELY MANAGED TO ESCAPE THE ONRUSHING POLICE...
EVERYTHING I TRY... EVERYTHING I DO...
SEEMS TO END IN... DISASTER!
MAYBE JAMESON WAS RIGHT! MAYBE I AM A MENACE!
SMILIN' STAN LEE, AUTHOR... JAZZY JOHNNY ROMITA, INNOVATOR... and JIM (MAD-MAN) MOONEY, ILLUSTRATOR... EAGERLY INVITE YOU
...TO SHARE THE EXTRAORDINARY, EPIC EXCITEMENT THAT LIES JUST AHEAD...
LETTERED BY: SAM ROSEN

NOW I'M STUCK WITH THIS SO-CALLED PRICE-LESS TABLET!
I STOPPED THE KINGPIN FROM STEALING IT--SO NOW I'M BLAMED FOR THE THEFT!
I DON'T KNOW HOW TO GET RID OF IT--
AND MY WHOLE WORLD WILL COME DOWN AROUND MY EARS IF IT'S FOUND HERE, WITH PETER PARKER!
WELL, THERE'S ONE PROBLEM I DON'T HAVE--
I DON'T HAVE TO WONDER WHY NOBODY CALLS ME LUCKY!!
SOMEONE AT THE DOOR!
MUST BE HARRY... COMING HOME!
THAT'S ALL I NEED--TO BE FOUND LIKE THIS!
KLIK!
THE LIGHT'S OUT... BUT I THOUGHT I HEARD SOMETHING!
IS THAT YOU, PETE? ARE YOU STILL UP?
GOTTA GET MY SHIRT BEFORE HE SWITCHES ON THE LIGHT!
NO ANSWER! I GUESS I WAS MISTAKEN!
2.

WHEW! JUST MADE IT!
BOY, AM I BUSHED!
CLICK!
MARY JANE COULD DANCE THE LEGS OFF ASTAIRE!
I DON'T DARE SHUT MY DOOR...
HE MIGHT HEAR IT CLICK!
I'LL HAVE TO GO TALK TO HIM!
ONLY ONE WAY TO KEEP HIM FROM GETTING SUSPICIOUS...
HI, PETEY! I THOUGHT YOU WERE ASLEEP!
I WAS... TILL YOU CAME STOMPIN' IN, TWINKLETOES!
HAVE A GOOD TIME, HARR?
WITH M.J.? YOU KNOW IT, SON!
SO FAR SO GOOD...
...LONG AS HE DOESN'T LOOK AT MY FEET!
SEEING MUCH OF GWEN THESE DAYS, ROMEO?
NOT REALLY! I'VE BEEN KEEPING KIND OF... BUSY!
ANY GUY WHO'S TOO BUSY FOR THAT CHICK NEEDS A GOOD HEAD-SHRINKER!
WELL, I'M HITTIN' THE HAY!
ME TOO!
THAT MAKES ONE MORE TIME I AVOIDED DISCOVERY... BY THE SKIN OF MY TEETH!
BUT I'VE GOTTA STOP FEELING SORRY FOR MYSELF!
BOY! WHAT A GREAT WAY TO LIVE!
I HAVE TO WORK THINGS OUT... SOMEHOW...
IF ONLY FOR THE SAKE OF AUNT MAY!
3.

HER RENT IS DUE IN A FEW DAYS, AND I'M FLATTER THAN...
MAYBE EVERYTHING ISN'T A TOTAL WASHOUT!
HEY! WAIT A MINUTE!
WHAT ABOUT THOSE PICTURES I TOOK...OF THE KINGPIN?!!
THEN, MINUTES LATER...
HEY! THESE ARE GREAT!
THEY'RE SHARP AND CLEAR!
AND, EVEN BETTER THAN THAT...
THEY MAY HELP TO SHOW THAT SPIDEY'S INNOCENT!
WAIT A MINUTE! I JUST REMEMBERED...
WITH JOLLY JONAH IN THE HOSPITAL...
WHO'S GONNA BUY THEM FROM ME??
BUT, SINCE WE CAN'T ANSWER THAT AT THE MOMENT, LET'S GO OUTSIDE, WHERE WE FIND...
WHAT'S HAPPENING?? MY PAPERS...THEY'RE ALL BLOWING AWAY!!
IT'S LIKE...A HURRICANE!
NEWS
SECONDS LATER, THE "HURRICANE" STOPS, REVEALING THE DRAMATIC FIGURE WHOM THE WORLD KNOWS AS...QUICKSILVER!!
I'VE REACHED THE CITY AT LAST!
I MUST EXPLAIN EVERYTHING THAT HAS OCCURRED...
AND HOPE THEY WILL UNDERSTAND!
AND NOW TO FIND---THE AVENGERS!
...BEGINNING WITH THE MOMENT MAGNETO'S ISLAND FORTRESS WAS DESTROYED...
AND WANDA AND I MANAGED TO ESCAPE...TOGETHER WITH THE MISSHAPEN TOAD! *
*AS SEEN IN AVENGERS #53! ...SMILEY!
4

"WE CRASH-LANDED ATOP AN ISOLATED PEAK IN THE ADIRONDACKS..."
THE SHIP IS WRECKED!! IT MAY NEVER FLY AGAIN!
UNLESS YOU'RE UP ON OUR OTHER MARVEL MAGS, THESE CHARACTERS ARE NEW TO YOU! BUT DON'T WORRY--YOU'LL STILL BE ABLE TO FOLLOW THE STORY WITH EASE! --SOLICITOUS STAN.
DO NOT BE CONCERNED, MY SISTER!
AT LEAST WE ARE SAFE!
SAFE, PIETRO? SAFE TO DO WHAT ...TO GO WHERE?
ARE WE NOT STILL... OUTCASTS?
IF ONLY WE COULD PROVE THAT WE ARE NOT EVIL!
EVERYTHING WAS THE FAULT OF MAGNETO!
WE HAD NO CHOICE BUT TO OBEY HIM!
THE TOAD SPEAKS THE TRUTH...
BUT WHO WOULD BELIEVE US?
THE AVENGERS WOULD BELIEVE! THEY WOULD UNDERSTAND!
DID THEY NOT ACCEPT US IN THE PAST?
BUT PIETRO ...THINK OF THE DANGER!
WHAT IS DANGER...TO THOSE WHO WOULD BE REDEEMED?!!
5.

WE CANNOT... WE SHALL NOT LIVE LIKE HUNTED BEASTS!!
REMAIN HERE, MY SISTER! REMAIN UNTIL...
...I RETURN ONCE MORE!!
THUS, WITH A SUDDEN BURST OF INCOMPREHENSIBLE SPEED, THE FASTEST LIVING BEING OF ALL HURTLES TOWARDS THE HEART OF NEW YORK---
---LEAVING HIS WAN AND LOVELY SISTER IN THE CARE OF THE TRAGIC TOAD..!
HE WILL NOT FAIL US, WANDA!
WE MUST BOTH HAVE FAITH!
MINUTES LATER, A METEORIC FIGURE ZOOMS TO THE TOP OF AVENGERS' HQ...
THE INTRUDER ALARM!
SOMEONE IS UPON THE ROOF!!
I MUST THROW THE REPELLOR-SWITCH... AT ONCE!
6.

QUICKSILVER!! YOU!!
NOT EVEN THE ELECTRIC REPELLOR-SCREEN COULD STOP ME!
MY SPEED WAS GREATER THAN THAT OF THE DEADLY CURRENT!
BUT IT IS THE AVENGERS I SEEK!
YOU MUST TAKE ME TO THEM!
BUT...THAT IS IMPOSSIBLE, PIETRO!! THEY ARE IN AFRICA!*
* DON'T TAKE OUR WORD FOR IT! SEE FOR YOURSELF IN AVENGERS # 62! ...SOFT-SELL STAN.
THEN... MY MISSION HAS BEEN... IN VAIN!
EVEN IF I COULD REACH THE DARK CONTINENT...HOW WOULD I FIND THEM?
HEY! WATCH IT THERE, MAC!
NO! THERE MUST BE SOME OTHER WAY!
AM I ATTACKED?!!
NO...IT IS ONLY THE MORNING NEWSPAPERS BEING DELIVERED!
SPIDER-MAN! A FUGITIVE FROM THE LAW??
I MUST LEARN MORE ABOUT THAT...!!
DAILY BUGLE
SPIDER-MAN WANTED!
7.

IN TRUTH, HE IS A WANTED CRIMINAL!
BUT WHO COULD HAVE THE POWER TO APPREHEND SUCH A MAN?
WHO... BUT QUICKSILVER?
THE DAILY BUGLE
SPIDER-MAN WANTED!
FATE HAS GIVEN ME THE MEANS TO REDEEM MYSELF AT LAST!
AND NOW, AS YOU BEGIN TO ANTICIPATE WHAT'S ABOUT TO HAPPEN NEXT, LET'S VISIT AN EXPENSIVE, EAST SIDE HOSPITAL, WHERE WE HEAR...
MR. JAMESON IS RESTING AT THE MOMENT...
HIS CONDITION IS LISTED AS FAIR, MR. ROBERTSON!
ACTUALLY, HE SUFFERED NOTHING MORE THAN A CASE OF SHOCK...
BUT HE'LL NEED COMPLETE REST FOR THE NEXT FEW WEEKS!
WEEKS DID YOU SAY?
THEN, THAT MEANS...
...I'LL HAVE TO TAKE OVER HIS DUTIES!
AS A MATTER OF FACT, HE MUMBLED SOMETHING TO THAT EFFECT, WHEN...
OH! IT'S JOHN JAMESON!
DOCTOR! HOW IS MY FATHER?
HE'LL BE ALL RIGHT, COLONEL!
HE'S RESTING COMFORTABLY!
GOOD TO SEE YOU, ROBBIE! I KNEW YOU'D BE AT HIS SIDE!
BUT, HOW DID IT HAPPEN? I CAN'T BELIEVE SPIDER-MAN REALLY ATTACKED HIM!
I DON'T BELIEVE HE DID, JOHN!
IT WAS MORE OF A THREAT... WHICH ACCIDENTALLY BACKFIRED!
I'D BETTER BE LEAVING NOW!
I'LL HAVE A HECTIC DAY TOMORROW... WITH YOUR FATHER ABSENT!
THINGS WILL BE IN GOOD HANDS, ROB... WITH YOU AT THE HELM!
BE SURE TO REMEMBER ME TO YOUR WIFE ... AND TO YOUNG RANDY!
YES! I'LL DO THAT, SON!
20-34
8

SOME TIME LATER...
I THOUGHT YOU WANTED TO GET TO SLEEP EARLY, DEAR?
I'M TOO TENSE, HONEY... I'M ALL KEYED UP!
MY MIND IS GOING A MILE-A-MINUTE... THINKING ABOUT A DOZEN THINGS!
I... DIDN'T HEAR RANDY COME IN YET!
HE'S HERE, ROB!
HE CAME IN QUIETLY... SO AS NOT TO DISTURB YOU!
WHY HAVE YOU BEEN SO CONCERNED ABOUT HIM LATELY?
I THOUGHT THAT CAMPUS PROTEST MATTER WAS ALL SETTLED?
IT'S NOT JUST THAT, MARTHA---
IT'S HIS FUTURE---IT'S THE WORLD HE'S GROWING UP IN!
HE'S TROUBLED... REBELLIOUS... FULL OF THE ANGRY IMPATIENCE OF YOUTH!
HE WANTS TO TAKE THE WORLD IN HIS HANDS... AND SHAPE IT INTO SOMETHING BETTER!
THAT'S WHAT'S IMPORTANT, MARTHA! THAT'S WHAT REALLY COUNTS!
IT'S THE WAY WE USED TO FEEL ...REMEMBER?
IT'S THE DREAM THAT BELONGS TO THE YOUNG... IT'S THE HOPE OF THE WORLD!
BUT, SLEEP HAS A WAY OF COMING... JUST AS NEXT MORNINGS HAVE A WAY OF ROLLING AROUND... AND SO WE FIND...
BETTER SCRATCH MY APPOINTMENTS FOR TODAY, BETTY!
WITH JJ OUT, IT'S A WHOLE NEW BALL GAME!
IT'LL START WITH NEW PIX!
PETER PARKER HAS BEEN WAITING TO SEE YOU, MR. ROBERTSON!
HE WOULDN'T BE THIS EARLY, UNLESS HE HAD SOMETHING SPECIAL! ASK HIM TO---
OH! HERE HE IS NOW!
FIRST TELL ME, MR. R... HOW'S JAMESON?
NOTHING SERIOUS, SON! HE'S ON THE MEND!
NOW, ABOUT THOSE PICTURES...
SAY! THESE ARE DYNAMITE!
MISS BRANT! DROP EVERYTHING! CALL THE PRESS ROOM!
THERE MAY STILL BE TIME TO CATCH THE EARLY EDITION!
9.

THESE SHOW... BEYOND A SHADOW OF DOUBT... THAT SPIDER-MAN TRIED TO PRE-VENT THE TABLET'S THEFT!
THEY ALSO PROVE... CONCLUSIVELY... THAT THE YOUNG CAMPUS PROTESTERS HAD NOTHING TO DO WITH IT!
SECONDS LATER...
CALL THE COMPOSING ROOM... AND GET ME REWRITE!
PARKER! WHAT ARE YOU MUMBLING ABOUT? ISN'T THAT CHECK BIG ENOUGH?
BIG ENOUGH? IT'S THE MOST BREAD I'VE SEEN IN YEARS!
MAN! OL' JAMESON WOULD HAVE FREAKED OUT IF HE EVER SIGNED SOMETHING LIKE THIS!
THERE GOES ONE HAPPY-LOOKING CITIZEN!
MR. R. MUST HAVE FLIPPED OVER HIS SNAPS!
NOW AUNT MAY CAN GO DOWN SOUTH FOR THE SUNSHINE SHE NEEDS!
AND I CAN FINALLY GIVE HARRY MY SHARE OF THE RENT!
FACE IT, PETEY...
THINGS ARE LOOKING UP... AT LAST!
10

NOW, ALL I HAVE TO DO IS GET RID OF THAT NUTTY TABLET!
AND I'VE FINALLY FIGURED OUT A WAY!
UPTOW
I CAN'T SIMPLY GO SKIPPING INTO MY FRIENDLY NEIGHBOR-HOOD POLICE STATION!
BUT, I'LL DO THE NEXT BEST THING...
I'LL LET SOMEONE ELSE DO IT FOR ME!
AND SO...
WHO'S THERE??
HAVE NO FEAR...
SPIDEY'S HERE!
11.

I'VE GOT THE STOLEN TABLET FOR YOU!
I FIGURE YOU'D KNOW HOW TO RETURN IT!
NOW MAYBE THE POLICE WILL BELIEVE I ONLY TOOK IT TO KEEP IT SAFE FROM THE KINGPIN!
WAIT! COME BACK!
I WANT TO TALK TO YOU!
SOME OTHER TIME, MISTER!
I'VE GOT THINGS TO DO!
HE'S TOO SHARP! I DON'T DARE TALK TOO MUCH---
--IN CASE HE RECOGNIZES MY MUFFLED VOICE... EVEN THRU THE MASK!
BUT, JAMESON'S ALIVE... SO I'M NOT A MURDERER!
AND I FINALLY GOT THE TABLET OFF MY BACK!
WHAT'S MORE... FOR THE FIRST TIME, I'VE GOT A WEB-FULL OF SPENDING MONEY!
AND MAN... AM I GONNA SPEND IT!
WAIT A MINUTE! WHY IS MY SPIDEY SENSE TINGLING??
THAT ONLY HAPPENS WHEN DANGER'S NEAR!
12

SOMETHING JUST ZOOMED AHEAD OF ME...
MOVING SO FAST THAT IT KEPT MY WEBBING FROM HITTING THE WALL!
WHICH MEANS, THERE'S ONLY ONE WAY FOR ME TO GO...
...AND THAT'S DOWN!

I AM SORRY, SPIDER-MAN!
IT WAS NOT MY INTENTION TO MAKE YOU FALL!
I WISH ONLY TO CAPTURE YOU...
TO BRING YOU TO JUSTICE!
QUICKSILVER!
13

I DID NOT REALIZE THE FAMOUS SPIDER-MAN WOULD BE SO VULNERABLE...
SO SEEMINGLY HELPLESS!
I SHALL HAVE TO SAVE YOU!
FROM UP THERE?
THAT I'VE GOTTA SEE!
NOTICE HOW MY GREAT SPEED PROVIDES UN-LIMITED CENTRIFUGAL FORCE---
---ENABLING ME TO DEFY GRAVITY ITSELF---!
SINCE YOU CLEVERLY BROKE YOUR FALL BY REPEATEDLY STRIKING THE BUILDING...
I NEED NOT WORRY ABOUT YOUR FATE!
PARK HOTEL
I SHALL ALLOW YOU TO LAND, AND THEN---AT MY LEISURE, I'LL---
WHA..? WHERE DID HE GO?
PARK HOTEL
DANCIN
CATER
14

IT IS IMPOSS-IBLE!
HE MUST BE HERE! HE MUST!
AHH! I MIGHT HAVE GUESSED!
YOU ARE MOST ELUSIVE!
NOW WHAT'S HE DOING?
BUT, BY WHIRLING AROUND, AT ULTRA-HIGH SPEED...
SEE HOW EASILY I CAN HURL YOU OFF-BALANCE!
I NOW CALL UPON YOU TO SURRENDER...
FOR I HAVE NO WISH TO HARM YOU!
IT IS MERELY MY PURPOSE TO BRING YOU TO JUSTICE!
BETTER CHECK YOUR SCORE CARD, SONNY!
I'M ONE OF THE GOOD GUYS!
15.

I WARN YOU, SPIDER-MAN! IT IS NOT WISE TO TRIFLE WITH QUICKSILVER!
I MUST BRING YOU TO JUSTICE... TO PROVE MYSELF WORTHY TO THE AVENGERS ONCE MORE!
THERE'S GOTTA BE AN EASIER WAY THAN THAT!
ON YOUR FEET, WEB-SLINGER! DO NOT TRY TO CATCH ME UNAWARES!
MY SPEED IS TOO GREAT FOR ANY SUCH MANEUVER!
WELL, JUST BETWEEN US, SPEEDY...
I'M NOT EXACTLY A SLOWPOKE MYSELF!
YOU THINK YOUR SPEED CAN COMPARE WITH MINE!
DON'T YOU REALIZE...TO ME, YOU'RE MOVING IN SLOW MOTION?!!
16

I CAN STRIKE YOU A DOZEN TIMES...
BEFORE YOU EVEN FEEL THE FIRST!
NOW SURRENDER ...SO THAT WE MAY END THIS FARCE!
ALL YOUR POWERS... ALL YOUR VAUNTED SPIDER STRENGTH
CANNOT SAVE YOU NOW!
BUT, SINCE WE HATE TO SHOW OUR HERO GETTING HIS LUMPS, LET'S GRAB OURSELVES A CHANGE OF SCENE...
DID YOU BRING THE LATEST EDITION FOR MY FATHER, LEEDS?
YES, COLONEL... BUT, PERHAPS YOU SHOULDN'T SHOW IT TO HIM YET!
NONSENSE! HE'S WELL ENOUGH TO READ NOW!
BUT, THAT EXPRESSION ON YOUR FACE
IS THERE ANYTHING IN THERE THAT'LL UPSET HIM?
IS THAT YOU, LEEDS?? WHERE'S MY BLASTED PAPER!!
DON'T JUST STAND THERE, MAN...
HAND IT OVER... WHILE IT'S STILL NEWS!
TOO LATE TO BACK OUT, NOW!
YEAH! MIGHT AS WELL GET IT OVER WITH!
C'MON! C'MON! C'MON!
IF YOU'RE GONNA DAY-DREAM... DO IT ON YOUR OWN TIME!
17

WHAT'S THIS??!! WHAT'S THIS??!!
"BUGLE PHOTOS SEEM TO VINDICATE SPIDER-MAN!"
MY PAPER ...PRINTING PICTURES THAT SHOW THE WALL-CRAWLER'S INNO-CENT!!??
NOW TAKE IT EASY, DAD!
EASY?? YOU EXPECT ME TO TAKE IT EASY... WHEN I'M SURROUNDED BY ASSASSINS?!
IF THIS IS ROBERTSON'S IDEA OF A JOKE ---I'LL HAVE HIS HIDE!!
BETTER GET THE DOCTOR, NED!
YES SIR!
I SURE DON'T WANNA BE AROUND WHEN OLD BLOOD 'N GUTS LEARNS WHAT ROBBIE PAID FOR THOSE PHOTOS!
I DON'T CARE WHAT THOSE PHOTOS SHOW!
SPIDER-MAN'S GUILTY!
HE'S GUILTY! GUILTY! GUILTY! GUILTY! GUILTY!
BUT, GUILTY OR NOT, WE'VE GOT TO ADMIT THAT IT TAKES A LOT TO KEEP HIM DOWN...
NO MATTER HOW I PUMMEL YOU, YOU CONTINUE TO BATTLE ON!
A PITY FOR ONE SO VALIANT TO BE A CRIMINAL!
I'M NO MORE A CRIMINAL THAN YOU ARE!!
YOU SHOULDN'T BELIEVE EVERYTHING YOU READ!
IF ONLY HE'D SLOW DOWN... SO I CAN NAIL HIM... JUST ONCE!
BUT, INSTEAD OF LESSENING HIS SPEED...
YOU ARE TOO POWER-FUL!
THERE IS BUT ONE WAY TO DEAL WITH SUCH AS YOU--!
MY SPEED SHALL CREATE A WHIRLPOOL OF AIR---
CAUSING A SUCTION UPDRAFT ...WHICH WILL LEAVE YOU BREATH-LESS!
18

NOT EVEN SPIDER-MAN CAN CONTINUE TO FIGHT...WITHOUT OXYGEN!
CAN'T... LET IT END... LIKE THIS!
CAN'T LET...THE POLICE...UN-MASK ME!
I'VE GOT TO... STOP HIM... SOMEHOW!
WHOOOPFFF!
IF MY STRENGTH... HOLDS OUT... THERE'S...STILL A CHANCE...
FAST...AS HE IS...HE CAN'T RUN...THRU AN OBJECT...
...AN OBJECT... SUCH AS...MY ARM!!
WHEW! ONLY MY SPIDEY STRENGTH KEPT IT FROM BEING SNAPPED IN TWO LIKE... UH OH!
JUST WHAT I DON'T NEED!
SPIDER-MAN!! STAY WHERE YOU ARE!
WE WANT BOTH OF YOU!
THAT'S REAL FLATTERING, FELLAS!
BUT, SINCE WE'RE BOTH SORTA SHY...
I'M BETTING THEY WON'T FIRE!
...SPECIALLY WITH ME CARRY-ING QUICK-SILVER!
DANCING, D CATERING
DON'T JUST STAND THERE, MEN... STOP HIM!
GLAD TO, SARGE...
JUST TELL US HOW!
19.

WHEN QUICKIE COMES TO, I'LL TRY TO EXPLAIN THINGS TO HIM!
THUS, A FEW SECONDS LATER...
YOU MIGHT HAVE SLAIN ME... BUT DID NOT...
I WILL NO LONGER PIT MY PROWESS AGAINST YOURS!
GROOVY! THAT SAVES ME THE TROUBLE OF TRYING TO CONVINCE YOU THAT I'M NOT ATTILA THE HUN!
I SHALL FIND ANOTHER WAY TO WIN MY REDEMPTION!
NOT AT THE EXPENSE OF ONE SUCH AS YOU!
IF ONLY SOME OF THAT...
WOULD RUB OFF ON JAMESON!
HOW ABOUT THAT?
MAYBE MY LUCK'S CHANGING AT LAST!
OR, IS THIS JUST A LULL...
BEFORE THE STORM?
WE'LL FIND OUT FOR SURE, NEXT, WHEN WE'RE SUDDENLY GONNA MEET:
THE MOST SHOCKING FOE OF ALL!
20

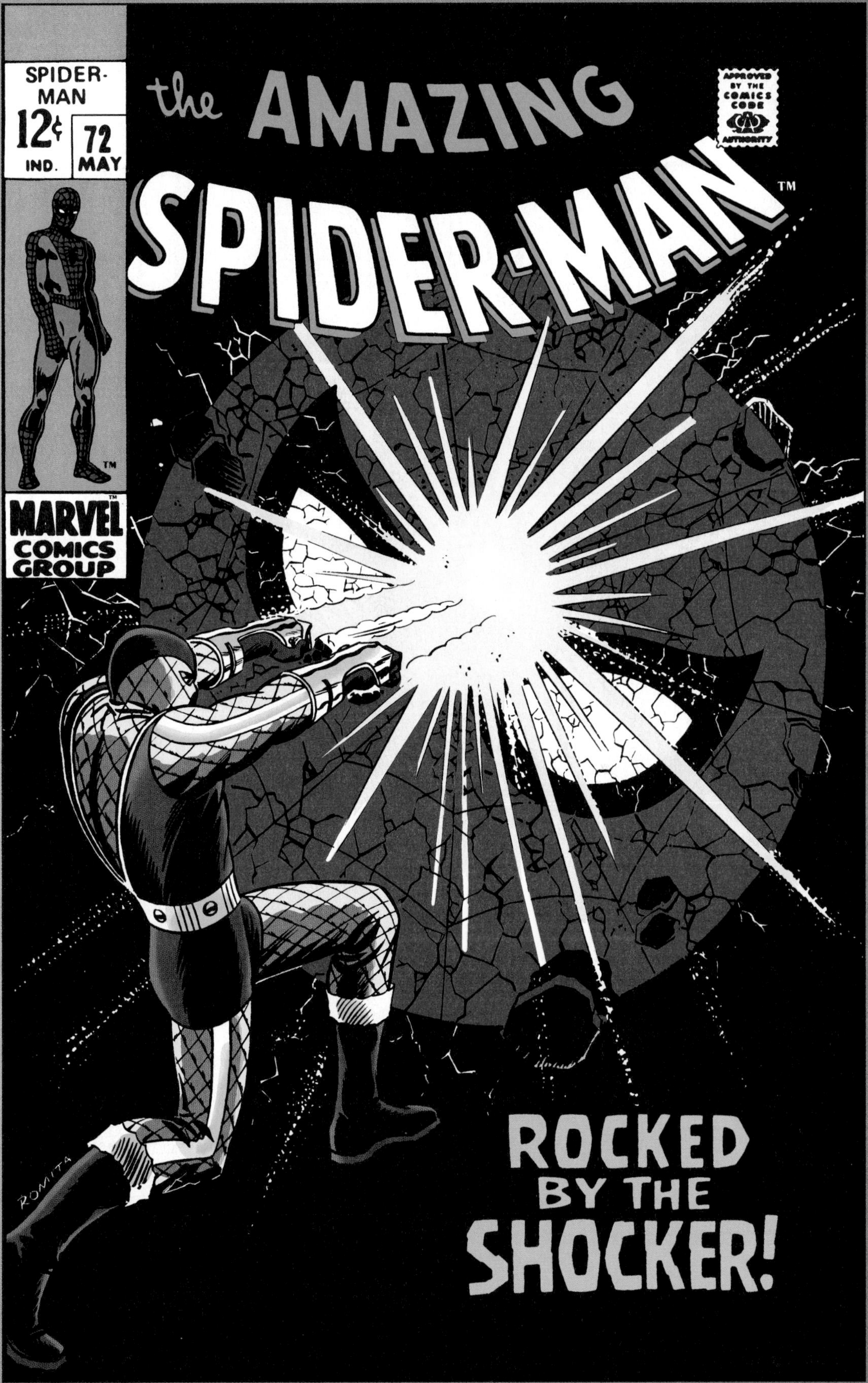
SPIDER-MAN
12¢
IND.
72
MAY
the AMAZING
SPIDER-MAN™
APPROVED BY THE COMICS CODE AUTHORITY
MARVEL COMICS GROUP
ROMITA
ROCKED BY THE SHOCKER!

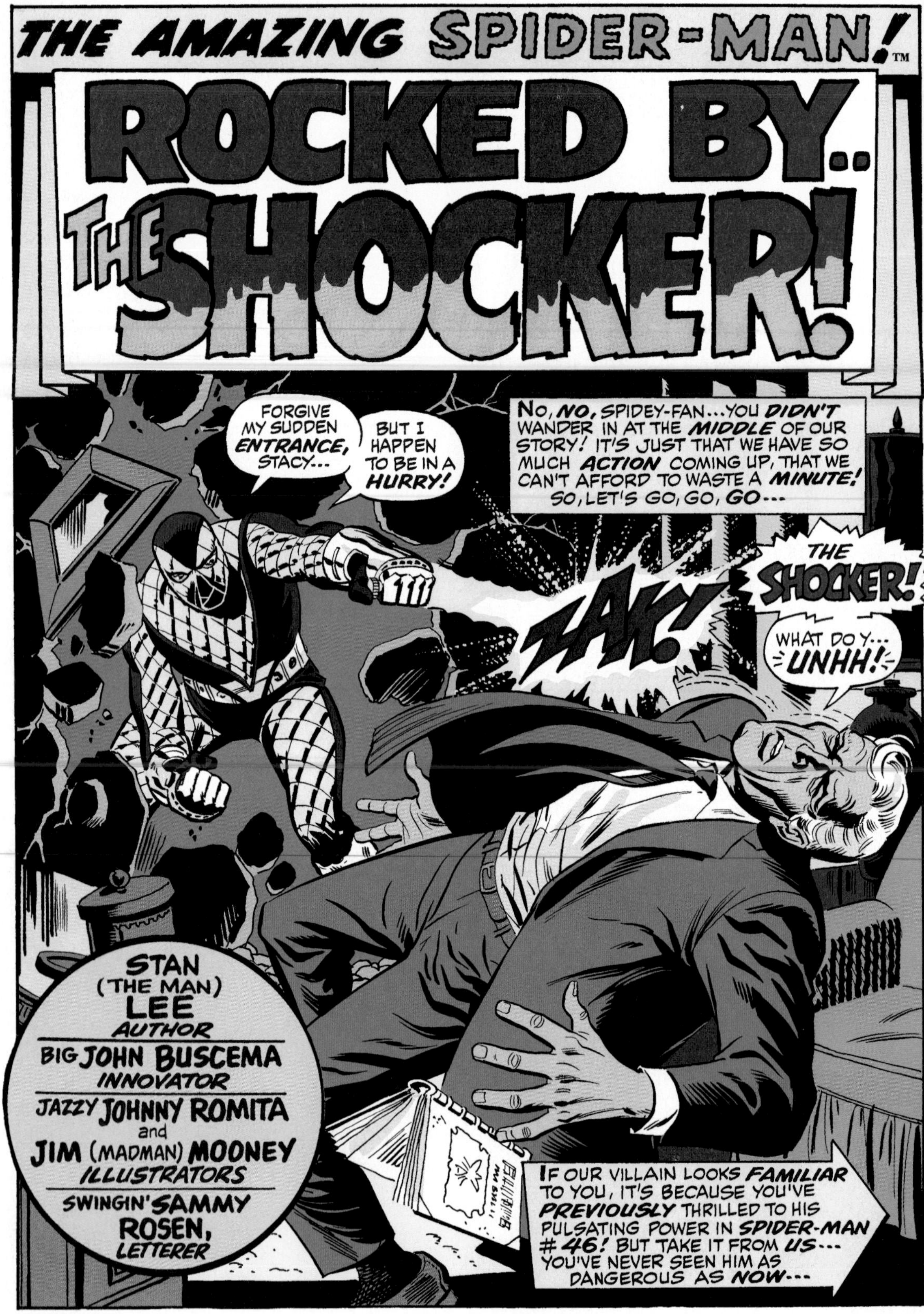
THE AMAZING SPIDER-MAN!™
ROCKED BY.. THE SHOCKER!
FORGIVE MY SUDDEN ENTRANCE, STACY...
BUT I HAPPEN TO BE IN A HURRY!
NO, NO, SPIDEY-FAN...YOU DIDN'T WANDER IN AT THE MIDDLE OF OUR STORY! IT'S JUST THAT WE HAVE SO MUCH ACTION COMING UP, THAT WE CAN'T AFFORD TO WASTE A MINUTE! SO, LET'S GO, GO, GO---
ZAK!
THE SHOCKER!
WHAT DO Y... UNHH!
STAN (THE MAN) LEE AUTHOR
BIG JOHN BUSCEMA INNOVATOR
JAZZY JOHNNY ROMITA and JIM (MADMAN) MOONEY ILLUSTRATORS
SWINGIN' SAMMY ROSEN, LETTERER
IF OUR VILLAIN LOOKS FAMILIAR TO YOU, IT'S BECAUSE YOU'VE PREVIOUSLY THRILLED TO HIS PULSATING POWER IN SPIDER-MAN #46! BUT TAKE IT FROM US--- YOU'VE NEVER SEEN HIM AS DANGEROUS AS NOW---

LUCKY FOR HIM I USED MY VIBRO-POWER AT ITS WEAKEST INTENSITY!
HE'LL BE CONSCIOUS AGAIN WITHIN A MATTER OF MINUTES!
VZZZAKK!
BUT, I'LL HAVE FOUND WHAT I SEEK BY THEN!
NO SAFE CAN RESIST MY VIBRATING BLAST!
ACCORDING TO THE NEWS-PAPERS, THE PRICELESS CLAY TABLET SHOULD BE IN HERE---
SINCE SPIDER-MAN WAS DUMB ENOUGH NOT TO KEEP IT, AND SELL IT FOR HIMSELF!
BUT THE SHOCKER HAS NO SUCH SCRUPLES!
THE TABLET MUST BE MINE!
I'M IN LUCK!
STACY HASN'T YET RETURNED IT TO THE COLLEGE!
THIS ANCIENT PIECE OF PETRIFIED STONE IS WORTH A KING'S RANSOM!
DAD! DAD! WHAT WAS THAT NOISE??
IT SOUNDED LIKE PART OF THE BUILDING CAVING IN!!
DAD! WHERE ARE YOU? WHY DON'T YOU ANSWER?
WHAT'S THAT? ...FOOT-STEPS... RUNNING TOWARDS ME!
2.

A GIRL! MUST BE HIS DAUGHTER!
OH, NO! NO!
YOU'RE IN LUCK, GORGEOUS!
I ALREADY GOT WHAT I WANT... SO I'M CUTTING OUT!
AND NO NEED TO STRAIN YOUR TONSILS...
EXCEPT FOR A HEADACHE, HE'LL BE AS GOOD AS NEW!
DAD... WHO WAS HE? WHAT DID HE DO?
I THOUGHT... THE TABLET WOULD BE SAFE... HERE WITH ME!
I DIDN'T COUNT ON BEING ATTACKED... BY SOMEONE AS POWERFUL ...AS THE SHOCKER!
GET TO THE PHONE, DEAR! CALL THE POLICE!
DAD, DIDN'T THE SHOCKER ONCE BATTLE SPIDER-MAN TO A STANDSTILL?
IF HE'S AT LARGE AGAIN...
HOW CAN ANYONE HOPE TO STOP HIM?
3.

WE MUST ADMIT THAT GROOVY GWENDY HAS POSED A MOST INTERESTING QUESTION! BUT, BEFORE TRYING TO ANSWER IT, LET'S VISIT A SEEDY LITTLE PAWNSHOP ON A SEEDY LITTLE SIDE-STREET---
WHOEVER THAT IS OUTSIDE, BEAT IT!
I'M CLOSIN' FOR THE NIGHT!
ZAKK!
DON'T COUNT ON IT, MISTER!
THE SHOCKER!
WH-WHAT'RE YOU DOIN' HERE?
I'M JUST SMALL POTATOES TO A GUY LIKE YOU!
TO ME YOU'RE NOTHING!
BUT YOU KNOW HOW TO REACH ---THE BIG BOYS!
I WANT YOU TO CONTACT THEM! TELL 'EM I HAVE THE STOLEN TABLET!
I'M GONNA FENCE IT TO THE HIGHEST BIDDER!
YOU CAN'T! IT'S TOO LATE!
EVER SINCE SPIDER-MAN SNATCHED IT FROM THE KINGPIN HIMSELF, NO ONE'LL TOUCH IT!
IT'S TOO HOT! NO ONE WANTS TO TANGLE WITH THE WALL-CRAWLER AGAIN!
THEY DON'T, HUH?
THBAMM
ZAK!
SO THEY'RE AFRAID OF THE WEB-SLINGER, ARE THEY?
I'LL GIVE 'EM SOME-THING TO REALLY BE SCARED OF!
ZAK
4.

AND JUST IN CASE NO ONE GETS THE MESSAGE...!
TKKLANGG!
HOLY SMOKE! IT LOOKS LIKE ANOTHER RIOT!
AND IN THE MIDDLE OF WINTER, YET!
HELP... POLICE!! ANYONE!!
A FEW MINUTES LATER...
...THE PUBLIC IS CAUTIONED TO AVOID THE EAST FORTIES...
WHERE POLICE ARE CONDUCTING A HOUSE-TO-HOUSE SEARCH FOR THE SHOCKER...
THE SHOCKER... AT LARGE AGAIN!
LIKE, DO THEY HAVETA BREAK IN ON THE SOUL PARADE JUST ON ACCOUNTA SOME COSTUMED NUT?
I THOUGHT HE WAS IN JAIL... BUT IF HE'S ON THE LOOSE ONCE MORE--
...THEN SPIDER-MAN BETTER MAKE THE SCENE... BUT FAST!
HEY! HE JUST GOT ON... A COUPLE OF BLOCKS AGO!
CRAZY TEEN-AGERS!
WHATEVER HAPPENS NEXT, BETTER HAPPEN FAST!
I FINALLY CONVINCED AUNT MAY TO GO SOUTH FOR HER HEALTH...
AND HER TRAIN LEAVES IN AN HOUR!
IF I'M NOT THERE TO SEE HER OFF...
SHE'LL BE SO WORRIED ABOUT ME, THAT SHE WON'T GO!
UH OH! SPIDEY SENSE IS STARTING TO TINGLE!
THE SHOCKER MUST BE NEARBY!
5.

WHILE, BACK AT THE PAWN SHOP...
ANY TRACE OF HIM, HARRIS?
NOT YET, INSPECTOR!
LOOKS LIKE WE JUST LOST HIM ON THE ROOFTOPS!
NO TRACE OF THAT TABLET, EITHER!
BUT THERE'S A MILLION PLACES HE COULD HAVE STASHED IT AWAY BY NOW!
IT ALL HAPPENED SO FAST!
THE SHOCKER AIN'T HUMAN! ---NO ONE CAN TAKE 'IM!
MAYBE NOT... BUT JUST ABOUT NOW, SOMEONE'S GONNA TRY...
HOLD IT, BIG BOY!
YOU'RE NOT GOING ANYWHERE!
WHO SAID THAT??
I'LL GIVE YOU A HINT, MAN...
IT'S NOT ARETHA FRANKLIN!
BTOK!
HE'S STILL CONSCIOUS!
MUST HAVE USED HIS VIBRATING POWER AGAIN, TO DEFLECT MY BLOW!
I ALMOST FORGOT WHAT A DEADLY OPPONENT THE SHOCKER CAN BE!
SPIDER-MAN! I THOUGHT YOU'D DROP BY!
HE DOESN'T EVEN SOUND HURT!
6

LAST TIME WE FOUGHT, YOU MANAGED TO ESCAPE WITH YOUR LIFE!
YOU SHOULD HAVE QUIT... WHILE YOU WERE AHEAD!
ZAK!
THERE'S ONE FOR STARTERS!
ZAK!
ANOTHER BLAST!
HE'S TRYING TO BRING THE CHIMNEY DOWN ON ME!
AHH! YOU'RE AS NIMBLE AS EVER, WALL-CRAWLER!
KRASH!
...NOT THAT IT WILL DO YOU ANY GOOD!
ALTHOUGH I COULD PROBABLY FINISH YOU OFF WITH A SUDDEN DOUBLE BLAST...
I PREFER TO TOY WITH YOU AWHILE!
...FOR OLD TIMES' SAKE!
HE BLASTED A HOLE... IN THE FLOOR OF THE ROOF... BELOW ME!!
I--I'M FALLING!
ZAK!
THWIPPP
BUT IF HE THINKS HE'S LOST ME...
HE'D BETTER THINK AGAIN!
7.

WHILE YOU'RE FALLING, WEB-HEAD... JUST THOUGHT I'D LET YOU KNOW...
I'VE HIDDEN THAT BLASTED TABLET IN A PLACE WHERE NO-BODY'LL EVER FIND IT AGAIN!
SO YOUR BATTLE WITH THE KING-PIN WAS A TOTAL WASTE OF TIME
AND BEFORE I FORGET--- HAPPY LANDINGS!
WHUPPFFF!
SAME TO YOU, BIG MOUTH!
THOP!
WHAT DO I DO NOW? DELIVER HIM TO THE LAW---
OR HOLD ON TO HIM---TILL I LEARN WHERE HE HID THE TABLET?
WHATEVER I DO...IT HAD BETTER BE QUICK...
IF I DON'T WANT TO MISS AUNT MAY!
FUNNY...I DIDN'T THINK THIS JOKER WOULD BE SO EASY TO...
I NOTICE YOU'VE THROWN CAUTION TO THE WINDS, YOU FOOL!
UH OH! I WAS RIGHT!
A DANGEROUS ERROR, WHEN BATTLING THE SHOCKER!
DESPITE YOUR PUNY POWERS, SPIDER-MAN..
IT'S A PITY YOU CAN'T FLY!
BOK!
8

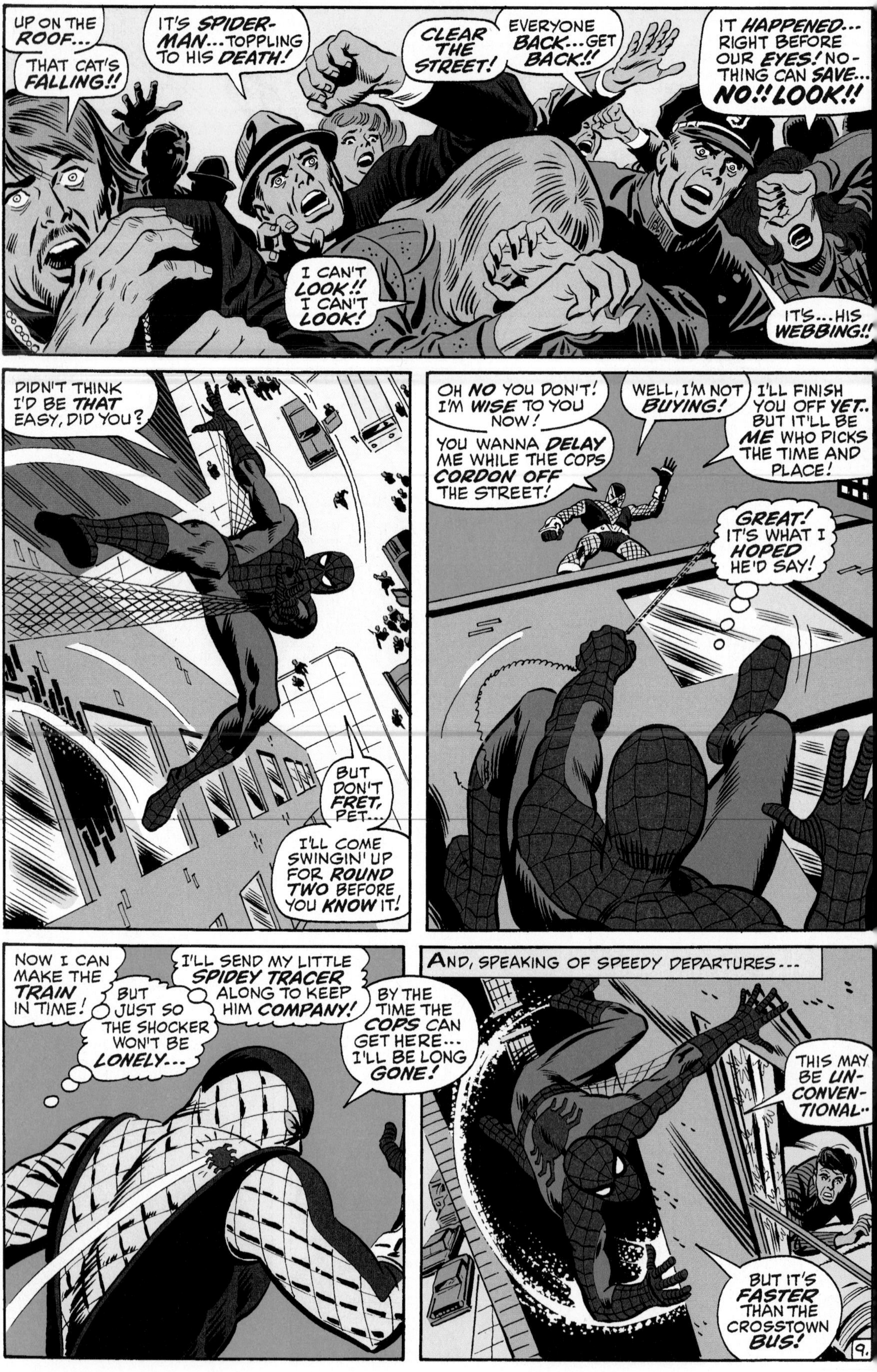
UP ON THE ROOF...
THAT CAT'S FALLING!!
IT'S SPIDER-MAN...TOPPLING TO HIS DEATH!
CLEAR THE STREET!
EVERYONE BACK...GET BACK!!
IT HAPPENED... RIGHT BEFORE OUR EYES! NO-THING CAN SAVE... NO!! LOOK!!
I CAN'T LOOK!! I CAN'T LOOK!
IT'S...HIS WEBBING!!
DIDN'T THINK I'D BE THAT EASY, DID YOU?
BUT DON'T FRET, PET...
I'LL COME SWINGIN' UP FOR ROUND TWO BEFORE YOU KNOW IT!
OH NO YOU DON'T! I'M WISE TO YOU NOW!
YOU WANNA DELAY ME WHILE THE COPS CORDON OFF THE STREET!
WELL, I'M NOT BUYING!
I'LL FINISH YOU OFF YET.. BUT IT'LL BE ME WHO PICKS THE TIME AND PLACE!
GREAT! IT'S WHAT I HOPED HE'D SAY!
NOW I CAN MAKE THE TRAIN IN TIME!
BUT JUST SO THE SHOCKER WON'T BE LONELY...
I'LL SEND MY LITTLE SPIDEY TRACER ALONG TO KEEP HIM COMPANY!
BY THE TIME THE COPS CAN GET HERE... I'LL BE LONG GONE!
AND, SPEAKING OF SPEEDY DEPARTURES...
THIS MAY BE UN-CONVEN-TIONAL..
BUT IT'S FASTER THAN THE CROSSTOWN BUS!
9.

AND NOW, FOR THE BENEFIT OF AUNT MAY'S COUNTLESS FANS, WE HAPPILY PRESENT ONE OF THE FEW SCENES WHICH DOESN'T SHOW HER AT DEATH'S DOOR---
PETER, DEAR... ARE YOU SURE YOU CAN AFFORD THIS TICKET TO FLORIDA WHICH YOU BOUGHT ME?
YOU KNOW IT, AUNT MAY!
WITH THE MONEY I GOT FOR THOSE NEWS PIX I SOLD TO THE BUGLE, I COULD SEND YOU TO THE MOON...
...BUT YOU WOULDN'T LIKE THE ALTITUDE!
HAVE A GREAT TIME...AND SOAK UP GOBS OF SUN--- LIKE THE DOC TOLD YOU TO, HEAR?
AND REMEMBER...NO DISCOTHEQUING PAST FOUR A.M.... AND DON'T OVERDO THE JOGGING AND KARATE!
SHE CAN'T HEAR ME THRU THE GLASS... BUT SHE GETS THE MES-SAGE!
BLESS HER HEART...THIS TRIP'S JUST WHAT SHE NEEDED!
SHE'S LOOKING HEALTHIER ALREADY!
AS FOR ME, I DON'T KNOW WHAT TO DO FIRST!
I STILL HAVE TO SQUARE MYSELF WITH GWEN ...AND THEN --- HEY!!
HOW ABOUT THIS! SPIDEY FINALLY GOT A DECENT WRITE-UP!
THINGS ARE REALLY LOOKING UP SINCE JOLLY JONAH'S IN THE HOSPI-TAL AND JOE ROBERTSON IS RUNNING THE PAPER!
DAILY BUGLE
SPIDER-MAN TACKLES SHOCKER!
RISKS LIFE IN VALIANT EFFORT TO CAPTURE
THEN, AS THE AMAZING YOUTH IDLY SCANS THE REST OF THE NEWSPAPER, HE SUDDENLY SEES A FATEFUL ITEM ---
A WRITE-UP ABOUT DR. CURT CONNORS!
HE'S WORKING ON SOME NEW, VITAL, HIGHLY-SECRET EXPERI-MENT AT HIS LAB IN THE FLORIDA EVERGLADES!
IT'S BEEN MONTHS SINCE OUR PATHS LAST CROSSED!
HE'S ONE OF THE GREATEST MEN I'VE KNOWN!
"BUT, EXCEPT FOR HIS WIFE,.. I'M THE ONLY OTHER PERSON WHO KNOWS THAT DOC CONNORS IS ALSO... THE DEADLY, SUPER-POWERFUL LIZARD!!"
10.

"HE CAN'T HELP BECOMING THE LIZARD--- HE DOESN'T WANT TO BE THE LIZARD--- BUT THAT DOESN'T MAKE HIM ANY THE LESS DANGEROUS!"
"I STILL REMEMBER THE LAST TIME WE FOUGHT..!"*
"IT WAS ALMOST THE END OF SPIDER-MAN!"
*IF YOU'VE FORGOTTEN ISH #45, YOU'LL HAVE TO TAKE OUR WORD FOR IT! ...SNIDE STAN.
"AND, WHAT MADE MY PREDICAMENT DOUBLY TOUGH WAS..."
"I KNEW IF I INJURED THE LIZARD, I'D BE INJURING DR. CONNORS!"
"BUT, I FINALLY TRICKED HIM INTO FOLLOWING ME INSIDE A REFRIGERATED CAR---"
"WHERE THE SUB-ZERO TEMPERATURE MADE HIM WEAK ENOUGH FOR ME TO OVERCOME!"
"AND THAT WAS THE LAST THAT I, OR ANYONE, EVER AGAIN HEARD OF THE LIZARD!"
BUT WOULDN'T IT BE A GAS IF I COULD GET A SUMMER JOB... WORKING FOR DR. CONNORS?
I COULD LEARN MORE WITH HIM THAN IN A DOZEN SCIENCE CLASSES!
ANYWAY, WHAT HAVE I GOT TO LOSE?
IF I GET A CHANCE LATER ON, MAYBE I'LL DROP HIM A LINE!
BUT RIGHT NOW... I BETTER START CONCEN-TRATING ON THE SHOCKER AGAIN!
11.

AND, SPEAKING OF CONCENTRATION, LET'S SEE WHAT JOLLY JONAH JAMESON IS COGITATING ABOUT RIGHT NOW---
WHAT'S THIS???!!
MY OWN NEWSPAPER CALLING SPIDER-MAN A HERO?!!
BUGLE
DAILY BU
SPIDER-M
THE WHOLE @**!!#!%@??!! COUNTRY'S GOING TO THE DOGS!
A MAN CAN'T EVEN ENJOY HIMSELF IN THE HOSPITAL ANYMORE!
I'M GONNA FIRE EVERY NINCOMPOOP ON THAT PAPER!!
MR. JAMESON! YOU'RE DELIRIOUS!
YOU'RE DING DONG RIGHT I AM!
WHEN I FIND OUT WHO WROTE THAT STORY..!!
DOCTOR! DOCTOR! HELP!
YOU CAN'T DO THIS TO ME! GET ME MY LAWYER!
YOU'LL NEED AN UNDERTAKER IF YOU DON'T CALM DOWN!
PRIVA
HELLO! HELLO! GET ME THE BUGLE!
NO! I DON'T WANT A DING-BUSTED MUSIC STORE... I MEANT THE DAILY BUGLE!
NOT BAGLE, DUMMY!! BUGLE!
MR. JAMESON! YOU SIMPLY MUST HOLD STILL!
HOW COME YOU DIDN'T GET ME A PET SHOP... WHERE THEY SELL BEAGLES?!!
NO! I DON'T WANT A DAD-BLASTED PET SHOP!!
GET THAT NIT-WITTED NEEDLE AWAY FROM ME!!
NO! NO! I DIDN'T MEAN YOU!
I THOUGHT I'D NEVER GET THAT TRANQUILIZER INTO HIM!
IS HE ALWAYS THAT EXCITABLE, DOCTOR?
ONLY WHEN HE'S AWAKE!
WHY DID I BECOME A PUBLISHER?
I'M TOO SENSITIVE... TOO GENTLE... FOR ALL THIS!
NOBODY... UNDERSTANDS ME... NOBODY... CARES... NOBODY...
ZZZZ
12

AND NOW THAT WE'VE SHARED A BRIEF CULTURAL MOMENT TOGETHER, LET'S RETURN TO OUR HARRASSED HERO, WHO SUDDENLY SPIES...
GWEN! GWEN... WAIT UP!
S'MATTER? I'M NOT EVEN GOOD ENOUGH TO TALK TO ANYMORE?
OH, PETER! I-- I'M SORRY!
I'M AFRAID I WAS SO BUSY THINKING ABOUT WHAT HAPPENED TO MY DAD---THAT I DIDN'T HEAR YOU!
YOUR DAD?
WHAT DID HAPPEN, GWENDY?
THEN, AFTER A BRIEF EXPLANATION...
HE'S ALL RIGHT NOW--- BUT HE MIGHT HAVE BEEN KILLED!
I'VE NEVER SEEN ANYONE AS MENACING AS THE SHOCKER!
NO? HOW ABOUT... SPIDER-MAN?
SPIDER-MAN IS--- DIFFERENT!
FOR ALL HIS POWER...HIS MYSTERY... HE'S SOMEHOW FASCINATING!
HEY! PERHAPS I SHOULD BE JEALOUS!
AT LAST SHE'S BEGINNING TO ACT MORE LIKE HER OLD YUMMY SELF!
LET'S GRAB A SODA TOGETHER LADY!
SURE, PETE... I---
LOOK! IT'S FLASH THOMPSON!
WELCOME HOME, SOLDIER!
GWEN! I HOPED YOU'D BE COMING BY, DOLL!
MAN! ARE YOU A SIGHT FOR THESE GAL-HUNGRY EYES!
BUT HOW COME YOU DIDN'T WRITE ME MORE OFTEN, BABY?
I THOUGHT MARY JANE WAS TAKING CARE OF THAT DEPARTMENT!
HAVE THINGS BEEN THAT BAD ON THE HOME FRONT?
AND, I'VE BEEN SEEING A LOT OF PETER!
HEY, JOHN WAYNE... JUST ONE DARN MINUTE..!
LAST TIME I SAW YOU, I THOUGHT THE ARMY HAD CHANGED YOU!
I COULDA SWORN YOU WERE ALMOST TURNING HUMAN!
BUT IF YOU THINK THOSE NEW STRIPES GIVE YOU THE RIGHT TO---
BUG OFF, SONNY BOY!
WHEN I NEED A CIVILIAN, I'LL ASK FOR ONE!
13

LOOK, THOMPSON, IF YOU'RE TRYING TO PUT ME DOWN IN FRONT OF MY GIRL---!
PETER! STOP IT! WHAT'S GOTTEN INTO YOU?
FLASH WAS ONLY KIDDING... THE WAY HE USED TO!
MAYBE I'M THE ONE WHO WAS WRONG ABOUT YOU, PARKER!
MAYBE YOU'RE STILL THE SAME OLD SQUARE I ALWAYS THOUGHT YOU WERE!
OKAY... OKAY! MAYBE I WAS TOO UPTIGHT!
BUT NO ONE LIKES TO SEE SOME OTHER GUY MAKING A PLAY FOR HIS GIRL!
FACE IT, FRIEND! ANY JOE WHO DOESN'T MAKE A PLAY FOR THAT CHICK IS READY FOR EMBALMING!
ANYWAY, I'M CUTTING OUT NOW!
THANKS FOR THE WARM WELCOME!
GWEN... I--I'M SORRY!
YOU SHOULD BE, PETER!
FOR A BOY WHO'S ALWAYS MISSING WHEN THERE'S ANY TROUBLE...
IT'S STRANGE HOW HOSTILE YOU CAN BE, TO A MAN WHO'S BEEN IN COMBAT!
SO... I CAN NEVER ESCAPE IT!
IN ORDER TO FUNCTION AS SPIDER-MAN, POOR PETER PARKER HAS TO TAKE OFF WHENEVER HE'S NEEDED!
THE OLD IDENTITY CONFLICT IS BACK TO HAUNT ME AGAIN!
SO HOW CAN GWEN HELP BUT THINK OF ME AS A FULL-TIME CHICKEN!
I EVEN CAUGHT THE WAY SHE CALLED ME A BOY, AND FLASH A MAN!
YEP, I REALLY BLEW IT THAT TIME!
AND NOT 'CAUSE FLASH WAS OUT OF LINE...
IT WAS BECAUSE---FOR THE FIRST TIME IN MY LIFE... I WAS JEALOUS... I WAS SCARED OF LOSING GWEN!
AND, THANKS TO MY STUPID TEMPER... I PROBABLY DID!
NUTS! I'M GONNA TACKLE THE SHOCKER NOW!
I'VE GOTTA DO SOMETHING TO MAKE ME FORGET WHAT A JACKASS I'VE BEEN!
IT WON'T TAKE LONG TO ZERO-IN ON MY LITTLE SPIDEY TRACER!
14

OKAY, SOAP OPERA TIME'S OVER NOW! SO HERE'S WHAT YOU'VE BEEN WAITING FOR---!
HEY, MARTY... LOOK OUT!
WHAT IN BLAZES IS THAT?
I DUNNO... BUT LOOK AT THE HOLE IT JUST BLASTED IN FRONT OF US!
SKREEECHHH!
ZAK!
SPTOOG!
A SECOND BLAST!!
IT TORE THE ARMORED DOOR... RIGHT OFF ITS HINGES!!
DON'T WORRY ABOUT THIS MONEY, GENTLEMEN!
I PROMISE YOU THAT THE SHOCKER WILL PUT IT TO VERY GOOD USE!
THE SHOCKER!! ...WE... SHOULDA GUESSED..!
I HATE TO SPOIL A GOOD THING FOR YOU, FELLA...
UNHHH!
BUT THIS KIND OF ENTRANCE APPEALS TO MY SENSE OF DRAMA!
15.

I'LL SAY ONE THING FOR YOU, SHOCKIE...
YOU SURE CAN TAKE YOUR LUMPS!
UH OH! HIS COSTUME AUTOMATICALLY VIBRATED AGAIN WHEN I ZONKED HIM...
ENABLING HIM TO SHRUG OFF THE BLOW ONCE MORE!
THAT CRUMMY VIBRATING POWER OF HIS MAKES HIM ONE TOUGH COOKIE TO BEAT!
I LET YOU LIVE, THE LAST TIME WE MET! BUT, NOW--
I WON'T BE SO MERCIFUL!
LUCKY HE TELEGRAPHED THAT BLAST!
I WAS ABLE TO LEAP OVER IT!
ZAK!
BUT I CAN'T KEEP DODGING ALL OF THEM!
ZZAKK!
THAT ONE WAS TOO CLOSE!
THINK, SPIDEY... THINK!
PTASK!
16

OH NO!
THE WHOLE WALL'S COMING DOWN ON ME!
BRRAKK
ZAK!
IF I CAN SHOOT OUT MY WEBS FAST ENOUGH...
I'LL USE THEM TO DEFLECT THE BRICKS!
...AND TO CUSHION MY FALL!
BY THE TIME HE GETS OUT OF THERE...
IF HE EVER DOES...
I'LL BE JUST A MEMORY ...WITH MY WELL-EARNED LOOT!
DON'T BET ON IT, SWEETIE!
THWIIPP!
PTHWAPP!
NOW WHAT'S HE DOING?
I CAN FREE MYSELF INSTANTLY!
...BY VIBRO-SHOCKING YOUR WEBS LOOSE!
ZZZZ
17.

NOW, TASTE A BLOW DELIVERED WITH VIBRO-SHOCK POWER...
POWER WHICH MAKES IT A DOZEN TIMES MORE POTENT THAN ANY NORMAL PUNCH!
NICE TRY, GUY!
BUT, SINCE I'M AT LEAST A DOZEN TIMES STRONGER THAN ANY NORMAL CUT-UP...
IT'LL TAKE MORE THAN THAT TO DOWN ME!
CAREFUL! WE DON'T WANNA HURT OUR TENDER LITTLE CLAWS NOW, DO WE?
HE'S FIGHTING MAD... REACHING UP AT ME AGAIN--!
ZAK!
NOW WASN'T THAT A SILLY THING TO DO?
THUPP!
18

ALL RIGHT, SPIDER-MAN!
YOU'VE TRIED TO MOCK ME FOR THE LAST TIME!
WADDAYA MEAN TRIED?
I THOUGHT I DID A PRETTY NEAT JOB OF IT!
HAVE TO MOVE FAST...
BEFORE HE ZAPS ANOTHER VIBRO-BLAST AT ME!
THERE, BIG MAN! YOU CAN'T HIT WHAT YOU CAN'T SEE!
MY FACE! ...COVERED WITH WEBBING!
KNOW SOMETHING? IT'S AN IMPROVE-MENT!
AND NOW... LET'S CUT THE KIDDING AROUND...!
BROP!
YOU SHOULDN'T HAVE TOLD ME HOW YOUR VIBRO-POWER DEFLECTS MY BLOWS!
...YOU CONVINCED ME TO USE MY SUNDAY PUNCH!
AND HERE IT IS NOT EVEN THE WEEKEND! TSK! TSK!
OH, BY THE WAY--- DON'T BOTHER TRYING TO VIBRATE YOURSELF LOOSE!
YOU'LL FIND IT AWFULLY FRUSTRATING...
...'SPECIALLY SINCE I COPPED YOUR WRIST POWER UNITS!
THEY'LL MAKE A SWINGIN' PAIR OF CUFF LINKS!
19

KRRAK!
RAK!
KRRAK!
FOR THE LUVVA MIKE! NOW WHAT??
IT'S THE DRIVER OF THE ARMORED CAR!
HE MUST THINK I WAS IN CAHOOTS WITH THE SHOCKER!
STAY WHERE YOU ARE, WEB-SLINGER!
HAND OVER THAT MONEY BAG!
I'D LIKE TO OBLIGE, PAL...
BUT A FELLA GETS MIGHTY TIRED OF BEING A FULL-TIME TARGET!
ANYWAY, IF YOU'LL TAKE A SQUINT AROUND THE CORNER...
YOU'LL REALIZE HOW YOU'VE BEEN WASTING BULLETS!
PTHIK!
PTHAK!
PTHOK!
IT'S THE SHOCKER... ALL GIFT-WRAPPED AND READY FOR MAILING!
AND HERE'S THE DOUGH HE GRABBED FROM THE TRUCK!
HOW ABOUT THAT? THE WALL-CRAWLER WAS ON THE LEVEL...HE GOT IT BACK FOR US!
SO HOW COME NO ONE EVER TRUSTS 'IM?
AND, THAT'S JUST WHAT SPIDEY WOULD LIKE TO KNOW---!
SO I FINALLY NAILED THE SHOCKER... BIG DEAL!
I'M IN THE DOGHOUSE WITH GWEN...THE TABLET IS GONE AGAIN... I JUST REMEMBERED SOMETHING ELSE...
I FORGOT TO TAKE A SINGLE PICTURE OF THE ENTIRE BATTLE!
SO ALL I GET OUT OF IT IS SOME SKINNED KNUCKLES!
IN OTHER WORDS, THE WONDERFUL PARKER LUCK IS STILL RUNNING TRUE TO FORM! NUTS!
NEXT
SPIDEY'S NEWEST SUPER-FOE!

SPIDER-MAN
12¢
IND.
73
JUNE
the AMAZING SPIDER-MAN™
APPROVED BY THE COMICS CODE AUTHORITY
MARVEL™ COMICS GROUP
FEATURING: MAN-MOUNTAIN MARKO!
ROMITA
THE WEB CLOSES!

THE AMAZING SPIDER-MAN!™
THE WEB CLOSES!
INTRODUCING: THE SENSATIONAL MAN-MOUNTAIN MARKO
IT'S MY FAULT THAT CAPTAIN STACY WAS INJURED BY THE SHOCKER!
IF I HADN'T LEFT THAT ANCIENT TABLET HERE, HE WOULDN'T HAVE BROKEN IN TO STEAL IT!
BUT, NOW THAT I SEE THAT GWEN'S DAD IS OKAY, I...
UH OH! SOMEONE'S COMING!
ARE YOU COMFORTABLE, DAD? CAN I BRING YOU ANYTHING?
I'M FINE, THANKS, HONEY! FEELING AS GOOD AS NEW AGAIN!
OKAY... BUT IF YOU WANT ANYTHING, JUST BELLOW, FELLOW!
IT'S GWENDY! BOY... SHE MUST HAVE TAKEN A DOUBLE DOSE OF PRETTY PILLS TODAY!
AUTHORED BY: STAN (THE MAN) LEE
INNOVATED BY: BIG JOHN BUSCEMA
COORDINATED BY: JOHN (RING-A-DING) ROMITA
ILLUSTRATED BY: JIM (MADMAN) MOONEY
LETTERED BY: SLEEPY SAM ROSEN

BY THE WAY, DAD... I DON'T SUPPOSE PETER PARKER HAS CALLED?
WHY, DEAR? WERE YOU EXPECTING HIM TO?
WELL, I DID THINK THAT HE...
OH, WHY WORRY ABOUT THAT? HE'S NOT THE ONLY BOY IN THE WORLD!
ANYWAY, I THINK HE'S STILL ANGRY ABOUT HIS MEETING WITH FLASH THOMPSON YESTERDAY!*
IF HE'S NOT THE ONLY BOY IN THE WORLD... WHY DO YOUR EYES GLOW THAT WAY WHEN YOU MENTION HIM, YOUNG LADY?
JUST MY LUCK TO HAVE A FATHER WHO'S AN EX-DETECTIVE!
NITEY NITE, MISTER CUPID!
*IF YOU MISSED IT LAST ISH, NO SWEAT! IT'S GOT NOTHING TO DO WITH THIS MONTH'S FESTIVITIES ANYWAY! STRAIGHT-TALKIN' STAN.
WHEW! ONLY A NUT LIKE ME WOULD BE HANGING AROUND ON THE CEILING WHEN HE COULD HAVE A DREAM-THING LIKE GWEN IN HIS ARMS!
WELL, IF THEY EVER GIVE MEDALS FOR STUPIDITY... I'LL GET A CHESTFULL!
SHE'S GONE! I CAN GO DOWN NOW!
CAPTAIN STACY ... DON'T BE ALARMED!
I'VE SOMETHING TO ASK YOU!
IT'S ABOUT THE STOLEN TABLET!
SPIDER-MAN!
YOU'VE GOT YOUR SIGNALS CROSSED, MISTER...
THIS ISN'T GRAND CENTRAL STATION!
JUST BECAUSE I DON'T THINK YOU'RE AS BAD AS YOU'RE PAINTED...
THAT DOESN'T MEAN I LIKE HAVING MY HOUSE BROKEN INTO!
SORRY ABOUT THAT!
ALL RIGHT... WHAT DO YOU WANT TO KNOW?
2.

IT'S ABOUT THE SHOCKER!
WHEN HE STOLE THE TABLET FROM YOU, DID HE LEAVE ANY CLUES?
DID HE MENTION ANY PLACE WHERE HE MIGHT HAVE INTENDED TO HIDE IT??
I'M AFRAID HE WAS TOO SMART FOR THAT!
I WAS LUCKY ENOUGH TO CATCH HIM, AND HAVE HIM GIFT-WRAPPED FOR THE COPS...
BUT NOBODY'S BEEN ABLE TO LEARN WHERE HE STASHED THE STOLEN TABLET!
WHY ARE YOU SO INTERESTED?
THERE ARE STILL SOME DIE-HARDS, LIKE JONAH JAMESON, WHO THINK I HAD A HAND IN STEALING IT!
THE ONLY WAY I CAN REALLY CLEAR MYSELF IS TO FIND THE TABLET AGAIN... AND RETURN IT!
BUT, SINCE THERE'S NOTHING MORE THAT YOU CAN TELL ME...
AND SINCE I FORGOT TO BRING MY CRYING TOWEL...
THIS IS AS GOOD A TIME AS ANY FOR ME TO SPLIT!
WAIT!
I JUST REMEMBER SOMETHING...
THE SHOCKER USED TO HAVE A GIRL FRIEND!
SHE PAID HIS BAIL ONCE OR TWICE!
WHAT BETTER PLACE TO HIDE THE TABLET THAN WITH HER??
TALK FASTER, MAN!
IT'S DRAFTY OUT HERE!
SHE USED TO BE IN SHOW BUSINESS... CALLED HERSELF AN EXOTIC DANCER!
SHE LIVED SOMEWHERE ON THE WEST SIDE... NEAR THE THEATRE DISTRICT!
KNOW SOMETHING? YOU'RE A REGULAR EARL WILSON!
THANKS FOR THE INFO, CAP! SEE YOU AROUND!
IF YOU RUN INTO TROUBLE... CALL THE POLICE!
DON'T TAKE THE LAW INTO YOUR OWN HANDS!
OH, PERISH FORBID!
3.

NOW ALL I HAVE TO DO IS FIND ONE SPECIAL FEMALE IN A CITY OF MILLIONS!
HOTEL
AND I DIDN'T EVEN THINK TO ASK IF HE KNEW HER NAME!
OH WELL... IT'LL BE MORE SPORTING THIS WAY!
AT LEAST STACY NARROWED IT DOWN TO ONE NEIGHBORHOOD!
THEN, AFTER ABOUT AN HOUR OF WEARISOME WEB-SWINGING---
AT LAST! MY SPIDEY SENSE IS STARTING TO TINGLE!
SO...IF IT ISN'T A FALSE ALARM...
I SHOULD BE ON TO SOME-THING!
THE TINGLING GETS STRONGER AS I COME CLOSER TO THAT WINDOW BELOW!
BUT WHAT'S ALL THAT RACKET I HEAR?
SOUNDS LIKE SOME KINDA FIGHT!
4.

VOICES... YELLING ABOUT A HIDDEN TABLET!
FOR ONCE I'M IN LUCK! I FOUND IT FIRST CRACK OUT OF THE BOX!
UH OH... WAIT A MINUTE!
MAYBE I'M NOT SO LUCKY! LOOK AT THE SIZE OF THAT GUY!!
I TELL YOU I DON'T KNOW ANYTHING!
THE SHOCKER NEVER GAVE ME ANY TABLET!
YOU'VE... GOT TO BELIEVE ME!
MAN-MOUNTAIN MARKO DON'T HAVE TO BELIEVE NOTHIN', SISTER!
THE MAGGIA'S TOP BRASS GOT WAYS OF FINDING THINGS OUT, SEE?
AND THEY SAY THE SHOCKER STASHED THAT HUNKA STONE HERE WITH YOU!
AND THEY DON'T PAY ME TO TAKE NO FOR AN ANSWER!
BUT... IF THE SHOCKER EVER LEARNS ...THAT I DOUBLE-CROSSED HIM...
YOU MEAN THAT'S WHAT YOU'RE WORRIED ABOUT?
HE'S ALL TUCKED AWAY IN JAIL NOW, AIN'T HE?
BUT ME... I'M ON THE LOOSE!
AND I AIN'T LEAVIN' TILL I GET WHAT I CAME FOR!!
NO! NO! DON'T..!!
5

RELAX, SISTER! YOU AIN'T GONNA GET HURT---
PROVIDIN' I FIND THAT TABLET!
IT'S GOTTA BE HIDDEN HERE SOMEWHERE!
YOU---TORE THAT HEAVY SEAT APART... WITH YOUR BARE HANDS!
HOLD IT, BIG MAN! HAVEN'T YOU HEARD ABOUT INFLATION?
DO YOU KNOW WHAT IT COSTS TO UPHOLSTER A CHAIR NOWADAYS?
SPIDER-MAN!!
YA THINK YOU CAN STOP ME?
WELL, I DID SORT OF NURTURE THAT HOPE!
YOU'RE A REAL WISE-GUY, HUH?
WELL, WISE-GUYS BUG ME, SEE?
AND MAN-MOUNTAIN MARKO DON'T LIKE TO BE BUGGED
ZOKK!

STILL AWAKE, HUH?
WELL, DON'T WORRY, SHORTY...
I'LL TAKE CARE OF THAT REAL FAST!
HEY!
MAN-MOUNTAIN, HUH?
BTAMM!
TO ME, CHARLIE... YOU'RE JUST AN ANT-HILL!
NOW, LADY... ABOUT THAT TABLET--!!
IF YOU'LL GIVE IT TO ME---YOUR TROUBLES WILL BE OVER!
YOU...HANDLED THAT GIANT... LIKE HE WAS A TOY!!
YOU'RE ...AS DANGER-OUS...AS THEY SAY YOU ARE!
AWW, I'M JUST A PUSSY-CAT WHEN YOU GET TO KNOW ME!
7.

THE POOR GAL'S TERRIFIED!
I DON'T KNOW IF IT'S ME...
...OR FEAR OF THE SHOCKER IN CASE SHE GIVES UP THE TABLET!
I'VE GOT TO CALM HER DOWN, SOMEHOW!
LOOK, MISS... THE SHOCKER CAN'T BLAME YOU FOR GIVING UP THE TABLET!
SINCE I ONCE MANAGED TO GET IT AWAY FROM HIM...
HE WOULDN'T EXPECT YOU TO HAVE ANY BETTER LUCK!
HE THOUGHT I'D BE OUT FOR GOOD!
WELL, HE'S GOT A LOT TO LEARN ABOUT MAN-MOUNTAIN MARKO'S POWER!
I'LL TACKLE HIM NOW.. WHILE HE'S TRYIN' TO CON THE CHICK!
THROPP!
THIS MAKES US EVEN, PANTY-WAIST!
WE HATE TO CUT OUT AT A TIME LIKE THIS, BUT WE JUST REMEMBERED... THERE'S SOMETHING ELSE GOING ON ACROSS TOWN WHICH WILL HAVE A GREAT EFFECT ON SPIDEY'S LIFE...!
FIRST THE KINGPIN STOLE THAT BLASTED TABLET... THEN SPIDER-MAN GOT IT... THEN THE SHOCKER... AND NOW, WHO KNOWS?
MAYBE I WAS A FOOL TO WORK FOR THE KINGPIN!
I GUESS HE'LL ALLOW ME TO LANGUISH IN HERE!
OKAY, WILSON.. LOOK ALIVE!
CLICK!
NOW WHAT?
8

WE NEVER THOUGHT YOU'D BE WORTH THAT MUCH TO ANYONE---
BUT SOMEONE JUST POSTED YOUR BAIL!
YOU MEAN... I'M GOING FREE?!!
SO THE KINGPIN DID COME THRU FOR ME AFTER ALL!
I SHOULD HAVE KNOWN I'M MUCH TOO VALUABLE TO BE JUST WRITTEN-OFF!
BUT THEN... WHO?
GUESS AGAIN, MISTER!
IT WASN'T THE KINGPIN!
THE NAME IS CICERO... CAESAR CICERO!
GET YOUR THINGS AND FOLLOW ME, WILSON!
I HAVEN'T GOT ALL DAY!
IF YOU'RE GOING OUT WITH A CHARACTER LIKE HIM, I'M FIGURING YOU'LL BE BACK HERE PRETTY SOON!
WHY NOT THINK IT OVER, WILSON?
MISTER, I'D TAKE OFF WITH TYPHOID MARY JUST TO GET OUT OF HERE!
CAESAR CICERO! YOU'RE THE BIG-TIME MOUTHPIECE FOR THE MAGGIA!
WHY WOULD YOU WANT TO BAIL ME OUT?
HMM...YOU'RE NOT EXACTLY A CHATTERBOX, ARE YOU?
THE CAR'S WAITIN', BIG C!
NOW LISTEN GOOD! I DON'T REPEAT THINGS!
YOU WERE THE KINGPIN'S BIGGEST BRAIN!
SO YOU KNOW MORE ABOUT THE TABLET THAN ANYONE!
THE TABLET?? BUT..I DON'T HAVE IT!
YEAH ---WE KNOW!
BUT IT'LL SOON BE OURS! AND WHEN IT IS---
SOMEONE'S GOTTA TELL US WHAT ITS SECRET IS!
AND THAT'S WHERE YOU COME IN!
BUT I... I DON'T KNOW THE SECRET!
THEN THAT'S JUST TOO BAD ---FOR YOU!
9.

AND NOW, BELIEVER--- BACK TO THE BUSINESS AT HAND...
I'M BEGINNIN' TO LOSE MY PATIENCE, LADY!
KRASH!
IF I DON'T LATCH ONTO THAT TABLET PRETTY SOON..!
HEY! WAIT, A MINUTE!
WELL, WELL! NOW AIN'T THIS REAL CLEVER ?!!
A COZY LITTLE WALL SAFE, JUST MINDIN' ITS OWN BUSINESS ...BEHIND A TWO-BIT PAINTING!
NO! YOU MUSTN'T OPEN IT! NO!
CLAM UP, SISTER... AND I MEAN NOW!
I CAN RIP THIS TOY OUTTA THE WALL WITH ONE HAND, JUST LIKE ---HEY!
DON'T YOU KNOW WHEN TO QUIT?
SURE, BIG MOUTH... BUT THIS ISN'T THE TIME!
IT AIN'T, HUH?
YOU HALF-PINT PUNK---I'LL MOP UP THE PLACE WITH YA!
WHEN I'M FINISHED THIS TIME, THEY'LL HAVETA SCOOP YA UP WITH A BLOTTER!
GOLLY GEE! I WISH YOU WOULDN'T TALK THAT WAY!
IT'S HARD FOR A FELLA TO FIGHT WHEN HE'S TREMBLING IN FEAR!
10.

BUT, I'LL TRY TO CONTROL MY LITTLE SURGE OF PANIC... AS ANY STALWART SUPER-HERO SHOULD!
YOU'RE REAL CUTE WITH THE WORDS, MASKED MAN---BUT IT'LL TAKE MORE THAN THEM TO GET YOU OUTTA THIS!
WHEW! WHAT DO THEY FEED THIS JOKER? HE'S AS STRONG AS A BULL!
GET ME OUT? I THOUGHT YOU WERE THE ONE WHO NEEDED A HELPING HAND!
AND, SPEAKING OF HELPING HANDS...
I'LL BE GLAD TO CONTRIBUTE A COUPLE...
SO LONG AS YOU KEEP GETTING THEM KNUCKLES UP!
THIS IS RIDICULOUS!
I KEEP SOCKING ---AND HE KEEPS STANDING!
BROK!
AWRIGHT, WALL-CRAWLER ---NOW THE PARTY'S OVER!
THIS WOULD PUT A CHARGIN' ELEPHANT TO SLEEP!
IF THEY HAD ANY BRAINS, THEY'DA GIVEN ME WHAT I WANTED RIGHT OFF THE BAT!
IT WOULDA SAVED EVERY-ONE A LOTTA TROUBLE!
'CAUSE MAN-MOUNTAIN MARKO ALWAYS GETS WHAT HE'S AFTER!
11.

THIS IS YOUR LUCKY DAY, WEBHEAD!
IF I HADN'T FOUND THE TABLET, I MIGHTA REALLY GOT MAD AT YA!
TOO BAD THE DAME AIN'T GONNA BE SO LUCKY!
WHA--WHAT DID YOU MEAN BY THAT??
I DON'T HAVETA WORRY ABOUT SPIDER-MAN--- HE CAN'T GO BLABBIN' TO THE COPS ANY MORE'N I CAN!
BUT THEY MIGHT LISTEN TO A PIGEON LIKE YOU...
AND LADY...YOU KNOW TOO MUCH!
MARKO, I'M SURPRISED AT YOU!
DON'T YOU KNOW IT'S IMPOLITE TO THREATEN A FEMALE?
IF YOU'RE STILL SPOILING FOR A FIGHT...
HOW ABOUT TRYING ME FOR SIZE?
BUT, LEST YOU THINK THAT SPIDEY'S THE ONLY GENT IN THE WORLD WITH TROUBLES, LET'S SEGUE OVER TO THE DAILY BUGLE FOR A MINUTE OR TWO, WHERE WE FIND---
I'VE ALWAYS GIVEN YOU YOUR HEAD, SON---LET YOU DO WHAT YOU THOUGHT WAS BEST!
BUT WHEN IT COMES TO QUITTING SCHOOL, I DRAW THE LINE!
A MAN WITHOUT AN EDUCATION IS LIKE...
I KNOW... I KNOW! I HEARD IT ENOUGH!
BUT WHAT'S THE POINT BEIN' A SUCCESS IN WHITEY'S WORLD?
WHY MUST WE PLAY BY HIS RULES?
12

THE RULES ARE THE SAME, RANDY...NO MATTER WHO THE PLAYERS ARE...NO MATTER WHERE THE GAME IS PLAYED!
YOU WANNA BE A MILITANT... FINE! MAYBE WE NEED MORE OF THAT STRIPE!
BUT THE NAME OF THE GAME IS POWER, SON...
AND EDUCATION IS THE GREATEST POWER OF ALL!
THE WHOLE WORLD'S CHANGING, RANDY...AND MAYBE THE PARADE'S JUST PASSING ME BY!
BUT I STILL WANT WHAT'S BEST FOR MY PEOPLE ...WHAT'S BEST FOR YOU!
JUST OUTSIDE THAT DOOR ...ALL AROUND US...EVERY-WHERE...THERE'S A WAR GOING ON...
A WAR AGAINST BIGOTRY, INJUSTICE AND WANT!
IT TAKES WEAPONS TO FIGHT A WAR, SON...
AND WITHOUT EDUCATION...YOU'RE A SOLDIER UNARMED!
LOOK, DAD...I DIG WHAT YOU SAY...
AND I KNOW YOU'VE GOT IT MADE HERE IN WHITEY'S WORLD!
BUT WHAT ABOUT THE OTHER BRO-THERS WHO PLAYED IT YOUR WAY...WHO GOT THEIR SHEEP-SKINS...AND STILL CAN'T MAKE IT ON THE OUTSIDE?
I... WASN'T PROMISING... UTOPIA!
ROBERTSON! WHERE'S ROBERTSON??
AH HA!! THERE YOU ARE!
YOU QUISLING! YOU BENEDICT ARNOLD!
YOU MADE A HERO OUT OF SPIDER-MAN WHEN MY BACK WAS TURNED!
NOW WHOA, JJ ...SIMMER DOWN!
THE BUGLE'S SUPPOSED TO TELL IT LIKE IT IS, RIGHT?
WRONG!!
YOU KNOW HOW THE BUGLE FEELS ABOUT THAT WEB-SLING-ING WEASEL...YOU KNOW HOW I FEEL ABOUT HIM!!
SURE! SO WRITE ALL THE EDITORIALS YOU WANT...IT'S YOUR PAPER!
BUT THE NEWS COLUMNS ARE MY DEPART-MENT!
AND I CALL 'EM AS I SEE 'EM!
YOU THINK I CAN'T FIRE YOU?
YOU WON'T HAVE TO SACK ME, MAN!
IF YOU WANT THE NEWS DISTORTED, BECAUSE OF YOUR OWN PARANOIC VENDETTA...GET YOURSELF ANOTHER JOE!
WITH HIS WHOLE FUTURE AT STAKE...EVERY-THING HE'S SPENT A LIFETIME WORK-ING FOR...
DAD'S STANDING RIGHT UP TO HIM!
NOW WAIT ONE DING-DONG MINUTE THERE, ROBBIE!
I ACCEPT YOUR APOLOGY!!
13.

DUNNO WHAT'S GOTTEN INTO YOU ANYWAY!
USED TO BE A MAN COULD ENJOY BLOWIN' HIS TOP ONCE IN A WHILE!
'SPECIALLY WHEN HE OWNED THE PLACE!!
DUNNO WHAT THE WORLD'S COMING TO THESE DAYS...
JUST REMEMBER ONE THING FROM NOW ON...
I PAY YOUR SALARY HERE... NOT THAT CRUMMY WEBHEAD!
THAT'S WHAT I MEAN, DAD!
WHY SHOULD YOU HAVETA TAKE ALL THAT BULL FROM A RACIST LIKE HIM?
AND THAT'S WHAT I MEAN, SON! YOU'VE GOT A GOOD BRAIN... USE IT!
JAMESON IS NO MORE A RACIST THAN LITTLE EVA!
HE'S A BIG, BLUNDERING BLOWHARD WITH A HANG-UP ABOUT SPIDER-MAN!
BUT JUST 'CAUSE HE'S WHITE, IT DOESN'T MAKE HIM A RACIST!
WE'LL NEVER GET ANYWHERE TILL WE RECOGNIZE WHO OUR REAL ENEMIES ARE!
HOWEVER, ON THE OTHER SIDE OF TOWN, A CERTAIN YOUNG LADY HAS ABSOLUTELY NO PROBLEM IN BEING ABLE TO TELL WHO HER ENEMY IS! VOILÁ...
YELL LOUDER, SISTER... SO SPIDER-MAN'LL HEAR YA!
NO! YOU CAN'T! NO!
HELP!! SOMEBODY... HELP!
GO ON, HALF-PINT... HERE'S YOUR CHANCE TO BE A HERO!
I HAVE TO REACH THAT WINDOW IN TIME!
NOW!
NICE TRY, LITTLE MAN!
BUT NOT NICE ENOUGH!
14

HAH! I FIGGERED YOU'D GO OUT THE WINDOW, TRYIN' TO SAVE 'ER!
WELL, LOTS OF LUCK, MASKED MAN! YER SURE GONNA NEED IT!
NO MATTER HOW YA MAKE OUT... I'M THE WINNER!
I GOT WHAT I CAME FOR!
SHE HASN'T REACHED THE GROUND YET!
IF I CAN JUST SHOOT MY WEB FAST ENOUGH---!
THWIPP!
GOT HER!
EASY NOW... EEEEASY!
I ONLY HAD TIME TO SHOOT OUT A REAL THIN STRAND!
IT JUST HAS TO HOLD!
15.

THEN, A FEW STRENUOUS, SUSPENSEFUL SECONDS LATER...
YOU'LL BE OKAY NOW, MISS...
WHICH IS MORE THAN THEY'LL SAY ABOUT THAT MAN-MOUNTAIN... WHEN I CATCH UP WITH HIM!
THE ROOM'S EMPTY INSIDE...WELL, I DIDN'T EXPECT HIM TO STILL BE THERE!
AND NOW, WHILE SPIDEY CATCHES HIS BREATH... LET'S SHIFT OUR SCENE ONCE MORE...
YOU SAY YOU WANT TO SOLVE THE MYSTERY OF THE TABLET!
SO I BRING YOU A MAN WHO CAN HELP TO DO IT!
YOU...YOU'RE THE MAN CALLED SILVERMANE...!
ONE OF THE LAST OF THE LEGENDARY, OLD-TIME LEADERS OF... THE MAGGIA!
AND YOU ARE BUT A WORTHLESS PAWN OF THE KINGPIN!
SO, CAESAR! ONCE AGAIN YOU ACTED WITHOUT MY ORDERS!
ONCE AGAIN YOU TRY TO SHOW THAT YOU ARE MORE SUITED FOR LEADERSHIP THAN THE AGING SILVER-MANE!
AND, PERHAPS YOU ARE... PERHAPS YOU ARE!
I AM OLD... AND I AM TIRED...
BUT THIS I TELL YOU, CAESAR...
SO LONG AS I DO LIVE... IT IS I WHO LEAD... AND YOU WHO FOLLOW!
NOW GO! I KNOW YOU ARE ANXIOUS TO RETURN TO YOUR PLOTTING...
AS YOU SCHEME ANEW FOR A MEANS TO DEPOSE ME!
SINCE YOU ARE HERE, WILSON, YOU WILL REMAIN!
THE TABLET IS ON ITS WAY... WE WILL STUDY IT TO-GETHER!
AND WHAT ABOUT ME?
NOT EVEN YOU CAN ORDER ME ABOUT THIS WAY, SILVERMANE!
DO NOT PROVOKE ME, CAESAR!
I AM OLD ...BUT THE POWER STILL IS MINE!
16

I GOT IT, BOSS! I SNATCHED IT OUTTA THE GIRL'S APARTMENT!
NOT EVEN SPIDER-MAN COULD STOP ME!
IT'S THE ANCIENT TABLET... THE MOST PRICELESS STONE OF ALL TIME!
YOU HAVE DONE WELL, MARKO!
BUT I KNEW YOU WOULD NOT FAIL ME!
WHAT MAKES THAT CRUMMY HUNKA ROCK SO VALUABLE, SILVERMANE?
THAT, MY GIGANTIC UNDERLING, IS WHAT I SOON INTEND TO LEARN!
WILSON! STUDY IT... MAKE CERTAIN IT IS GENUINE!
IT'S THE McCOY, ALL RIGHT! I'D KNOW IT ANYWHERE!
WHAT DO ALL THEM NUTTY-LOOKIN' SCRATCHES ON IT MEAN?
THEY ARE ANCIENT HEIRO-GLYPHICS...
WHICH NO MAN HAS YET BEEN ABLE TO TRANSLATE!
BUT, THEY ARE THE KEY TO ONE OF THE GREATEST SECRETS OF ALL TIME!
YEAH? AND WHAT'S THAT, BOSS?
AHH... IF I TOLD YOU, THEN IT WOULD BE A SECRET NO LONGER!
17.

BUT, SINCE THE NAME OF THE MAG IS SPIDER-MAN, LET'S SEE WHAT OUR SWINGIN' SUPER-HERO IS DOING RIGHT NOW---
IT WOULD TAKE ME A WEEK TO COVER THE WHOLE CITY, STREET BY STREET---
AND EVEN THEN, THERE'D BE NO GUARANTEE OF FINDING MAN-MOUNTAIN MARKO!
MY BEST BET IS TO HANG LOOSE ---AND WAIT TILL I GET A LEAD!
ONE THING'S FOR SURE... IT WON'T BE EASY FOR A JOKER LIKE HIM TO STAY HIDDEN FOR LONG!
SO I MIGHT AS WELL HEAD FOR HOME NOW!
NO ONE'S APT TO SEE ME SWINGING INTO THE WINDOW AT THIS TIME OF NIGHT!
AND EVEN IF THEY DID... WHAT WOULD THEY DO ABOUT IT?
18

LOOKS LIKE HARRY'S OUT ON ANOTHER DATE!
BOY... NOTHING'S BETTER FOR A DOUBLE-IDENTITY DO-GOODER THAN A REAL PLAYBOY ROOMMATE!
BUT, SPEAKING OF PLAYBOYS... IT'S ABOUT TIME I DUG UP SOME MORE DOUGH TO PAY FOR AUNT MAY'S FLORIDA VACATION!
I HAVEN'T HAD A CHANCE TO TAKE ANY GOOD PIX LATELY, AND---
HEY! WAIT A MINUTE---!
I JUST REMEMBERED ... I'VE BEEN WANTING TO CALL DR. CONNORS ... DOWN IN FLORIDA!
IT WOULD BE A GAS IF I COULD GET A SUMMER JOB, WORKING FOR HIM!
NOT ONLY WOULD I BE ABLE TO LOOK AFTER AUNT MAY...
BUT I COULD LEARN MORE NATURAL SCIENCE FROM CURT CONNORS THAN ANYONE I KNOW!
I'LL JUST INVEST IN ONE LONG-DISTANCE CALL!
HE'S USUALLY WORKING IN HIS LAB LATE AT NIGHT!
OH! SORRY I WOKE YOU, MRS. CONNORS!
WHAT? YOU SAY THE DOC ISN'T THERE?
HE JUST LEFT UNEXPECTEDLY WITH A COUPLE OF MEN... WHOM YOU'VE NEVER SEEN BEFORE?
WELL, I.. I'M SORRY I BOTHERED YOU!
STRANGE... DOC CONNORS ALMOST NEVER LEAVES HIS LAB IN THE EVERGLADES!
HE KNOWS THE DANGER... IN CASE SOMETHING SHOULD GO WRONG AGAIN...
--IF HE SHOULD HAPPEN TO TURN INTO... THE LIZARD!
19

SOMEHOW, I CAN'T GET HIM OUT OF MY MIND...
AND I CAN'T STOP WONDERING WHO THOSE TWO MEN WERE...
OR WHERE HE WENT WITH THEM... IN THE MIDDLE OF THE NIGHT ...OR WHY??
Love Gwen
HOWEVER, IT SEEMS THAT WE SHALL LEARN THE ANSWER BEFORE PETER PARKER DOES, AS WE RETURN TO THE LUXURIOUS HEADQUARTERS OF THE MAN CALLED SILVERMANE...
SO...YOU WANT THE SECRET OF THE TABLET, EH?
ALL IT TOOK WAS ONE PHONE CALL TO OUR BOYS DOWN SOUTH...
TO GET THEM TO PUT DR. CONNORS ON THE FIRST PLANE TO NEW YORK!
AGAIN YOU PROVE YOURSELF MORE CAPABLE OF DE-CISION THAN THE AGED SILVER-MANE, EH, MY FRIEND?
I PROVE NOTHING... EXCEPT MY LOYALTY TO THE MAGGIA!
THE MAGGIA!! WHAT DO YOU WANT WITH ME?
LOOK...I'M JUST A DIME-A-DOZEN RESEARCH SCIENTIST FROM THE EVERGLADES!
I DON'T KNOW WHAT YOU'RE AFTER, BUT YOU GRABBED YOURSELF THE WRONG MAN!
YOU UNDERESTIMATE YOURSELF, DOCTOR! YOU ARE JUST THE MAN WE NEED!
BUT YOU CAN'T KEEP ME HERE! IT... IT ISN'T SAFE!
IS THAT A FACT?
AND JUST WHY ISN'T IT SAFE, CONNORS?
I... CAN'T ANSWER THAT!!
NEXT
ALL BEDLAM BREAKS LOOSE!
20

SPIDER-MAN
12¢
IND.
74
JULY
the AMAZING
SPIDER-MAN
APPROVED BY THE COMICS CODE AUTHORITY
MARVEL COMICS GROUP
ROMITA
FEATURING:
THE FANTASTIC
SECRET
OF THE
PETRIFIED
TABLET!

THE AMAZING SPIDER-MAN!
IF THIS BE BEDLAM!
YOU BETTER DO WHAT SILVERMANE WANTS, SEE?
EVEN IF YA DON'T CARE ABOUT YOURSELF... REMEMBER---
WE ALSO "INVITED" YER WIFE AND KID UP HERE TO KEEP YA COMPANY!
SO, IF THE OLD MAN WANTS YA TO TRANSLATE THAT TABLET OF HIS---
--YOU BETTER START TRANSLATIN'!
MARKO! YOU MUST NOT YET HARM HIM!
THE MAGGIA HAS MUCH USE FOR DR. CONNORS!
STOP! YOU DON'T KNOW THE DANGER!
YOU DON'T REALIZE... WHAT CAN HAPPEN!
STAN (the MAN) LEE, SCRIPT WRITER
JOHNNY (RING-A-DING) ROMITA, INNOVATOR
JIM (MADMAN) MOONEY, ILLUSTRATOR
SAM (ROSY) ROSEN, LETTERER
...ALL REQUEST YOU TO ENJOY THIS DAZZLING DONNYBROOK!

MARKO! IF YOU INJURE HIM, HE WILL BE USELESS TO US!
LOOK... IF YA WANNA CONVINCE THE PUNK... LEMME DO IT MY WAY!
AIN'T NOBODY CAN ROUGH A GUY UP LIKE MAN-MOUNTAIN MARKO!
JUST STAND BACK, SILVERMANE... AND I'LL SHOW YA!
THAP!
YOU THINK YOU SPEAK TO SOME CHEAP, STREET-CORNER HOOD?
I MAY BE OLD ...BUT I AM STILL LEADER HERE!
NO ONE BUT SILVERMANE GIVES THE ORDERS!
YOU HAD NO CALL TO SHAME ME THAT WAY... IN FRONT OF EVERYBODY!
WE WILL SPEAK OF IT NO MORE!
I MUST... PAUSE FOR A MOMENT! THE EXERTION HAS ...CAUSED MY PAIN ...TO RETURN!
A PITY... THAT CAESAR CICERO... IS NOT HERE!
HOW MY SCHEMING RIVAL WOULD ENJOY... THIS EVIDENCE OF... AN OLD MAN'S FRAILTY!
SECONDS LATER...
THE PAIN HAS SUBSIDED... BUT WE HAVE LOST TOO MUCH TIME!
THE TABLET! GIVE IT TO CONNORS! WE MUST BEGIN AT ONCE!
ARE YA DONE WITH ME, SILVERMANE?
I'M ITCHIN' TO GO OUT 'N TANGLE WITH SPIDER-MAN AGAIN!
NO! HERE YOU WILL STAY ...TILL I DISMISS YOU!
OKAY! BUT NEXT TIME I LEAN ON 'IM... IT'LL BE FOR GOOD!
2.

MARKO! YOU WILL STAND GUARD, OUTSIDE THE DOOR!
I WILL LEAVE WILSON, OUR OTHER CAPTIVE, IN HERE WITH YOU!
AND I WARN YOU BOTH... THE MAGGIA DOES NOT TOLERATE FAILURE!
CONNORS! YOU MAY HAVE FREE USE OF THIS FULLY-EQUIPPED LABORATORY!
YOU HAVE 24 HOURS TO TELL ME THE SECRET OF THE ANCIENT TABLET!
SO LONG AS MY WIFE... MY SON ...ARE HOSTAGES ...I MUST COMPLY!
THIS IS INSANE! NO ONE CAN TRANSLATE THIS TABLET!
SOME OF THE GREATEST HIEROGLYPHIC EXPERTS IN THE WORLD HAVE TRIED IT!
SHUT UP, WILSON! YOU'RE BABBLING LIKE A HYSTERICAL CHILD!
MY EX-BOSS...THE KINGPIN...SPENT A FORTUNE TRYING TO LEARN THE SECRET!
THERE IS FAR GREATER DANGER HERE ...THAN YOU SUSPECT!
HUH? WHAT DO YOU MEAN, CONNORS? WHAT ARE YOU TALKING ABOUT?
IT'S STARTING TO HAPPEN AGAIN... JUST AS I FEARED!
BUT I MUST FIGHT IT... I MUST REMAIN NORMAL... I CAN'T CHANGE...TO THE LIZARD ...NOT NOW... NOT NOW!
YOUR FACE! THAT LOOK OF PAIN!
WHAT'S WRONG WITH YOU, MAN??
MARTHA AND BILLY... IF I CAN JUST KEEP THINKING OF THEM...CONCENTRATING ON THEM... IF I CAN DRIVE EVERYTHING ELSE FROM MY MIND...!
IT...IT WORKED! THE MOMENT PASSED! MY FINGERS ARE HUMAN ONCE MORE!
BUT...FOR HOW LONG? FOR HOW LONG??
IT'S NOTHING, WILSON! JUST... A HEAD-ACHE!
AND NOW... I'VE GOT TO WORK...AS I'VE NEVER WORKED BEFORE!
3.

I'VE HEARD ABOUT THE TABLET...AND READ ABOUT IT!
THEN THAT'S WHY THEY CAPTURED YOU... BECAUSE YOU'RE A BIOLOGIST!
WHATEVER FANTASTIC SECRET IT CONTAINS... HAS SOMETHING TO DO WITH BIOLOGY... WITH THE MYSTERY OF LIFE ITSELF!
BUT, WHAT DO WE DO NEXT? HOW DO WE UNRAVEL THE SECRET?
LET ME WORRY ABOUT THAT!
JUST TAKE OFF YOUR COAT ...AND STAND BY TO HELP!
SOME TIME LATER, IN ANOTHER PART OF THE CITY...
HUH?? ONE OF MY PAPERS... FLOATING UP... INTO THE AIR!
AND A DIME... COMING DOWN... OUT OF NOWHERE!!
NEWSPAPERS
NO... NOT EXACTLY OUT OF NOWHERE... AS WE SHALL SEE..
MAYBE THERE'S SOMETHING IN THE BUGLE THAT'LL GIVE ME A LEAD ON MAN-MOUNTAIN MARKO!
SAY! WHAT'S THIS...?
SOMEONE SPRUNG THE KINGPIN'S RIGHT-HAND MAN!
BUT... IT DOESN'T MAKE SENSE..!
IT WASN'T FAT STUFF WHO PUT UP THE BAIL...
IT WAS CAESAR CICERO ... THE BIG-TIME MAGGIA MOUTHPIECE! BUT... WHY?
KINGPIN'S CRIME LIEUTENANT BAILED OUT BY MAGGIA LAWYER
POLICE PONDER CONNECTION
CAESAR CICERO
LOUIS WILSON
4

I REMEMBER MARKO SAYING IT WAS A MAGGIA TIP THAT LED HIM TO THE TABLET!
AND SO... IF THE SYNDICATE'S MIXED UP IN THIS...
...THEN CAESAR CICERO IS THE LEAD I WANT!
HIS OFFICE IS JUST BELOW!
I'M IN LUCK! HE'S JUST LEAVING!
ANOTHER FEW MINUTES AND I'D HAVE MISSED HIM!
HE CAN'T BE MORE THAN FIVE FEET TALL!
IT FIGURES THEY'D NICK-NAME HIM BIG C...
5.

FORGIVE THE FLAMBOYANCY, COUNSELOR...
BUT I'M JUST AN OLD SHOW-MAN AT HEART!
WHA..?? THE SPIDER SIGNAL!!
GLAD YOU NOTICED IT FAST, BIG C!
I NEVER KNOW WHEN THESE DIME STORE BATTERIES'LL GO DEAD!
SPIDER-MAN!
WHAT DO YOU WANT WITH ME?
JUST A LITTLE CONVERSATION, MISTER!
WEB-SWINGING AROUND TOWN CAN MAKE A FELLA MIGHTY LONELY!
SO HOW ABOUT ANSWERING A FEW SIMPLE QUESTIONS?
QUESTIONS?? ABOUT WHAT?
WOULDJA BELIEVE...MAN-MOUNTAIN MARKO ...AND A CERTAIN STOLEN TABLET?
FTIK!
NOW WHAT DID YOU WANNA DO THAT FOR?
ALL THAT IT MEANS IS...YOU'LL HAVE TO TELL ME WHAT I WANT TO KNOW EVEN FASTER THAN EVER!
NO! I CANNOT BETRAY THE MAGGIA!
WHAT WE HAVE HERE IS A FAILURE TO COMMUNICATE!
6

NOW LOOK... I KNOW THAT MAN-MOUNTAIN MARKO WORKS FOR THE MAGGIA...
SO ALL YOU HAVE TO DO IS TELL ME WHERE TO FIND HIM!
AND YOU HAPPEN TO BE THEIR TOP LEGAL EAGLE!
--AND I'LL SKIP OFF INTO THE NIGHT... WIGGLING MY WEBBING BEHIND ME!
I CAN'T TELL YOU... I CAN'T!
AWW-- TRY!
UH OH! THERE GOES MY SPIDEY SENSE... TINGLING LIKE SIXTY!
CICERO'S GOON SQUAD MUST BE JET PROPELLED!
A BOOKCASE DOOR... SLIDING OPEN!
AND THAT'S NO PEACE PIPE START-ING TO POKE THRU!
OKAY, CAESAR.. I CAN TAKE A HINT!
I KNOW WHEN I'M NOT WANTED!
BUT YOU SHOULD HAVE TOLD ME YOU WERE HAVING A PARTY!
I'D HAVE WORN MY BEADS!
GOOD OL' SPIDER SPEED! WHAT WOULD I DO WITHOUT YOU?
KRAK!
WE GOT HERE AS SOON AS WE COULD, BIG C!
YOU TAKE COVER, CICERO! WE GOT ENOUGH MUSCLE TO NAIL 'IM!
TALK IS CHEAP, MY FRIEND!
DO IT!
7.

HE MUSTA COME TO FREE THAT CONNORS DAME AND HER KID!
BUT HOW'D HE FIND OUT THAT WE'RE HOLDIN' 'EM AS HOSTAGES?
CONNORS! HE MUST MEAN THE WIFE AND SON OF CURT CONNORS!
ZAP!
KRAK!
SUDDENLY, IT'S ALL BEGINNING TO ADD UP!
THE MAGGIA HAS THE TABLET... BUT DOESN'T KNOW WHAT ITS SECRET IS...
AND THAT'S WHERE DOC CONNORS COMES IN!
HERE, GUYS...
YOU CAN USE SOME BOOK LEARNING!
I OUGHT TO THROTTLE THAT PANICKY FOOL FOR BABBLING ABOUT OUR CAPTIVES!
THERE WAS NO REASON FOR SPIDER-MAN TO SUSPECT THEIR PRESENCE ...BUT NOW HE KNOWS!
THAT MEANS THERE MUST BE A SPEED-UP OF THE PLAN!
THE WEB-SPINNER MUST NOT LEAVE HERE ALIVE!
8

BUT, WHILE THE OTHERS KEEP HIM BUSY, I MUST TAKE NO CHANCES!
THE WOMAN AND HER SON CAN REMAIN HERE NO LONGER!
I WILL NOT BOTHER TO CLEAR IT WITH THE DODDERING SILVERMANE!
IT WILL BE INTERESTING... TO SEE HIS RE-ACTION!
HOW ABOUT THAT?!!
WHILE I WAS BUSY LULLING HIS GORILLAS TO SLEEP--
BIG C DECIDED TO TAKE A POWDER!
THE BOOKCASE... IT'S COVERING THE PASSAGE AGAIN!
I'D BETTER JUST... UH OH! SOME-THING'S WRONG! I CAN FEEL IT!
FRACK!
HEY! HOW UNFRIENDLY CAN YOU GET?!!
THWIPP!
DON'T BOTHER ANSWERING...
IT WAS JUST A RHETORICAL QUESTION!
9.

BIG C MUST BE COUNTING ON THESE MAGGIA MUSCLE-MEN TO DELAY ME WHILE HE SKIPS OUT WITH HIS CAPTIVES!
WHICH MEANS I'VE GOTTA HAUL ANCHOR AND REALLY START MOVING!
THE BOOKCASE... THAT WAS THE WAY HE GOT OUT!
AND, WHAT'S GOOD ENOUGH FOR CAESAR..!
10.

A STEEL DOOR... SLIDING DOWN...TO BLOCK THE PASSAGE-WAY!
HAVE TO REACH IT... BEFORE IT CLANGS SHUT!
THERE'S JUST... TOO MUCH AT STAKE...
...FOR ANYTHING...
...TO STOP ME...
NOW!!
11.

AHEAD OF ME... IN THE CORRIDOR... VOICES!
THEY SOUND LIKE A WOMAN ...AND A YOUNG TEEN-AGER!
THERE'S NO DOUBT ABOUT IT! I'D KNOW MRS. CONNORS' VOICE ANYWHERE!
BUT WHY DIDN'T BIG C GET THEM OUT OF HERE YET?
VBOOOM!
IT WORKED!
THE WALL-CRAWLER NEVER EVEN HAD A CHANCE!
I KNEW THOSE LITTLE TAPE RECORDINGS OF YOUR VOICES WOULD CATCH HIS INTEREST...
LONG ENOUGH TO LET HIM LINGER JUST OUTSIDE MY BOOBY-TRAPPED DOOR!
THIS IS WHY IT IS I... AND NOT THE AGING SILVERMANE... WHO SHALL LEAD THE MAGGIA!
MOM! IF SPIDER-MAN WAS... STANDING NEAR THAT BLAST..!
DON'T SAY IT, BILLY! DON'T... EVEN THINK IT!
IT'S ALL LIKE SOME FEAR-FUL, ENDLESS NIGHTMARE!
12

BUT, AS THE SMOKE SLOWLY CLEARS, BEHIND THE RAPIDLY DEPARTING SEDAN...
IT'S LUCKY I WAS SUSPICIOUS ENOUGH TO STAND BACK...
--AND USE MY WEBBING TO YANK OPEN THE DOOR FROM A SAFE DISTANCE!
BUT, WHILE I'M BUSY CONGRATULATING MYSELF...
...BIG C MANAGED TO MAKE HIS GETAWAY!
AND THAT MEANS DOC CONNORS' WIFE AND SON ARE STILL IN DANGER!
BUT SOONER OR LATER I'LL TRACK CICERO DOWN...
AND WHEN I DO...!!
MEANWHILE, AT THE SUMPTUOUS HEAD-QUARTERS OF THE MAN CALLED SILVERMANE...
THIS TIME, CAESAR CICERO, YOU HAVE GONE TOO FAR!
BY BRINGING OUR CAPTIVES DIRECTLY TO ME, YOU WILL INEVITABLY LEAD SPIDER-MAN TO THIS VERY SPOT!
YOU GROW TOO FEAR-FUL IN YOUR OLD AGE, MY FRIEND!
AT ANY RATE, I HAD NO OTHER CHOICE!
DON'T WORRY, SILVERMANE...
THAT WEB-SWINGIN' WEAKLING WON'T GIT PAST ME... NO MATTER WHAT!
13

I AM OLD, CICERO... AND THE STRENGTH HAS LONG SINCE FADED FROM MY ONCE-POWERFUL BODY---
BUT, THIS I DO TELL YOU... I SHALL YET LIVE TO MAKE YOU REALIZE... YOU HAVE PUSHED ME TOO FAR!
WHY PICK ON BIG C, BOSS?
TOO MUCH TALK MAKES ME WEARY!
HE GOT THAT CONNORS DAME AND HER KID AWAY FROM THE WALL-CRAWLER, DIDN'T HE?
I DID MORE THAN THAT!
SPIDER-MAN WILL NEVER BOTHER US AGAIN!
I MUST SEE TO A MATTER OF FAR GREATER URGENCY..!
CONNORS! I WARN YOU... YOUR TIME IS RUNNING OUT!
I MUST HAVE WHAT I SEEK... AND I MUST HAVE IT SOON!
WITH EACH PASSING MINUTE MY HEART GROWS WEAKER!
IF I SHOULD DIE BEFORE YOU HAVE FINISHED... YOU WILL NOT LIVE TO GLOAT!
IN THAT EVENT... I HAVE ORDERED THAT YOU ARE NOT TO LEAVE HERE ALIVE!
HE MEANS IT, CONNORS! OUR LIVES AREN'T WORTH A NICKEL IF YOU DON'T SOLVE THE SECRET OF THAT BLASTED TABLET!
QUIET... ALL OF YOU!
I FINALLY HAVE THE ANSWER! IT'S JUST WHAT I GUESSED!
YOU WERE ON THE RIGHT TRACK, SILVER-MANE!
THE REASON IT'S BEEN A MYSTERY SO LONG IS THAT LANGUAGE EXPERTS TRIED TO SOLVE THE TABLET'S MESSAGE... INSTEAD OF A BIOLOGIST!
THE HIEROGLYPHICS STAND FOR BIO-CHEMICAL SYMBOLS... NOT FOR WORDS!
BUT YOUR TASK IS ONLY HALF DONE!
YOU STILL MUST CREATE A SERUM!
AT MY AGE... IN MY CONDITION... EVERY MINUTE... EVERY SECOND... IS OF VITAL IMPORTANCE!
I MUST HAVE THE SERUM NOW... DO YOU HEAR?? NOW!!
THE STRAIN... IS BEGINNING TO TELL AGAIN! HOW MUCH LONGER... CAN I HOLD BACK THE CHANGE?
14

I DIDN'T KNOW YOU HAD BEATEN IT, CONNORS!
WHAT IS THE TABLET'S SECRET? WHY IS IT SO IMPORTANT TO HIM?
NO MORE TALK! YOU WILL WORK NOW... WORK! WORK!
DO NOT FORGET... YOUR WIFE... AND YOUR SON!
EVEN NOW... THEY SIT WONDERING ABOUT THEIR FATE... THE FATE THAT IS IN YOUR HANDS ALONE!
DON'T CRY, MOM! DAD'LL GET US OUT OF THIS... SOMEHOW! I KNOW HE WILL!
BUT THEY'RE SO RUTHLESS... SO MERCILESS!
AND... THE MORE THEY THREATEN YOUR FATHER... THE MORE DANGER THERE IS... OF SOMETHING HAPPENING TO HIM...
...SOMETHING THAT NO ONE... NOT EVEN YOU... COULD EVER SUSPECT!
YOU'VE TRIED TO KEEP IT FROM ME, MOM...'CAUSE I WAS SO YOUNG...
BUT, I KNOW ABOUT DAD... I GUESS I'VE KNOWN IT FOR YEARS!
YOU KNOW, BILLY? YOU KNOW WHAT??
HOW COULD I LIVE WITH HIM ALL THESE YEARS... AND NOT REALIZE...?
MY DAD IS... THE LIZARD!
BUT DON'T WORRY, MOM ...THE SECRET'S SAFE WITH ME!
IF ONLY SPIDER-MAN HADN'T BEEN KILLED IN THAT BLAST...
HE'D HAVE FOUND SOME WAY... TO HELP US!
HELP US? HOW CAN ANYTHING HELP US NOW?
MILES AWAY, A WEARY COSTUMED FIGURE IS ASKING HIMSELF THAT VERY SAME QUESTION...
I'VE BEEN SEARCHING FOR HOURS... AND STILL NOTHING!
WHEREVER CICERO MAY BE HOLED UP... IT'S HIDDEN TOO WELL FOR MY SPIDEY SENSE TO SPOT IT!
BUT HOW DO I HELP THE DOC... AND HIS FAMILY... IF I CAN'T FIND THEM?
15

IT'S ALMOST DAWN NOW! HAVE TO GET SOME SLEEP BEFORE CLASS!
MUSTN'T FORGET TO CALL AUNT MAY IN FLORIDA AND SEE HOW SHE IS!
MY SPIDER-MAN'S WEB-INS HAVE KEPT ME TOO BUSY FOR ANY-THING!
Call Aunt May
HAVEN'T EVEN HAD A CHANCE TO PHONE GWENDY AND TRY TO SQUARE THINGS WITH HER!
THIS BUSINESS OF BEING A LONER IS FOR THE BIRDS!
IF ONLY THERE WAS SOMEONE I COULD TALK TO... SOMEONE I COULD CONFIDE IN!
I WISH HARRY WAS BACK FROM HIS DATE...
BUT... I'M TOO SLEEPY ...TO WAIT UP FOR HIM...
THE NEXT MORNING...
IF I DON'T SHOW UP FOR SOME CLASSES THEY'LL FORGET WHO I AM!
BUT, HOW CAN I DO IT... WHEN I SHOULD BE OUT FINDING DOC CONNORS?
HEY! WHAT'S BUGGIN' PARKER?
IS HE SUDDENLY TOO GOOD FOR US?
PARKER'S OKAY, MAN!
HE DON'T HAVETA DO THE RAH RAH BIT TO PROVE HE'S GOT SOUL!
THERE WAS A TIME ...WHEN THE DOC WAS THE ONLY FRIEND I HAD!
AND NOW... WHEN HE NEEDS SPIDER-MAN THE MOST...
HI, ROOM-MATE! I WAS HOPING I'D SEE YOU!
HOW DO YOU LIKE THE NEW OSBORN IMAGE, PETE?
OH... HI, HARRY...
CAN'T FIGHT IT! I HAVE TO START SEARCHING AGAIN!
16

HI, HARRY? IS THAT ALL YOU SAY TO A PAL WHO'S SPORTING HIS NEW FU MANCHU FACE FUZZ?
I'VE BEEN IN HIDING FOR WEEKS, JUST TO... HEY!
SORRY, HARR! CAN'T TALK ANYMORE!
THERE'S SOMETHING... IMPORTANT... THAT I'VE GOTTA DO!
GWEN! DID YOU SEE THAT? DID YOU HEAR HIM?
I'M BEGINNING TO THINK FLASH THOMPSON'S BEEN RIGHT ABOUT THAT JOKER ALL THE TIME!
THEN THINK AGAIN, MR. OSBORN!
THE MAN IS UPTIGHT! HE NEEDS HELP... NOT HOSTILITY!
IF YOU'RE HIS FRIEND... THEN ACT LIKE ONE!
AND, SPEAKING OF FRIENDSHIP...
NO MATTER WHAT IT TAKES... I'VE GOT TO KEEP SEARCHING TILL I FIND CURT CONNORS!
I OWE HIM THAT MUCH!
...AND I COULDN'T LIVE WITH MYSELF IF I LET HIM DOWN!
BUT, THE CITY'S SO BIG... AND TIME IS SO SHORT!
I'VE GOT TO MOVE FAST!
FASTER THAN EVER BEFORE!
I'LL KEEP GOING TILL I'VE COVERED EVERY STREET... EVERY ALLEY ...EVERY ROOFTOP...!
17

COME ON, SPIDEY SENSE ...WHAT ARE YOU WAITING FOR?
START YOUR TINGLING, BLAST IT!
I'M NOT QUITTING TILL YOU DO!
MEANWHILE, IN A NOT-TOO-DISTANT BUILDING---
YOU'VE GOT IT! YOU GOT THE SERUM ...AT LAST!
QUICKLY... I MUST HAVE IT... I MUST DRINK IT! IT MEANS EVERY-THING IN THE WORLD TO ME...!
WAIT! IT HASN'T BEEN TESTED YET! WE STILL DON'T KNOW WHAT THE RESULTS WILL BE!
YOU FOOL!! AT MY AGE---WHAT HAVE I TO LOSE!
GIVE IT TO ME!
FOR YEARS I HAVE STUDIED THE LEGEND OF THE ANCIENT TABLET!
THE OLDER I GROW... THE MORE CERTAIN I BECOME ...THAT IT MUST BE MINE!
TODAY, NONE WOULD BELIEVE! BUT, YEARS AGO---IN THE OLD COUNTRY... THEY KNEW WHAT THIS SERUM CAN DO!... JUST AS I KNOW... NOW!
BUT...IT'S STILL ONLY GUESS-WORK! IT COULD BE DANGER-OUS!
DANGER? YOU SPEAK TO SILVERMANE ---OF DANGER?!!
YEARS AGO---WHEN IN MY PRIME... I COULD HAVE HUMBLED CAESAR CICERO...AND A DOZEN LIKE HIM... WITH ONE BLOW!
AND SOON...I SHALL BE ABLE TO DO SO---AGAIN!
NO! DON'T DRINK IT! IT'S A TRICK! WHAT IF HE POISONED YA---?!!
SILENCE, MARKO! THERE ARE NONE WHO CAN OUTSMART SILVERMANE!
18

NONE!
ARGHHHH!
MARKO! MARK--- UHHHH---
THUMP!
YOU KILLED 'IM!
YOU THOUGHT IT WOULD SAVE YA, DIDN'T YA?
WELL, NOW YA'LL SEE HOW MUCH GOOD IT'S GONNA DO YA..!
HANDS OFF, MARKO!
YOU DON'T KNOW... WHAT YOU'RE TAMPERING WITH---!
MARKO!
THERE IS NO LONGER ANY NEED FOR YOUR STRONGARM TACTICS!
NO! IT--IT CAN'T BE!
19.

YOU'RE... STILL ALIVE!
BUT... YOU'RE NOT THE SAME! YOU'RE YOUNGER... STRONGER!!
OF COURSE I AM! THAT WAS THE PURPOSE... THAT WAS THE PLAN!
I GAMBLED EVERYTHING ON BEING RIGHT ABOUT THE TABLET'S SECRET... THE ONLY SECRET THAT COULD SAVE ME...
...THE SECRET OF... THE FOUNTAIN OF YOUTH!
NEXT
SPIDEY SLAMS INTO ACTION AS DEATH STRIKES AGAIN!

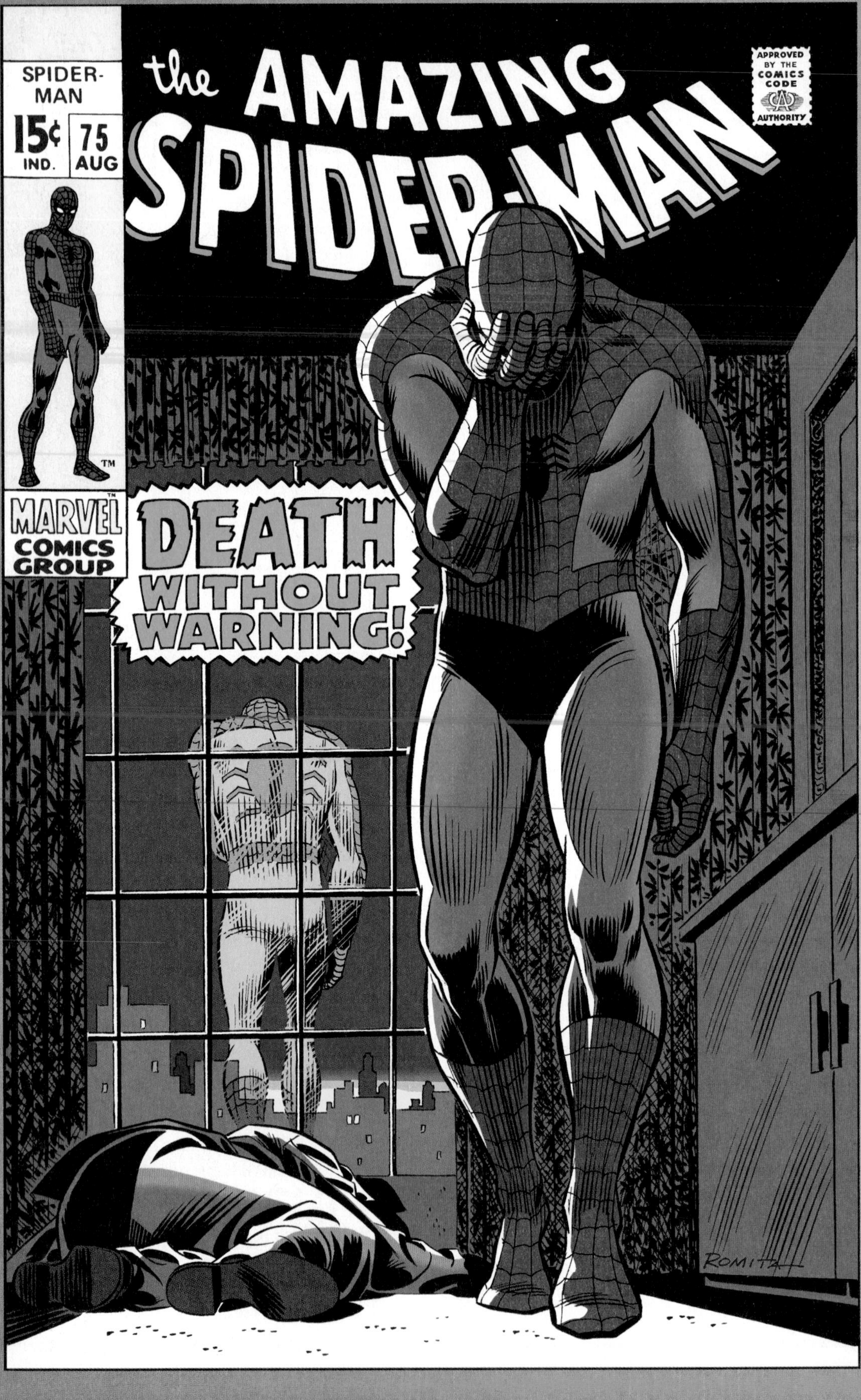
SPIDER-MAN
15¢
IND.
75
AUG
the AMAZING SPIDER-MAN
APPROVED BY THE COMICS CODE AUTHORITY
MARVEL COMICS GROUP
DEATH WITHOUT WARNING!
ROMITA

THE AMAZING SPIDER-MAN! TM
"DEATH WITHOUT WARNING!"
AUTHOR: STAN (THE MAN) LEE
INNOVATOR: JOHN (RING-A-DING) ROMITA
ILLUSTRATOR: JIM (MADMAN) MOONEY
LETTERER: ARTIE (SWEET LIPS) SIMEK
I'VE GOT TO FIND DOC CONNORS!
I KNOW THAT HE AND HIS FAMILY ARE IN THE DEADLIEST DANGER!
--DANGER WHICH IS SOMEHOW TIED UP WITH THE MAGGIA CRIME LORDS!
AND, AT THE ROOT OF IT ALL IS THE MYSTERIOUS ANCIENT TABLET!
BUT, I'LL FIND HIM YET--AND SOLVE THE MYSTERY--
IF IT'S THE LAST THING I DO!

MY BEST BET IS TO COVER THE HIGH CRIME AREAS OF THE CITY--
IF I CAN JUST ONCE GET A GLIMPSE OF MAN-MOUNTAIN MARKO--OR ANY OTHER KNOWN HOOD--
ALL I NEED DO IS FIND ONE OF THEM!
AND THEN GET HIM TO LEAD ME TO THE MAGGIA HEADQUARTERS!
A COUPLE OF SMALL-TIMERS, MAKING BOOK!
MAYBE THEY HAVE THE INFO THAT I NEED!
HOLD IT, BLACKIE!
THERE'S SOME-THING OUT THE WINDOW!
YA SOUND LIKE A NUT! WE'RE 20 STORIES HIGH!
I TELL YOU I SAW SOME-THING! BUT--
YEAH! YEAH! WHAT ELSE IS NEW?
HOW'S THIS FOR STARTERS, GUYS?
LOOK OUT! WE--WE'LL FALL!
SPIDER-MAN!
2

TALK FAST, GROUP-- BEFORE MY ARMS GET TIRED!
I'M LOOKING FOR THE MAGGIA HQ-- AND I KNOW YOU WANT TO HELP ME!
WE'LL TELL YOU ANYTHING-- ANYTHING!
JUST GET US BACK INSIDE!
BUT I DON'T WANT TO KNOW "ANYTHING"!
--JUST ONE ITTY BITTY ADDRESS!
IT'S-- RIGHT ACROSS TOWN-- THE GALBY BUILDING!
THANKS, KIDDIES!
WHO SAYS NEW YORKERS ARE TOO SELFISH TO HELP A LONESOME STRANGER?
NOW FOR DOC CONNORS --IF ONLY I'M NOT TOO LATE!
I'VE GOT TO LEARN WHY THE MAGGIA CAPTURED HIM--
AND HOW THE STOLEN TABLET FIGURES IN TO ALL-- UH OH!
MY SPIDEY SENSE IS STARTING TO TINGLE!
THAT MEANS IT'S TIME FOR THE OL' WEB-SLINGER TO GO INTO ACTION!
3

AND, SPEAKING OF ACTION--LET'S JUMP THE GUN A BIT AND REACH SPIDEY'S GOAL BEFORE HIM--
I TOLD YOU I DIDN'T KILL SILVERMANE!
LET GO OF ME, MARKO--WHILE YOU STILL CAN!
SILVERMANE--NO! IT--IT CAN'T BE YOU! IT CAN'T!
YOU'RE--AN OLD MAN--WITH ONE FOOT--IN THE GRAVE!
USE YOUR HEAD, YOU OVERSIZED SIMPLETON!
THIS WAS THE PRICELESS SECRET OF THE ANCIENT TABLET--!
THE SECRET COUNTLESS MEN HAD LIVED--AND DIED FOR--
THE SECRET OF--ETERNAL YOUTH!

WHAT'RE YA HANDIN' ME, MISTER?
NOBODY CAN GIT 40 YEARS YOUNGER--JUST ON ACCOUNTA SOME NUTTY FORMULA!
YER IN CAHOOTS WITH CONNORS, THAT'S WHAT!
STAY WHERE YOU ARE, YOU BLUNDERING OAF!
STUDY MY FACE--IS IT NOT THE SAME--ONLY YOUNGER?
NOW TELL ME WHAT HAPPENED TO SILVERMANE--OR I'LL TAKE YA APART!
IS MY VOICE NOT THE VOICE THAT HAS EVER COMMANDED YOU?
I AM STILL SILVERMANE! I AM STILL YOUR LEADER!
BUT NOW--I POSSESS BOTH THE YOUTH--AND THE STRENGTH--TO BE THE GREATEST MAGGIA CHIEFTAIN OF ALL!
4

BUT, WHILE WE STAND HERE ARGUING-- WHAT OF DR. CONNORS?
HE ALONE KNOWS THE SECRET OF THE TABLET'S FORMULA!
HE MUST NOT ESCAPE US!
HOW CAN A ONE-ARMED PUNK LIKE HIM GIT OUTTA THIS JOINT?
HE AINT GOT A CHANCE!
ANYWAY, --WE'RE HOLDIN' HIS WIFE AND KID HOSTAGE!
AND, EVEN AS MAN-MOUNTAIN MARKO SPEAKS... IN AN ADJOINING ROOM--
I WARN YOU, MR. CICERO-- IF ANY HARM COMES TO MY HUSBAND--
EASY, MOM --WE CAN'T THREATEN THEM!
SHUDDUP, BOTH OF YOU!
I'VE GOT TO FIND OUT WHAT CAUSED ALL THAT NOISE ON THE OTHER SIDE OF THE WALL!
SILVERMANE IS OLD--IF ANYTHING HAPPENED TO HIM--
THE COMMAND MUST PASS TO ME!
ALLOW NO ONE TO ENTER OR LEAVE THAT ROOM--
YA CAN COUNT ON ME, BIG C!
OR YOU YOU WILL ANSWER TO CAESAR CICERO!
EVERY DAY THAT PASSES BRINGS THE AGING SILVERMANE CLOSER TO DEATH!
ALL I NEED DO IS PLAY MY CARDS RIGHT--AND WAIT HIM OUT--
THEN, ONE DAY, CAESAR SHALL LEAD-- AS I WAS BORN TO DO!
COME IN, CAESAR-- COME IN! I HAVE BEEN EAGERLY AWAITING YOU!
NO! IT CANNOT BE! IT IS-- MADNESS!
JUST AS YOU HAVE BEEN SO PATIENTLY AWAITING MY CERTAIN DEMISE!
HE GOT YOUNGER, BIG C-- ON ACCOUNTA THE TABLET!
AND NOW, TREACHEROUS ONE--WE HAVE MANY SCORES TO SETTLE!
5

MARKO! IT'S A TRICK! HE'S NOT SILVERMANE-- HE CAN'T BE!
YEAH--SURE! THAT'S WHAT I THOUGHT, BIG C! HE CAN'T FOOL US!
HE MUST BE IN LEAGUE WITH THE POLICE! THEY'RE TRYING TO TRAP US-- TO MAKE US TIP OUR HAND!
IT WON'T WORK, CAESAR!
YOU CANNOT TURN US AGAINST EACH OTHER --TO SERVE YOUR OWN AMBITIOUS ENDS!
SILENCE HIM, MARKO-- BEFORE IT'S TOO LATE!
I DON'T KNOW WHAT HAPPENED-- OR HOW--
BUT IF I CAN GET THEM BOTH TO CRUSH EACH OTHER-- THEN NO ONE WILL STAND IN MY WAY!
DON'T WORRY, BIG C --I'LL TAKE CARE OF 'IM!
YOU BRAINLESS, MUSCLE-BOUND BUNGLER--
NOT EVEN YOUR STRENGTH WILL HELP YOU NOW!
I AM THE SILVERMANE THAT WAS--
THE SILVERMANE WHO YEARS AGO FOUGHT HIS WAY TO THE TOP OF THE MAGGIA--OVER MANY SUCH AS YOU!
DESPITE YOUR BESTIAL POWER--YOU HAVE NOT THE SPEED--NOR THE SKILL--TO HANDLE THE LIKES OF SILVERMANE!
THAT IS WHY I AM THE LEADER-- WHY I SHALL EVER BE THE LEADER!
NOW THAT THE SECRET OF THE TABLET IS MINE--
I SHALL STAY YOUNG AND STRONG-- FOREVER!

THE WAY YA TALK--THE WAY YA USE YER DUKES--JUST LIKE THE STORIES I USEDTA HEAR--OF HOW NOBODY COULD EVER BEAT SILVERMANE!
THE STORIES WERE TRUE! IT WAS I WHO HELPED ORGANIZE THE MAGGIA IN THIS CITY--
I, WHOSE RUTHLESS-NESS AND MIGHT HELPED CREATE THE GREATEST CRIME CARTEL OF ALL!
AND NOW THAT I HAVE REGAINED MY YOUTH--
I WILL DESTROY ANY WHO OPPOSE ME--AS I LEAD THE MAGGIA IN THE MOST DARING CRIMES OF ALL!
NOW SPEAK, MARKO--LET ME HEAR YOU SWEAR THAT YOU WILL OBEY ME BLINDLY!
LET ME HEAR YOU SAY THAT YOU BELIEVE --THAT YOU KNOW, BEYOND ALL QUESTION OR DOUBT--
--THAT I, AND I ALONE--AM SILVERMANE!
YEAH! YEAH! YOU ARE--YOU GOTTA BE SILVERMANE!
I CAN SEE IT NOW--RIGHT THERE --IN FRONT OF MY EYES--YOU DID GIT YOUNGER--
IT WUZ THE STUFF YOU DRANK--FROM THE FORMULA ON THE TABLET--THAT'S WHAT DID IT!
IN FACT--IT'S STILL DOIN' IT!! YOU'RE STILL GETTIN' YOUNGER --RIGHT IN FRONT OF MY EYES!
YER HAIR--IT AINT GREY NO MORE! YOU--YOU'RE EVEN YOUNGER--THAN ME!
IT--IT'S LIKE MAGIC! IT AINT POSSIBLE--BUT I SEE IT--I SEE IT HAPPENIN'--
JUST LIKE AS IF A CLOCK--IS MOVIN' BACKWARDS--JUST FOR YOU!
7

MARKO-- LOOK OUT BEHIND YOU--!
KRASH!
I KNEW I'D FIND YOU, BIG MAN-- SOONER OR LATER!
SPIDER-MAN!
STOP 'IM! IF HE MANAGES TO-- UNHHH!
HE'S ALL ALONE! HE CAN'T-- ARHHH!
RELAX, GENT'S!
I'LL HANDLE THINGS FROM HERE ON IN!
NOW, THE FIRST THING I WANT IS DR. CONNORS!
IF ANYTHING'S HAPPENED TO HIM--OR HIS FAMILY--
SHUT HIM UP, MARKO--AND DO IT NOW!
I WAS HOPIN' YA'D ASK ME, SILVERMANE!
SILVERMANE? THAT CAN'T BE HIM! HE SHOULD BE EIGHTY YEARS OLD!
8

I WENT EASY ON YOU LAST TIME, MARKO--
--'CAUSE I HAD OTHER THINGS ON MY MIND--
AND THERE WAS A LADY PRESENT!
TOOM!
BUT JUST IN CASE YOU THINK YOU'RE REALLY A MATCH FOR ME--
I'D BETTER CLUE YOU IN TO THE FACTS OF LIFE --BUT FAST!
YER LIFTIN' ME--WITH ONE HAND--LIKE I DON'T EVEN WEIGH NOTHIN'!
I'VE GOTTA HAND IT TO YOU, PAL--
FOR A DUMMY, YOU CATCH ON QUICK!
AND NOW, SONNY BOY, I WANT SOME ANSWERS!
BTHMM!
NO! IT CAN'T BE! BUT--IT IS--!
I'M GETTING YOUNGER STILL!!
HUH? WHAT'S THAT?
9

HE'S THE ONE MARKO CALLED SILVERMANE!
BUT HE LOOKS EVEN YOUNGER NOW THAN A FEW MINUTES AGO!
THE FORMULA SUCCEEDED BEYOND MY WILDEST HOPES!
I'M LIKE A MAN IN HIS EARLY TWENTIES --IN THE VERY PRIME OF LIFE!
AND, THE YOUNGER I GET--THE HEALTHIER I GET--THE MORE ALIVE--THE MORE POWERFUL I BECOME!
THERE IS NOTHING I CANNOT DO--NO ONE I CANNOT DEFEAT!
NOT EVEN SPIDER-MAN CAN HOPE TO OPPOSE ONE WHO HAS DRUNK FROM THE WATERS OF THE FOUNTAIN OF YOUTH!
HE--REALLY MEANS IT!
MEANWHILE--
I DON'T KNOW WHERE SPIDER-MAN CAME FROM--BUT THIS IS MY CHANCE TO ESCAPE!
ALL RIGHT, WALL-CRAWLER --LET'S SEE WHAT YOU'RE MADE OF!
THEY FORCED ME TO MAKE THAT POTION--FROM THE FORMULA INSCRIBED UPON THE ANCIENT TABLET!
BUT, WHEN THE MAGGIA FINDS OUT WHAT THE TRUE RESULT WILL BE--MY LIFE WON'T BE WORTH A NICKEL!
I'VE GOT TO FIND MARTHA--AND BILLY--AND GET THEM OUT OF HERE!
BECAUSE, IT'LL BE TOO LATE FOR ANYTHING --IF THE LIZARD SHOULD APPEAR!
10

IF THE CHANGE OCCURS--
NO! I MUSTN'T EVEN THINK OF IT--NOT WITH MY WIFE AND SON SO NEAR!
THE LIZARD HAS NO MEMORY--NO FEELINGS OF LOVE--NOT EVEN FOR THEM!
THE SPASMS--THEY'RE STARTING! I-I CAN'T STOP THEM!
MY MISSING ARM--BEGINNING TO THROB--TO PAIN ME!
IT'S GROWING BACK--BACK!
I HAVE TO TURN--RUN--GET AWAY FROM HERE--AWAY FROM MY FAMILY--WHILE--I STILL CAN!
I'LL--FIND A ROOM--AND LOCK MYSELF INSIDE--AND THEN--AND THEN--
HAH! THEY COULDN'T STOP ME! COULDN'T KEEP ME HUMAN ANY LONGER! I WAS TOO STRONG FOR THEM!
WHAT AM I DOING HERE? WHY AM I CLOSED IN--BY WALLS--DOORS--?
THIS IS NO FIT PLACE FOR ME! I NEED ROOM--SPACE--FREEDOM!
I THOUGHT I HEARD SOMEONE OUT HERE!
HOLD IT RIGHT THERE, MISTER--TILL I SEE WHO YOU ARE!
ZWAK!
I AM THE LIZARD!
THAT'S ALL YOU'LL EVER NEED TO KNOW!
11

THIS TIME I MUST NOT WASTE MY MATCHLESS POWER!
I MUST USE IT TO THE FULLEST!
ONLY THEN CAN I REMAIN THE LIZARD--FOREVER!
MUST GET OUT!
MUST HAVE TIME TO PLAN--TO STALK--AND THEN--TO STRIKE!
I CAN'T BEAR THE WAITING ANY LONGER!
I HAVE TO KNOW--WHAT'S HAPPENING OUT THERE!
NO, MOM! DAD WOULD WANT YOU TO STAY HERE!
HE'D WANT ME TO PROTECT YOU!
LISTEN! THEY'RE OUTSIDE THE DOOR!
WHAT DO YOU MEAN IT LOOKED LIKE A HUMAN LIZARD?
DO YOU THINK YOU CAN PLAY GAMES WITH CAESAR CICERO?
YA GOTTA BELIEVE ME, BIG C! HE WUZ DRESSED LIKE A MAN--BUT--UNHHH!
THE DAME AND THE KID ARE STILL SAFE IN THERE, CICERO!
IT'S A TRICK OF SILVERMANES! ADMIT IT! ADMIT IT!
GET YOUR GUNS--ALL OF YOU!
I DON'T KNOW WHAT HE'S UP TO--BUT IT'S TIME FOR THE FINAL SHOWDOWN!
AND, SPEAKING OF SHOWDOWNS--
NOT EVEN SPIDER-MAN CAN STAND UP TO THE INVINCIBLE POWER OF ETERNAL YOUTH!
THERE'S TOO MUCH AT STAKE HERE FOR ME TO TAKE ANY CHANCES!
MY FIRST JOB IS TO FIND DOC CONNORS--AND HIS FAMILY!
THEN I'LL GET BACK TO THIS OVERSIZED PETER PAN!
12

NO! YOU WILL NOT ESCAPE ME! NOBODY WILL EVER ESCAPE ME AGAIN!
ALL THE GANGLAND KILLINGS I HAVE ORDERED IN THE PAST WILL BE AS NOTHING TO THE REIGN OF TERROR THAT IS YET TO COME!
A BEAKER OF CHEMICAL ACID!
IF I HADN'T AVERTED MY FACE IN TIME--!
SPKLANNG!
I AM SILVERMANE! I ROSE TO THE TOP OVER THE SHATTERED REMAINS OF THOSE I HAD TO CRUSH IN MY CLIMB TO POWER!
AND NOW, I AM STRONGER, WISER, YOUNGER THAN EVER!
NOW, ALL WHO LIVE SHALL LEARN HOW MERCILESS THE MAGGIA CAN BE!
COULD BE JUST MY IMAGINATION--
BUT I COULD SWEAR HIS VOICE IS GETTING SHRILLER--YOUNGER--WITH EVERY WORD!
THIS IS HOW I BATTLED ONCE BEFORE--WHEN I WAS IN MY PRIME!
NO ONE WAS SAFE FROM THE SAVAGERY OF SILVERMANE!
WHY DON'T YOU FALL? WHY DON'T YOU COLLAPSE IN A PAROXYSM OF FEAR?
MAYBE IT'S 'CAUSE YOU'RE WEAKER THAN YOU THINK!
NO! NO! I'M THE DEADLY SILVERMANE!
I'M THE STRONGEST ONE OF ALL!
13

THERE'S NO DOUBT ABOUT IT! HE IS GETTING YOUNGER-- BY THE SECOND!
EACH BLOW HAS LESS WEIGHT-- LESS POWER BEHIND IT!
NOW STAY THERE, MISTER! I'VE STILL GOT A JOB TO DO!
UH OH! I'M STARTING TO TINGLE AGAIN! THERE'S NEW DANGER NEAR!
WHEN I GIVE THE WORD--YOU ALL RUSH INSIDE!
AND SHOOT ANYTHING THAT MOVES!
GET READY-- HERE WE GO--!
NOW!
YOU SURE HAVE A WAY OF MAKING A FELLA FEEL UNWANTED!
IT'S SPIDER-MAN! BUT-- HE WUZ EXPECTIN' US!
HE'S HIGH-TAILIN' IT AWAY!
STOP HIM! HE MUST NOT LEAVE THIS PLACE ALIVE!
FTNNG!
14

YOU SHOULD REALLY TRY TO CONTROL THOSE ANTI-SOCIAL TENDENCIES!
--'CAUSE THEY COULD BE HABIT-FORMING!
ZAK!
STAY WITH HIM--ALL OF YOU--UNTIL HE'S FINISHED!
IT IS TIME TO PUT AN END TO THE CAREER OF SILVERMANE--
AND THAT IS ONE TASK I SHALL PERFORM ALONE!
WHAT IS THIS? HAS SOMEONE ALREADY BEATEN ME TO IT?
SILVER-MANE! YOU SHALL NOT ROB ME OF MY VICTORY!
NO! NO!
IT CANNOT BE! IT IS IMPOSSIBLE! IT IS MADNESS!
I DID NOT KNOW-- THERE'D BE-- NO STOPPING IT!
WITH EVERY HEARTBEAT --I GROW YOUNGER-- YOUNGER--
BUT-- WHERE WILL IT END???
15

MY VOICE-- THE VOICE OF--A TEENAGER!
MY BODY-- GETTING SLIMMER-- WEAKER-- SMALLER-- WITH EACH PASSING SECOND!
THIS IS NOT THE WAY I PLANNED IT!
I WANTED LIFE ETERNAL-- POWER OVER ALL WHO LIVE--
THAT ALONE WAS MY GOAL!
BUT-- NOT THIS! NOT THIS!
NOT THIS!
THAT SCREAM-- COMING FROM THE SPOT WHERE I LEFT SILVER-MANE!
16

A BOY-- RUSHING FROM THE ROOM-- AS THOUGH SATAN HIMSELF IS AT HIS HEELS!
BUT--THE CLOTHES HE'S WEARING --THERE CAN BE NO MISTAKING THEM!
THAT YOUTHFUL FIGURE--JUST SECONDS AGO-- WAS THE MURDEROUS SILVERMANE!
SORRY, SWEETIES! IT'S TIME TO TAKE OFF THE KID GLOVES!
I'LL HAVE TO FINISH YOUR BOXING LESSON SOME OTHER TIME!
BUT DON'T WORRY! I'LL TELL CICERO YOU FOUGHT LIKE SAVAGES!
--'CAUSE I KNOW HOW HE TAKES THESE THINGS TO HEART!
STILL NO TRACE OF CONNORS!
BUT HE HAS TO BE HERE SOMEWHERE!
WHAT'S THAT-- IN THE ROOM BEHIND ME--?
SOUNDS LIKE-- A CHILD SOBBING--
CRRRAAKK!
17

THE SOBS-- ARE FADING AWAY--INTO NOTHINGNESS--!

SILVERMANE FOUND THE YOUTH HE SOUGHT--
AND THE PRIZE WILL BE HIS-- FOREVER!
18

THAT WAS WHY THE TABLET'S SECRET HAD TO BE COUCHED IN HIEROGLYPHICS--
IT WAS A SECRET TOO DANGEROUS-- TOO DEADLY--FOR ANY MAN TO POSSESS!
UP AHEAD-- THOSE VOICES THRU THE DOOR! I'D KNOW THEM ANYWHERE!
MRS. CONNORS! BILLY! GET BACK-- STAND AWAY FROM THE DOOR--!
SMASH!
MOM--LOOK! IT'S SPIDER-MAN! HE'S ALIVE--HE FOUND US!
YOUR FATHER, BILLY-- WHERE IS HE? WHAT HAPPENED TO DR. CONNORS?
WE DON'T KNOW! FOR A MOMENT-- I DARED TO HOPE--HE WAS WITH YOU!
ANYWAY, YOU CAN BOTH COME OUT NOW!
THERE'LL BE TIME ENOUGH LATER FOR EXPLANATIONS!
BUT NOW, THE IMPORTANT THING IS--YOU'RE BOTH ALIVE--AND UNHARMED!
AND A PORTION OF THE MAGGIA'S POWER HAS BEEN STRIPPED AWAY-- FOR GOOD!
BUT WHY ISN'T MY HUSBAND HERE? WHAT CAN HAVE HAPPENED TO CURT?
THERE'S ONLY ONE THING THAT COULD KEEP HIM FROM US-- EITHER HE'S BEEN INJURED-- OR--
NO! I-I CAN'T EVEN SAY IT!
WE KNOW WHAT YOU MEAN, MOM! BUT, IF HE DID BECOME THE LIZARD --AT LEAST SPIDER-MAN IS HERE TO HELP US!
19

YET, LAST TIME THEY FOUGHT--SPIDER-MAN WAS ALMOST DEFEATED BY THE SUPER-POWERED LIZARD! AND NOW--THE SCALY-SKINNED STALKER IS WISER, MORE POWERFUL THAN EVER--
BUT SUDDENLY--HE HAS A FLASH OF SANITY--AS HE REMEMBERS--
MUST BOARD MYSELF IN--SO THEY'LL BE SAFE FROM ME!
MY WIFE--MY SON--I MUST NOT HARM THEM!
THOOM!
BUT THEN, THE MOMENT OF LUCIDITY SOON PASSES--
NO! NO! NOTHING MUST KEEP ME TRAPPED! NOTHING!
THE LIZARD WAS BORN TO FIGHT--TO ATTACK!
THE LIZARD MUST THINK OF NOTHING ELSE!
DEEP BENEATH THE BESTIAL EXTERIOR, THE ESSENCE OF DR. CONNORS STRUGGLES FOR CONTROL--STRUGGLES FOR REASON--
BUT, WITH EACH PASSING MOMENT, HIS IDENTITY FADES--UNTIL IT IS FELT NO MORE!
UNTIL, AT LAST--
ONLY THE BEAST REMAINS!
20
NEXT
THE LIZARD LIVES!

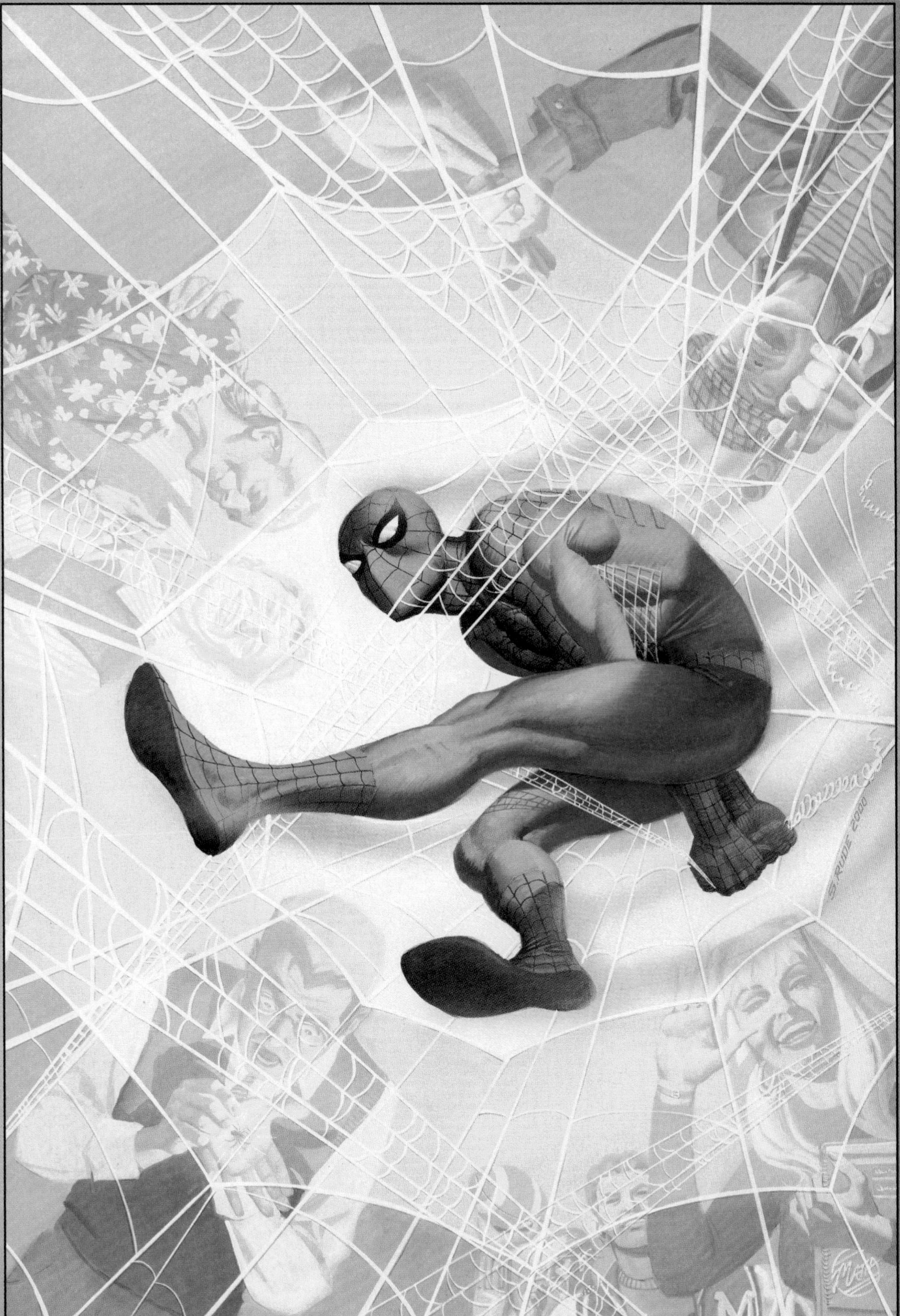

SPIDER-MAN: LIFELINE #1

Accidentally bitten by a common spider exposed to radiation, Peter Parker soon discovered he had miraculously gained the arachnid's powers and had, in effect, become a human spider! But with great power... also comes great responsibility!
Stan Lee presents:
THE AMAZING SPIDER-MAN!
LIFELINE Part 1
PIECES of FATE
THIS IS WEIRD... MY SPIDER-SENSE IS TINGLING!
BUT WHAT KIND OF TROUBLE COULD THERE BE AT A MUSEUM OPENING PRESS PARTY?
DUMB QUESTION, PARKER...
AFTER BEING BITTEN BY A RADIOACTIVE SPIDER YEARS AGO, PETER PARKER HAS PUT ON TIGHTS AND PROTECTED THE BIG APPLE--
--AS YOUR FRIENDLY NEIGHBORHOOD SPIDER-MAN...
...AND TROUBLE'S HAD A WAY OF FINDING HIM EVER SINCE!
A WEB-SPINNING TALE OF ADVENTURE BROUGHT TO YOU BY:
"FABULOUS" FABIAN NICIEZA & STEVE "THE DUDE" RUDE
BOB WIACEK-INKER
JOHN COSTANZA-LETTERER
GREG WRIGHT-COLORIST
RALPH MACCHIO-EDITOR
JOE QUESADA EDITOR IN CHIEF

THE BUSTLING GALA CROWD HUSHES AS A MAN STEPS TO THE PODIUM...
LADIES AND GENTLEMEN OF THE PRESS--WELCOME TO THE OPENING OF THE LIFELINE TABLET--
--THE SINGLE MOST SIGNIFICANT ARCHAEOLOGICAL FIND REGARDING LOST LANGUAGES AND THE MEDICINAL PRACTICES OF PRE-SUMERIAN CIVILIZATIONS!
I AM YOUR HOST, LOUIS WILSON, THE PREEMINENT SCHOLAR OF THE ORIGINAL LIFELINE TABLET.
I'VE ALSO SPENT THE LAST TWO YEARS UNEARTHING SIX ADDITIONAL FRAGMENTS OF THE ANCIENT STONE WE HAVE ON DISPLAY TONIGHT!
THE Miraculous ANCIENT STONE TABLET
STONE TABLET
BUT DON'T MENTION THE STINT YOU SPENT IN PRISON IN BETWEEN, LOUIE!
I HATE IT WHEN MY SPIDER-SENSE GOES OFF IN A BIG CROWD...
I SHOULDN'T BE SURPRISED SO MANY PEOPLE TURNED OUT FOR THIS--
--OL' J.J.J. WAS RIGHT--RUMORS OF AN IMMORTALITY FORMULA COMBINED WITH WILSON'S SHADY REPUTATION--
--WOULD CERTAINLY DRAW OUT THE ART WORLD GOSSIP-MONGERS!

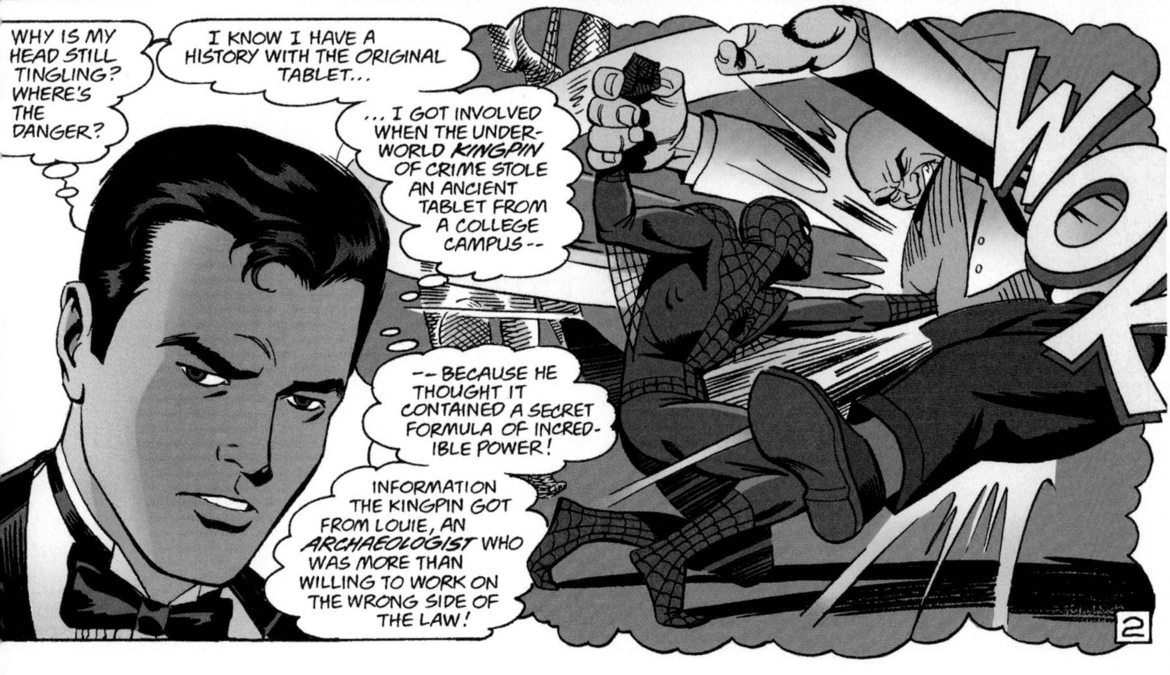
WHY IS MY HEAD STILL TINGLING? WHERE'S THE DANGER?
I KNOW I HAVE A HISTORY WITH THE ORIGINAL TABLET...
...I GOT INVOLVED WHEN THE UNDER-WORLD KINGPIN OF CRIME STOLE AN ANCIENT TABLET FROM A COLLEGE CAMPUS--
WOK
--BECAUSE HE THOUGHT IT CONTAINED A SECRET FORMULA OF INCRED-IBLE POWER!
INFORMATION THE KINGPIN GOT FROM LOUIE, AN ARCHAEOLOGIST WHO WAS MORE THAN WILLING TO WORK ON THE WRONG SIDE OF THE LAW!

"THINGS GOT EVEN MORE COMPLICATED--
"--WHEN THE SHOCKER TOOK THE TABLET FROM THE MAN I'D TURNED IT OVER TO--CAPTAIN GEORGE STACY...
"...HURTING HIM IN THE PROCESS AND MAKING IT A PERSONAL MATTER FOR ME! I KNEW GEORGE STACY.
"THE TABLET BECAME THE OBJECT OF A SCAVENGER HUNT INVOLV ING ALL KINDS OF UNDERWORL MAGGIA TYPES-
"--INCLUDING THUG-FOR-HIRE, MAN MOUNTAIN MARKO--
"--AND MOB LAWYER, CAESER CICERO, WHO BAILED OUT WILSON FROM PRISON--
"--SO THAT HE COULD DECIPHER THE TABLET FOR THE MAGGIA BIG BOSS, SILVERMANE!
"SILVERMANE, LIKE KINGPIN, BELIEVED THAT WHEN THE TABLET'S ANCIENT WRITING WAS TRANSLATED--
"--IT WOULD CREATE A FORMULA THAT WOULD GIVE SOMEONE RENEWED LIFE--A FOUNTAIN OF YOUTH, SO TO SPEAK.
"WILSON DECIPHERED THE TEXT BUT IT WAS MY OLD FRIEND, DR. CURT CONNORS WHO TURNED IT INTO A CHEMICAL FORMULA--
"--THAT ENDED UP WORKING TOO WELL! SILVERMANE DRANK IT AND GOT RENEWED LIFE, ALL RIGHT.
"TURNING YOUNGER BY THE SECOND UNTIL HE DEVOLVED--"

--INTO NOTHINGNESS!
THAT WAS YEARS AGO. WILSON DID HIS TIME IN PRISON AND TRIED TO GO LEGIT...
...AND I NEVER FOUND OUT WHAT BECAME OF THE ORIGINAL TABLET.
NOW WILSON CLAIMS THAT THESE ADDITIONAL FRAGMENTS HE UNCOVERED WILL HELP COMPLETE THE ORIGINAL TABLET'S WRITINGS!
I GUESS I SHOULDN'T BE SURPRISED THAT EVERYONE IS CURIOUS ABOUT AN OBJECT THAT COULD MAKE YOU LIVE FOREVER.
AS IF THIS LIFE HASN'T BEEN HARD ENOUGH, RIGHT?
MAYBE NOT FOR THEM... LOOK AT MY BOSS, JONAH, SCHMOOZING WITH HIS WIFE, MARLA--
--DAILY BUGLE EDITOR ROBBIE ROBERTSON WITH HIS SON, AND MY ROOMMATE, RANDY--
--AND... HEY... WAIT A SEC--
--MAYBE THAT'S WHY MY SPIDER-SENSE WAS GOING OFF.
CLIK
THAT WAITER LOOKS LIKE MAN MOUNTAIN MARKO!
COULD HE BE TRYING TO GO LEGIT?
IS IT JUST A COINCIDENCE THAT HE'S WORKING AS A WAITER HERE AND HE WAS ALSO INVOLVED IN THE ORIGINAL TABLET SCHEME?
4

NAAAH!!
TIME TO BREAK OUT THE RED AND BLUE SPANDEX!
GOOD THING I WASHED MY COSTUME LAST NIGHT!
I'D HATE TO MAKE A MALODOROUS IMPRESSION ON THE GLITTERATI!
CLIK CLIK
OH, C'MOOON-- THE BATHROOM IS TAKEN?
THIS NEVER HAPPENS TO CLARK KENT!
MR. WILSON-- TAKE COVER!
NO ONE HAS T'GET HURT!
I GOT WHAT I WANTED-- NOW EVERYONE JUST BACK AWAY!
WAIT! NO-- THOSE FRAGMENTS ARE PRICELESS!
NO DUH!
HUH--?
Y'KNOW, MANNY, WE REALLY HAVE TO WORK ON YOUR REPARTEE!
SAYS THE REFUGEE FROM EASTER ISLAND?
WRONG! LEARN YOUR TRIBAL ACCOU-TERMENTS!
WAKANDA GUY YOU THINK I'D BE TROTTING OUT INAPPROPRIATE HEADGEAR TO A FANCY-SCHMANCY BALL LIKE THIS?
SPIDER-MAN, RIGHT?
I'D KNOW THAT DOPEY SENSE OF HUMOR ANYWHERE!
HEY! I RESEMBLE THAT REMARK!

YOU LIKE MY NEW COSTUME?
IF THE WASP CAN SPORT A DIFFERENT LOOK EVERY DAY, WHY CAN'T THE WORLD'S FAVORITE WALL-CRAWLER?
CLIK
THWIPP
STILL RATED *NUMERO UNO* FOR CATCHING FLEEING FELONS!
THUP!
OH, CRUD...
ELOQUENT, AS ALWAYS, MANNY--
--HEY-- DON'T DROP THE--
CYCLOPS
--AH, WHAT KIND OF SPANKING WOULD *WE* BE IN FOR IF IT WEREN'T FOR MY *SPEEDY REFLEXES*?
WHO ELSE COULD LEAP LIKE THIS IN A SINGLE BOUND?
CELTIC MONOLITH
OH, WONDERFUL, I HAVE TO SAVE THE TABLET--
--THEN SAVE MYSELF--
--WHILE MARKO GETS AWAY!
HEY BIG FELLA, YOU *GRUESOME* SINCE LAST TIME I SAW YOU!
I CRACK ME UP.
Sigh

OKAY, HAIRY SCARY IS AS SECURED AS HE'S GOING TO GET...
...I HAVE TO GET THE TABLET BACK INTO THE RIGHT HANDS--WITHOUT BEING SEEN--
--WHICH COULD GET DICEY CONSIDERING THE COMMOTION GOING ON IN THE MAIN LOBBY!
WHO CALLED 911?
I DID--J. JONAH JAMESON--PUBLISHER OF THE DAILY BUGLE--
--AND A CITIZEN THREATENED BY THE DEADLIEST KILLER THIS CITY HAS EVER SEEN!
DON'T TELL ME, SPIDER-MAN'S IN THE BUILDING?
TEARING IT APART IS MORE LIKE IT!
DID ANYONE ELSE SEE HIM?
LOOK AT THE WEBS HE LEFT ALL AROUND! HE WAS IN DISGUISE! AN IDIOT COULD SEE THAT!
HE WAS WEARING A TUXEDO!
MR. JAMESON... EVERYONE'S WEARING A TUX--INCLUDING YOU!
WHY YOU'RE NOT INSINUATING--
WELL, WHOEVER IT WAS, THEY RETURNED THE FRAGMENTS TO US!
WHA--? BUT HE--WELL, IT MUST BE A PART OF A BIGGER SCHEME.
GOOD OL' JONAH, ALWAYS READY TO STICK HIS FOOT IN HIS MOUTH WHEN IT COMES TO SPIDEY!

LATER...
GOTTA FIGURE MARKO'S GOING TO MAKE ANOTHER GO FOR THOSE FRAGMENTS.
SO, IN THE MEANTIME, I'LL CATCH UP ON SOME SCIENCE JOURNALS...
...MY LIFE'S BEEN SUCH A MESS LATELY, THAT I'VE FALLEN WAY BEHIND IN THE LATEST STUDIES
...WOWP...WILSON'S LEAVING THE MUSEUM NOW...
WE CHECKED THE ENTIRE SQUARE BLOCK AND YOU'RE ALL CLEAR TO GO, MR. WILSON.
THANKS. THE ATTACK LEFT ME VERY NERVOUS ABOUT THE SAFETY OF THE FRAGMENTS.
ANCIENT TABLET
GO FIGURE, WILSON'S REALLY COMING ACROSS AS CLEAN NOW.
IS HE UP TO SOMETHING--
--OR AM I JUST TOO SUSPICIOUS IN MY OLD AGE?
WHATEVER THE CASE...
STREETS ARE PRETTY CLEAR TONIGHT.
NY NY 88-4612
MAYBE MARKO--
--OR WHOEVER HIRED HIM, SINCE THE BIG LUG COULD NEVER COOK UP ANY KIND OF SCHEME ON HIS OWN--
--ISN'T GOING TO TRY AGAIN FOR THE FRAGMENTS?
OR THEN AGAIN...
8

WOW! IN THE GOOD OLD DAYS, MARKO WOULD HAVE JUST LET THE CAR RUN RIGHT INTO HIM!
KLUMP
SKREEEEEEEEEEEE
PRETTY SPLASHY MOVE THERE, MANNY!
I GUESS THE MATRIX MOVIE REALLY HAS UPPED THE ANTE FOR EVERYONE IN THE BIZ!
HEY?
WHERE'D LURCH BY WAY OF THE SOPRANOS GO?
STOP!
WHAT'RE YOU DOING?
UH-OH DON'T TELL ME I FELL FOR THE OLD
--BAIT AND SWITCH!
YUP, I DID. TEN DEMERITS ON MY SUPER-HERO REPORT CARD!
WHOEVER GRABBED THE FRAGMENTS IS MOVING PRETTY FAST...
237

HOLD ON, WILSON-- I'LL GET YOU OUT!
KRUNCH
FORGET ABOUT ME-- GET THE FRAGMENTS!
SPIDER-MAN CODE OF CONDUCT-- PEOPLE BEFORE THINGS.
'CEPT IF IT WERE A FLAT-SCREEN TV, THOSE LOOK COOL.
COULD YOU PLEASE GO GET THE FRAGMENTS?
ON MY WAY.
HEY, I KNEW HE WAS RUNNING INTO A GATED ALLEY--
THUP
THUP
BNKK
--HOW COULD WHOEVER IT WAS GET THROUGH THE BARS SO EASILY?
DISPOSAL
DISTRICT B
HE'D HAVE TO BE AS SLIPPERY AS AN... OH, D'OH-- IT WAS THE EEL!
NYPD'S COMING... I HAVE A FEW QUESTIONS TO ASK LOUIE, SO...
HEY--WHAT'S GOING ON-- IS HE THE ACCIDENT VICTIM?
BIG PROBLEM-- I CHECKED HIS HEALTH INSURANCE--
--WOULDN'T 'CHA KNOW, HMO-- SINCE NO ONE WILL TREAT HIM, I'LL HAVE TO PERFORM MAJOR SURGERY MYSELF...
POLICE
POLICE
HE WAS KIDDING... WASN'T HE?
OKAY, LOUIE--
--EEL AND MARKO HAVE BOTH WORKED FOR MAGGIA LAWYER CAESER CICERO--
--WHO BAILED YOU OUT ONCE BEFORE, SO I'M ADDING TWO AND TWO...
NO! NO--I HAVE NOTHING TO DO WITH ANY OF THEM ANYMORE!
AND I BELIEVE YOU BECAUSE I'M A GULLIBLE GUY?
10

BECAUSE I STAND TO GAIN MORE FROM THOSE FRAGMENTS ON MY OWN--THAN I EVER WOULD--
--WORKING AS A PATSY FOR ONE OF THOSE CLOWNS AGAIN!
AND I DON'T JUST MEAN MONEY, EITHER! THE LIFELINE TABLET IS EXACTLY WHAT WE ALWAYS THOUGHT IT WAS--
--A FOUNTAIN OF YOUTH--BUT IT'S A WHOLE LOT MORE, TOO!
AFTER MY PAROLE, I SPENT YEARS SEARCHING FOR THE MISSING PIECES OF THE ORIGINAL TABLET--
"--EXHAUSTIVELY LINKING IT TO THE HYBORIAN AGE THROUGH THE CIVILIZATIONS OF LEMURIA AND ATLANTIS!
"I REALIZED THAT THE LIFE-LINE FORMULA DIDN'T WORK CORRECTLY FOR SILVERMANE--
"--BECAUSE SMALL--BUT CRUCIAL--PARTS OF THE EQUATION WERE MISSING!"
AND IF YOU FIGURED THIS OUT, THEN IT STANDS TO REASON...
THAT THE PEOPLE INVOLVED IN THE ORIGINAL ESCAPADE WOULD HAVE AS WELL!
OKAY, I'LL BUY IT FOR NOW.
THE POLICE'LL BE UP IN A SECOND--
"--I'M GOING TO TRACK DOWN EEL AND MARKO!"
AT THAT MOMENT INSIDE A FOREBODING ESTATE ON LONG ISLAND...
WE DID YA TO THE GOOD, BOSS. THE ROCKS ARE IN THE SACK!
BOTH OF YOU HAVE DONE VERY WELL INDEED.
THIS WILL MAKE ME A BIG MAN IN THE MAGGIA HIERARCHY!

BEIN' THEIR GO-TO SHYSTER WASN'T GOOD ENOUGH FOR YOU, CAESER?
DO YOU HAVE ANY RESPECT FOR LAWYERS, MARKO?
NOPE.
PROVES MY POINT, THEN.
IF A BRAINLESS SIDE OF BEEF LIKE YOU CAN'T RESPECT THE LEGAL ACUMEN OF CAESER CICERO--
--THEN HOW CAN I EXPECT THE REAL MOVERS AND SHAKERS TO?
THESE FRAGMENTS ARE GOING TO MAKE ME VERY RICH--AND VERY POWERFUL!
KRASH
OR NOT!
WAP
SHOULD'VE PLAYED IT SMART THEN, LIKE MY BOSS DID--
--BY HIRING BOOMERANG T'GET THE JOB DONE RIGHT!
MY ROCKS!
IT'S A SHAME, MATE...
SSSSSS
SSS
...WHAT WITH YOU PAYIN' OUT SO MUCH MONEY FOR SUCH FEEBLE HELP.
12

CORRECTION, SHORTY...
...MY ROCKS!
OR, ACTUALLY, T'BE PROPER ABOUT IT--
THUK
--"THE ROCKS BELONGING TO THE MAN GIVING ME A SUITCASE FULL OF CASH T'GET THEM FOR HIM!"
I'LL DOUBLE WHATEVER HE'S PAYING YOU!
TRIPLE IT!
NEVER BID AGAINST YOURSELF, SHORTY-- I WAS SERIOUSLY CONSIDERING THE "DOUBLE IT" OFFER!
OOPS, SHOULD'VE EXPECTED HE'D SLIDE THROUGH THE RUBBLE...
OUCH
KILL HIM, EEL! TAKE HIS BOOMERANG AND--
NOW, NOW, NO REASON T'GET GRAPHIC ABOUT IT...
...EVEN GREASED LIGHTNING LIKE THE EEL--
--IS A SITTING DUCK IN MID-LEAP!
FSSHH
THE GLUEME-RANG SHOULD DISSOLVE... EVENTUALLY.
G'DAY!
HEY-- GET BACK HERE!

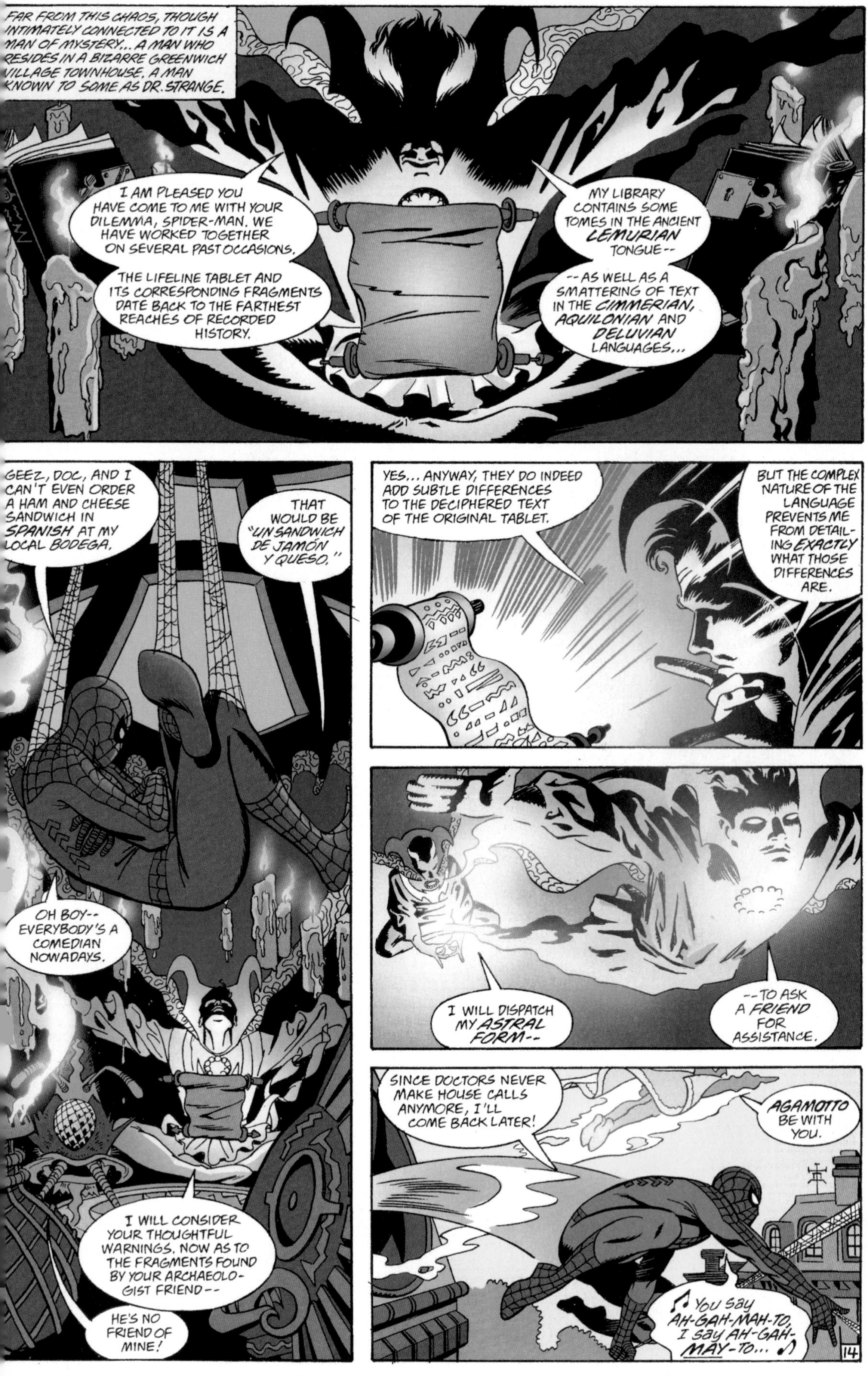
FAR FROM THIS CHAOS, THOUGH INTIMATELY CONNECTED TO IT IS A MAN OF MYSTERY... A MAN WHO RESIDES IN A BIZARRE GREENWICH VILLAGE TOWNHOUSE, A MAN KNOWN TO SOME AS DR. STRANGE.
I AM PLEASED YOU HAVE COME TO ME WITH YOUR DILEMMA, SPIDER-MAN. WE HAVE WORKED TOGETHER ON SEVERAL PAST OCCASIONS.
THE LIFELINE TABLET AND ITS CORRESPONDING FRAGMENTS DATE BACK TO THE FARTHEST REACHES OF RECORDED HISTORY.
MY LIBRARY CONTAINS SOME TOMES IN THE ANCIENT LEMURIAN TONGUE--
--AS WELL AS A SMATTERING OF TEXT IN THE CIMMERIAN, AQUILONIAN AND DELUVIAN LANGUAGES...
GEEZ, DOC, AND I CAN'T EVEN ORDER A HAM AND CHEESE SANDWICH IN SPANISH AT MY LOCAL BODEGA.
THAT WOULD BE "UN SANDWICH DE JAMÓN Y QUESO."
OH BOY-- EVERYBODY'S A COMEDIAN NOWADAYS.
I WILL CONSIDER YOUR THOUGHTFUL WARNINGS. NOW AS TO THE FRAGMENTS FOUND BY YOUR ARCHAEOLOGIST FRIEND--
HE'S NO FRIEND OF MINE!
YES... ANYWAY, THEY DO INDEED ADD SUBTLE DIFFERENCES TO THE DECIPHERED TEXT OF THE ORIGINAL TABLET.
BUT THE COMPLEX NATURE OF THE LANGUAGE PREVENTS ME FROM DETAILING EXACTLY WHAT THOSE DIFFERENCES ARE.
I WILL DISPATCH MY ASTRAL FORM--
--TO ASK A FRIEND FOR ASSISTANCE.
SINCE DOCTORS NEVER MAKE HOUSE CALLS ANYMORE, I'LL COME BACK LATER!
AGAMOTTO BE WITH YOU.
♪ You say AH-GAH-MAH-TO, I say AH-GAH-MAY-TO... ♪
14

LATER IN THE QUEENS HOME OF SECURITY CONSULTANT ARTHUR STACY... A GENTLEMAN THE WEB-SPINNER HAS HAD NUMEROUS DEALINGS WITH...
NOK NOK
WHAT-- OH.
WHO ELSE WOULD BE UPSIDE DOWN KNOCKING ON MY WINDOW...
SORRY TO BUG YOU AT HOME THIS LATE--
NO, YOU'RE NOT.
OKAY, I'M NOT--BUT I NEED YOUR HELP--OR RATHER, YOUR BROTHER'S!
WHO HA BEEN DEAD FOR YEARS SO I'M ASSUM ING IT'S IN REGARDS TO A CASE HE WORKED ON
--OR THE DETAILED JOURNALS HE KEPT ABOUT THEM?
YUP ON ALL COUNTS.
I HAVE HIS JOURNALS KEPT IN A SAFE.
AND YOU KNOW WHERE THEY ARE? I DON'T CARE WHAT ANYONE SAYS, YOU'RE JUST AS GOOD A DETECTIVE AS HE WAS.
HUMPH.
OKAY, SPIDEY, EASE UP HERE--
--ALWAYS FEEL ON EDGE WITH ARTHUR...
...BECAUSE HE'S A LIVING CONNECTION TO HIS BROTHER GEORGE STACY--
--AND GWEN...

HIGH SCHOOL. WHO CREATED THAT FOUR-YEAR TORTURE CHAMBER? BUT I FINALLY GRADUATED. AND THEN IN COLLEGE-- I MET HER, GWEN STACY.
I TRIED TO NEVER EVEN LOOK HER WAY.
SCIENCE NERDS AREN'T ALLOWED TO DATE THE GORGEOUS GIRL.
BUT SHE WAS MORE THAN JUST A PRETTY FACE... AND GO FIGURE, SHE THOUGHT THAT I WAS MORE THAN JUST A NERD.
AN INSECURE, ANGST-RIDDEN BAG OF WORRY, THAT'S WHAT I WAS!
WORRY ABOUT AUNT MAY'S HEALTH ALL THE TIME--MONEY WOES--PILED ON TOP OF MY SPIDEY RESPONSIBILITIES...
...IT'S AMAZING SHE SAW THROUGH THAT WALL OF WEIRD I BUILT AROUND MYSELF--
--MUCH LESS THAT WE FOUND THE TIME TO ACTUALLY HAVE SOME KIND OF A REAL RELATIONSHIP!
AND THROUGH IT ALL, GWEN'S FATHER WAS A ROCK--SUPPORTING HER IN EVERYTHING SHE DID--
--AND GIVING ME THE FATHER-FIGURE I'D BEEN MISSING SINCE UNCLE BEN'S DEATH.
GEORGE STACY WAS ONE OF THE GREATEST MEN I'VE EVEN KNOWN...
16

...WHICH MAKES MY FAILURE TO PREVENT DOCTOR OCTOPUS FROM TOPPLING THE ROOFTOP CHIMNEY THAT KILLED HIM AS HE TRIED TO PUSH A CHILD OUT OF THE WAY--
--ALL THE HARDER TO EVER ACCEPT.
AND AS IF LOSING HIM WEREN'T BAD ENOUGH, THE LAST THING HE SAID TO ME MADE IT EVEN WORSE...
IT--IT'S GWEN! AFTER I'M--GONE--THERE'LL BE NO ONE--TO LOOK AFTER HER--
NO ONE, PETER--EXCEPT --YOU!
BE GOOD TO HER--SON! BE GOOD--TO HER--
SHE LOVES YOU--SO VERY MUCH--
HE KNEW. MAYBE HE'D ALWAYS KNOWN.
SO NOT ONLY DID THE GIRL I LOVE LOSE HER FATHER--
--NOT ONLY DID THE CITY LOSE ONE OF ITS LEADING CITIZENS--
--BUT I LOST A MAN WHO COULD HAVE HELPED GUIDE ME--TEACH ME...
...TO BE SO MUCH MORE THAN I MIGHT HAVE EVER BEEN ON MY OWN...
HOW DIFFERENT WOULD MY LIFE HAVE BEEN HAD GEORGE STACY LIVED?

"GWEN LOST HER LIFE NOT LONG AFTERWARDS AT THE HANDS OF THE GREEN GOBLIN...
"...WHO WAS NORMAN OSBORN, A MONSTER WHO CAST A SHADOW OF EVIL ON HIS SON, MY BEST FRIEND, HARRY--
"--WHICH IN TURN COST HARRY HIS LIFE WHEN HE LATER ASSUMED THE MANTLE OF THE GOBLIN.
"AND HAVING RECENTLY LOST MY WIFE MARY JANE TO A TRAGIC AIRPLANE ACCIDENT...
...I BEGIN TO REALIZE WHY--
--SOMETHING LIKE THIS LIFELINE TABLET IS SO... SEDUCTIVE.
WHO COULDN'T PUT A MIRROR TO THEIR LIVES AND SEE REFLECTIONS OF THINGS THEY'D LIKE TO CHANGE?
UNDO MISTAKES THAT WERE MADE, PREVENT ACCIDENTS THAT HAPPENED...
POWER LIKE THAT... I'VE SEEN IT USED AND ABUSED BEFORE.
BUT THAT DOESN'T CHANGE THE FACT THAT WANTING TO WIELD SUCH POWER IS TOTALLY UNDERSTANDABLE...
...IF IT MEANT...
...A SECOND CHANCE AT HAPPINESS...

THEN AGAIN, WITH MY TRACK RECORD, I'D SCREW IT UP AND REMAKE THE WORLD INTO THE PLANET OF THE APES OR SOMETHING...
HERE IS GEORGE'S JOURNAL.
DOES IT SAY ANYTHING ABOUT THE TABLET AFTER SILVERMANE TURNED INTO PUDDING?
IT MENTIONS IT WAS "USED AS EVIDENCE TO CONVICT LOUIS WILSON"--
--AND WAS "PLACED INTO POLICE STORAGE."
SO AN ANCIENT ROCK THAT COULD BE A FOUNTAIN OF YOUTH IS SITTING IN A WAREHOUSE SOMEWHERE?
ONE WAY TO KNOW FOR SURE IS TO MAKE SOME CALLS TO FRIENDS I HAVE ON THE FORCE...
MINUTES LATER...
IT'S MISSING?!
WHEN? FOR HOW LONG? WHAT DO YOU MEAN YOU CAN'T TELL?
APPARENTLY, THE EVIDENCE LOCKER WAS REMOVED FROM ITS SHELF SPACE SOMETIME AFTER THE LAST INVENTOR CHECK SIX MONTHS AGO.
COMMON SENSE DICTATES IT WAS TAKEN RECENTLY, WHEN NEWS OF THE MUSEUM EXHIBIT HIT THE PAPERS.
BUT WHO--?
I GOT A LIST OF THE USUAL SUSPECTS, ARTHUR.
I'LL TRY TO NARROW THEM DOWN ON MY END, IF YOU COULD HELP ON YOURS--
--MAKE SOME MORE CALLS, SEE WHOSE FINGERS MIGHT HAVE DIPPED INTO THE PD'S ARCHIVE DEPARTMENT--
--I'D APPRECIATE IT. MAYBE EVEN BRING YOU SOME FLOWERS.
NOTHING SAYS, "THANK YOU" LIKE FLOWERS. CIAO FOR NOW!
19

AS SPIDEY SWINGS AWAY, WE TURN OUR ATTENTION TO A HEAVILY GUARDED BUILDING IN BROOKLYN...
THERE'S BOOMERANG.
'BOUT TIME. BOSS WAS GETTIN' ANTSY.
DID'JA GET THE ROCKS?
DO YOU NEED TO ASK?
YEAH, I DO.
AN' HOW MANY TIMES I TOL' YOU NOT TO USE THE ROOF?
I GOT ENOUGH FEDS CHASIN' 'ROUND MY BLOCK I SHOULD BE CHARGIN' 'EM RENT!
YOU OWN THE NEIGHBORHOOD, MATE--
--SO I'M SURE YOU MAKE MORE 'N ENOUGH BACK SELLIN' THEM YOUR BAD COFFEE, NEWSPAPERS AN' CIGS.
HERE'S YOUR PEBBLES.
AWRIGHT, OPEN UP THE CASE--
--LET'S SEE WHAT THE CICCY--
--HAD--?

THAT'S IT?!
YOU BETTER NOT BE HOLDIN' OUT ON HAMMERHEAD, OUT-BACK, OR ELSE I'LL--
BAM
DON'T ROUGH UP THE LINGUINI, BOSS.
WHAT YOU SEE IS WHAT HE HAD.
YOU AND EINSTEIN HERE WERE EXPECTING MORE?
WERE WE?
NOT NECESSARILY.
THOUGH OF COURSE, THE MORE THAT EXISTS, THE EASIER IT WOULD BE TO DECIPHER THE FULL TEXT OF THE TABLET FORMULA.
THESE FRAGMENTS SHOULD PROVIDE ENOUGH TO IMPROVE UPON THE ORIGINAL CHEMICAL COMPOUND.
THEY BETTER!
DON'T FORGET, WE KNOW WHERE YOUR FAMILY IS, AN' LET'S JUST SAY--
--SOMETIMES, ACCIDENTS HAPPEN, EVEN TO NICE GUYS, YOU GIT WHAT I'M SAYING--

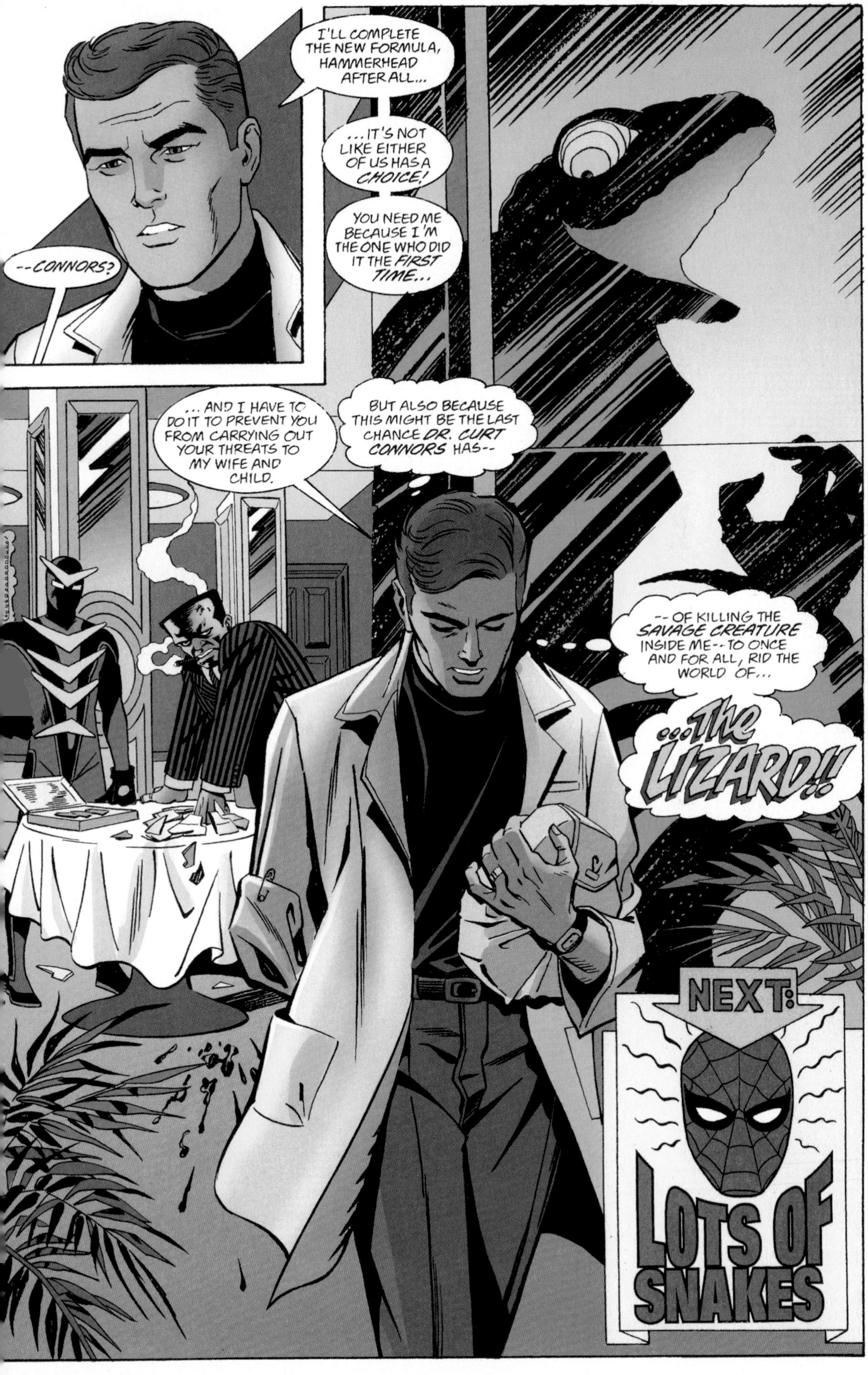

I'LL COMPLETE THE NEW FORMULA, HAMMERHEAD AFTER ALL...
--CONNORS?
...IT'S NOT LIKE EITHER OF US HAS A CHOICE!
YOU NEED ME BECAUSE I'M THE ONE WHO DID IT THE FIRST TIME...
...AND I HAVE TO DO IT TO PREVENT YOU FROM CARRYING OUT YOUR THREATS TO MY WIFE AND CHILD.
BUT ALSO BECAUSE THIS MIGHT BE THE LAST CHANCE DR. CURT CONNORS HAS--
--OF KILLING THE SAVAGE CREATURE INSIDE ME--TO ONCE AND FOR ALL, RID THE WORLD OF...
...The LIZARD!!
NEXT:
LOTS OF SNAKES

SPIDER-MAN: LIFELINE #2

LIFELINE
part 2
SNAKES IN THE GRASS
IN ORDER TO ADVANCE IN THE MAGGIA CRIMINAL ORGANIZATION, MOB-LAWYER CAESAR CICERO NEEDED MORE POWER!
MAN MOUNTAIN MARKO, THUG FOR HIRE, STOLE FRAGMENTS OF AN ANCIENT TABLET THAT WOULD GIVE CICERO THE POWER HE CRAVES!
THE EEL IS A SLIPPERY THIEF WHO HELPED MARKO WITH THE HEIST!
BOOMERANG IS THE MERCENARY WHO TRASHED CICERO'S LONG ISLAND HOME AND TOOK THE FRAGMENTS FROM HIM, DELIVERING THEM TO--
--HAMMERHEAD, A BOSS IN THE MAGGIA CRIME EMPIRE WHO WANTS THE TABLET FOR UNKNOWN REASONS!
AND STUCK IN THE MIDDLE OF ALL OF THIS IS YOUR FRIENDLY NEIGHBORHOOD SPIDER-MAN, WHO IS PROBABLY WONDERING WHY THE FOLLOWING FOLKS HAVE MADE HIS LIFE SO MISERABLE...
FABIAN NICIEZA and STEVE RUDE
writer · storytellers · penciler
BOB WIACEK - inker
JOHN COSTANZA - lettering
GREG WRIGHT - colorist
BRIAN SMITH - asst. editor
RALPH MACCHIO - editor
JOE QUESADA - editor in chief

MANHATTAN
BILLY NEUHAUS IS TIRED, COMING HOME OFF AN EXTRA SHIFT.
HE WORKS THE EVIDENCE LOCK-UP FOR THE NEW YORK CITY POLICE DEPARTMENT.
IT'S EITHER PULL DOUBLE SHIFTS OR TEND BAR. HE FIGURED THE DESK JOB WAS SAFER.
HE FIGURED WRONG...
PARKING
136
POLICE
C'MON, YOU STUPID KEY!
TWENTY YEARS ON THE JOB AN' ALL I GOT TO SHOW FOR IT IS A LOUSY APARTMENT, LOUSY PAY AND A LOUSIER PENSION!
WHICH WOULD EXPLAIN THE BRIBE YOU TOOK...?
HUH--?
AAH!
NO, "AAH" IS WHAT YOU SAY TO YOUR DENTIST.
WHAT YOU SAY TO A GUY WHO STICKS TO WALLS AND HAS THE PROPORTIONATE STRENGTH OF A SPIDER IS...
...ANYTHING HE WANTS YOU TO SAY!
WAAAAHH!
WHO DID YOU TAKE THE PAYOFF FROM?
I-I DON'T KNOW WHAT YER TALKIN' ABOUT--

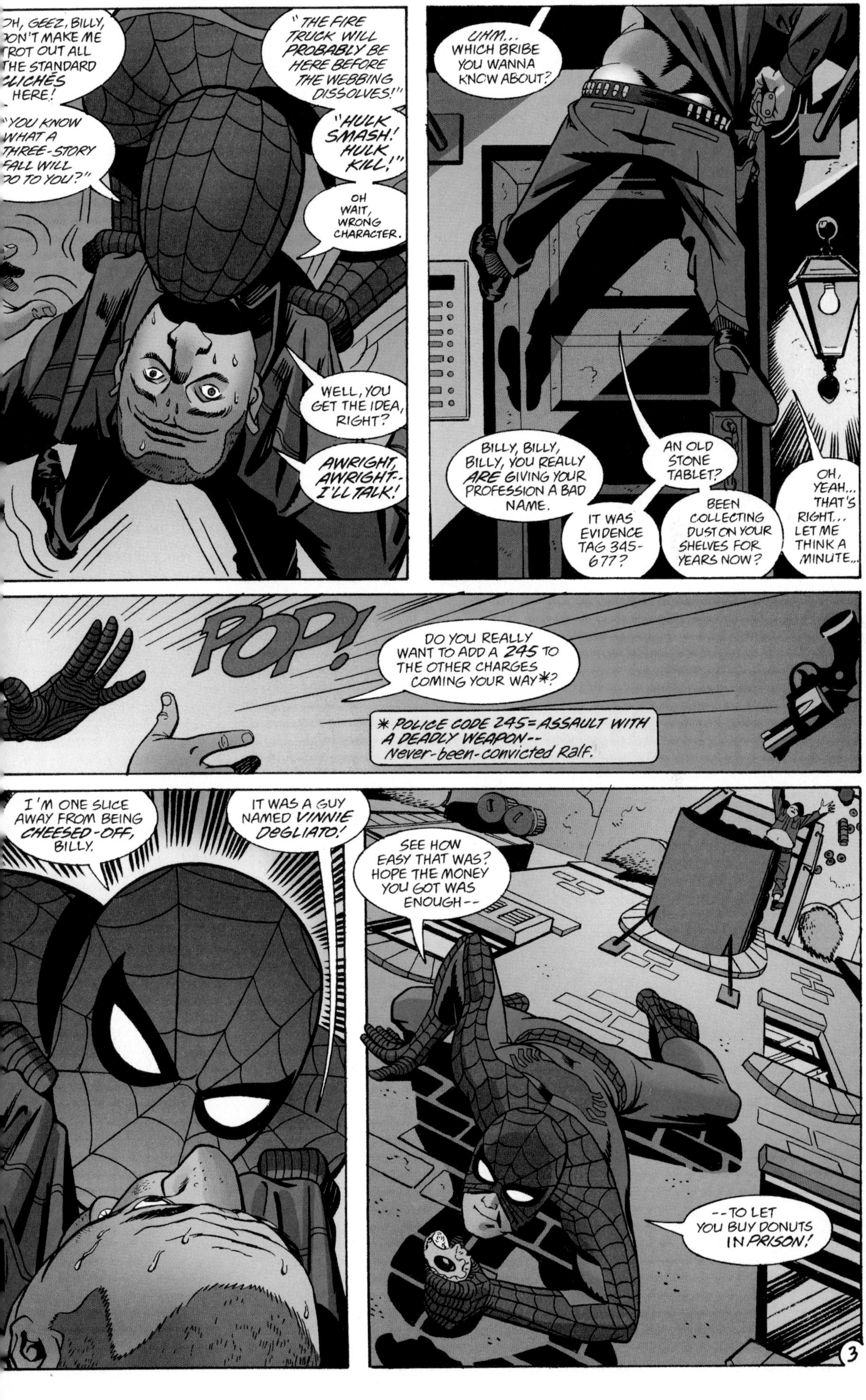
OH, GEEZ, BILLY, DON'T MAKE ME TROT OUT ALL THE STANDARD CLICHÉS HERE!
"YOU KNOW WHAT A THREE-STORY FALL WILL DO TO YOU?"
"THE FIRE TRUCK WILL PROBABLY BE HERE BEFORE THE WEBBING DISSOLVES!"
"HULK SMASH! HULK KILL!"
OH WAIT, WRONG CHARACTER.
WELL, YOU GET THE IDEA, RIGHT?
AWRIGHT, AWRIGHT-- I'LL TALK!
UHM... WHICH BRIBE YOU WANNA KNOW ABOUT?
BILLY, BILLY, BILLY, YOU REALLY ARE GIVING YOUR PROFESSION A BAD NAME.
AN OLD STONE TABLET?
IT WAS EVIDENCE TAG 345-677?
BEEN COLLECTING DUST ON YOUR SHELVES FOR YEARS NOW?
OH, YEAH... THAT'S RIGHT... LET ME THINK A MINUTE...
POP!
DO YOU REALLY WANT TO ADD A 245 TO THE OTHER CHARGES COMING YOUR WAY*?
* POLICE CODE 245=ASSAULT WITH A DEADLY WEAPON-- Never-been-convicted Ralf.
I'M ONE SLICE AWAY FROM BEING CHEESED-OFF, BILLY.
IT WAS A GUY NAMED VINNIE DEGLIATO!
SEE HOW EASY THAT WAS? HOPE THE MONEY YOU GOT WAS ENOUGH--
--TO LET YOU BUY DONUTS IN PRISON!

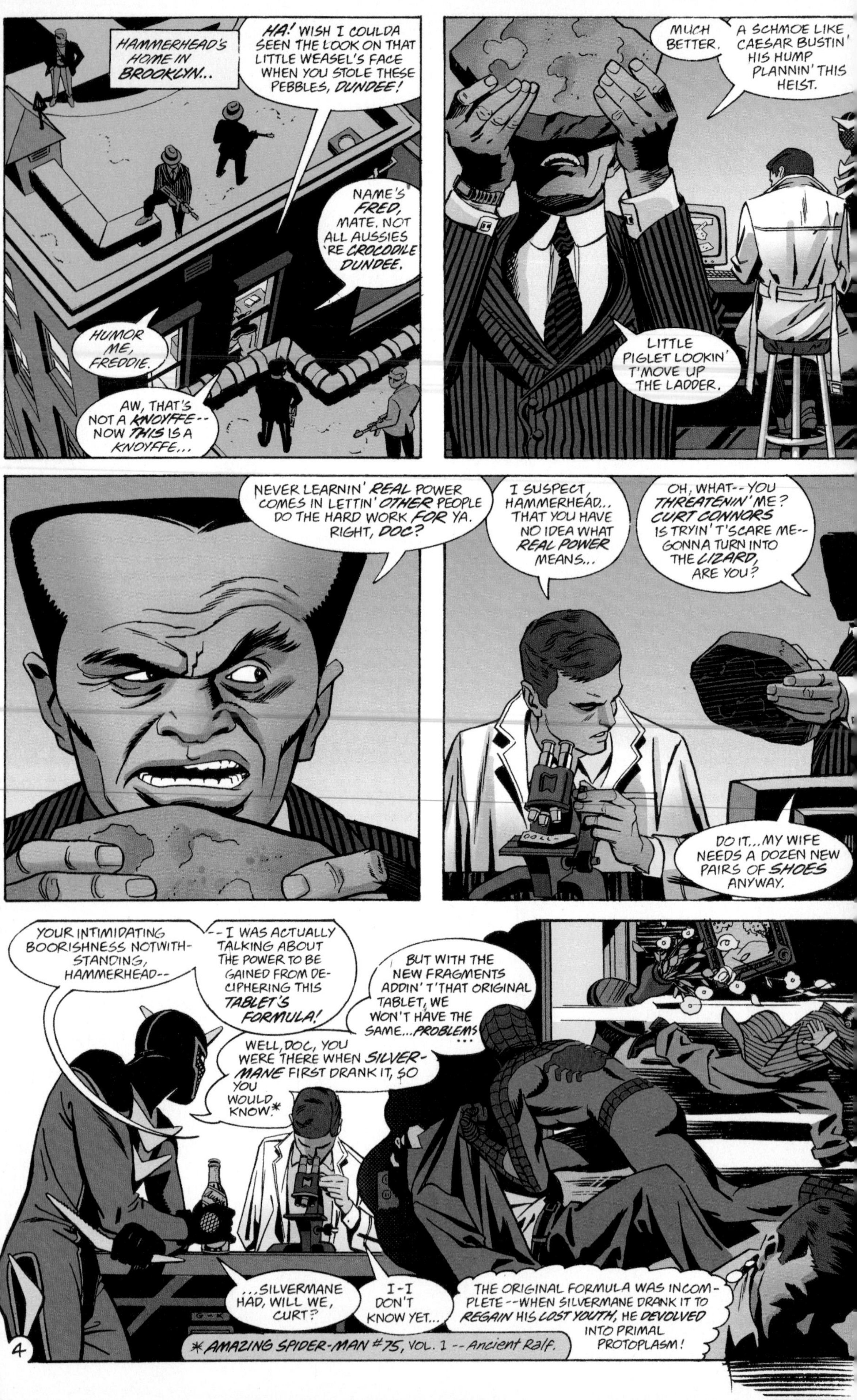
HAMMERHEAD'S HOME IN BROOKLYN...
HA! WISH I COULDA SEEN THE LOOK ON THAT LITTLE WEASEL'S FACE WHEN YOU STOLE THESE PEBBLES, DUNDEE!
NAME'S FRED, MATE. NOT ALL AUSSIES 'RE CROCODILE DUNDEE.
HUMOR ME, FREDDIE.
AW, THAT'S NOT A KNOYFFE-- NOW THIS IS A KNOYFFE...
MUCH BETTER.
A SCHMOE LIKE CAESAR BUSTIN' HIS HUMP PLANNIN' THIS HEIST.
LITTLE PIGLET LOOKIN' T'MOVE UP THE LADDER.
NEVER LEARNIN' REAL POWER COMES IN LETTIN' OTHER PEOPLE DO THE HARD WORK FOR YA. RIGHT, DOC?
I SUSPECT, HAMMERHEAD... THAT YOU HAVE NO IDEA WHAT REAL POWER MEANS...
OH, WHAT--YOU THREATENIN' ME? CURT CONNORS IS TRYIN' T'SCARE ME--GONNA TURN INTO THE LIZARD, ARE YOU?
DO IT... MY WIFE NEEDS A DOZEN NEW PAIRS OF SHOES ANYWAY.
YOUR INTIMIDATING BOORISHNESS NOTWITH-STANDING, HAMMERHEAD--
--I WAS ACTUALLY TALKING ABOUT THE POWER TO BE GAINED FROM DE-CIPHERING THIS TABLET'S FORMULA!
BUT WITH THE NEW FRAGMENTS ADDIN' T'THAT ORIGINAL TABLET, WE WON'T HAVE THE SAME... PROBLEMS...
WELL, DOC, YOU WERE THERE WHEN SILVER-MANE FIRST DRANK IT, SO YOU WOULD KNOW.*
...SILVERMANE HAD, WILL WE, CURT?
I-I DON'T KNOW YET...
THE ORIGINAL FORMULA WAS INCOM-PLETE--WHEN SILVERMANE DRANK IT TO REGAIN HIS LOST YOUTH, HE DEVOLVED INTO PRIMAL PROTOPLASM!
* AMAZING SPIDER-MAN #75, VOL. 1 --Ancient Ralf.

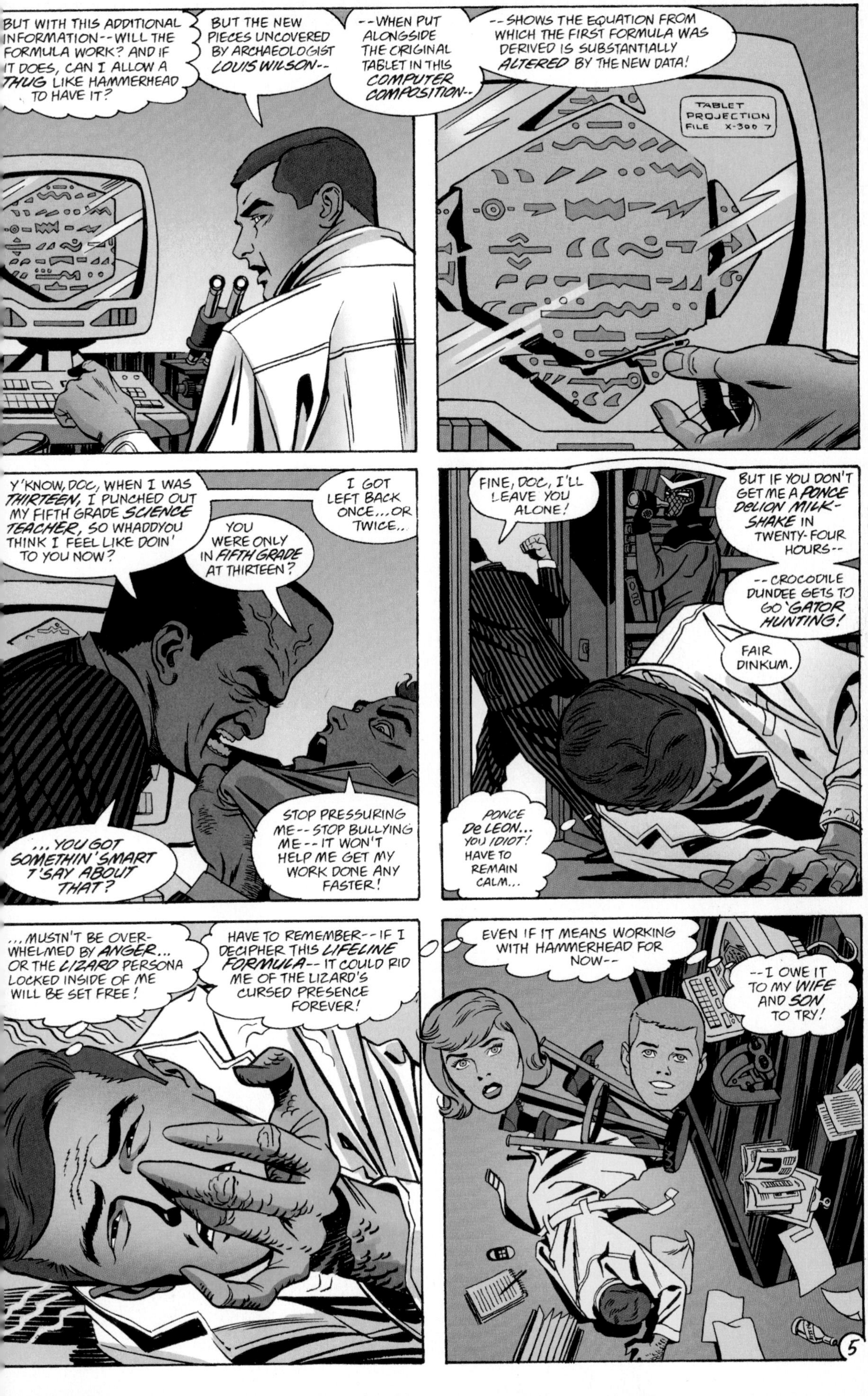
BUT WITH THIS ADDITIONAL INFORMATION--WILL THE FORMULA WORK? AND IF IT DOES, CAN I ALLOW A THUG LIKE HAMMERHEAD TO HAVE IT?
BUT THE NEW PIECES UNCOVERED BY ARCHAEOLOGIST LOUIS WILSON--
--WHEN PUT ALONGSIDE THE ORIGINAL TABLET IN THIS COMPUTER COMPOSITION--
--SHOWS THE EQUATION FROM WHICH THE FIRST FORMULA WAS DERIVED IS SUBSTANTIALLY ALTERED BY THE NEW DATA!
TABLET PROJECTION FILE X-300 7
Y'KNOW, DOC, WHEN I WAS THIRTEEN, I PUNCHED OUT MY FIFTH GRADE SCIENCE TEACHER, SO WHADDYOU THINK I FEEL LIKE DOIN' TO YOU NOW?
YOU WERE ONLY IN FIFTH GRADE AT THIRTEEN?
I GOT LEFT BACK ONCE...OR TWICE...
...YOU GOT SOMETHIN' SMART T'SAY ABOUT THAT?
STOP PRESSURING ME--STOP BULLYING ME--IT WON'T HELP ME GET MY WORK DONE ANY FASTER!
FINE, DOC, I'LL LEAVE YOU ALONE!
BUT IF YOU DON'T GET ME A PONCE DeLION MILK-SHAKE IN TWENTY-FOUR HOURS--
--CROCODILE DUNDEE GETS TO GO 'GATOR HUNTING!
FAIR DINKUM.
PONCE De LEON... YOU IDIOT! HAVE TO REMAIN CALM...
...MUSTN'T BE OVER-WHELMED BY ANGER... OR THE LIZARD PERSONA LOCKED INSIDE OF ME WILL BE SET FREE!
HAVE TO REMEMBER--IF I DECIPHER THIS LIFELINE FORMULA--IT COULD RID ME OF THE LIZARD'S CURSED PRESENCE FOREVER!
EVEN IF IT MEANS WORKING WITH HAMMERHEAD FOR NOW--
--I OWE IT TO MY WIFE AND SON TO TRY!

MANHATTAN
SO VINNIE DEGLIATO PAID OFF THE EVIDENCE COP?
YOU KNOW HIM, ARTHUR?
KNOW OF HIM.
FOCUS.
sigh DEGLIATO IS CONNECTED.
HAMMER-HEAD'S FAMILY.
WHICH HELPS EXPLAIN SOME OF THE THINGS I LEARNED...
PAROLE AND PROBATION REPORTS ON MARKO AND THE EEL?
THEY WERE BOTH REPRESENTED BY CAESAR CICERO?
WANTED
MARKO DELL AGE 38 HEIGHT 6'11 WEIGHT 270
WANTED BY NYPD
WANTE
REAL NAME alias THE EEL
YOU THINK "THE BIG C" IS WORKING FOR BLOCKHEAD?
NO. MY GUT TELLS ME THEY'RE PLAYING A GAME AGAINST EACH OTHER.
MINE IS SAYING I SHOULD'VE DROPPED THE CHALUPA.
HAMMY HAS THE ORIGINAL TABLET, CAESAR HAS THE NEW FRAGMENTS--
--AND THEY'RE USELESS WITHOUT EACH OTHER!
AND THEY BOTH KNOW THAT.
SO EXPECT CAESAR TO USE HIS AS BARGAINING CHIPS AGAINST HAMMER IN A BID FOR MORE POWER IN THE MAGGIA.
UNLESS HAMMER-HEAD ALREADY MADE HIS MOVE!
SPROING
THANKS, ARTHUR--DON'T BE A STRANGER, THOUGH YOU CAN'T GET MUCH STRANGER THAN ME!
SOMEDAY, I HAVE TO FIGURE OUT HOW HE DOES THAT.
THEN AGAIN AT MY AGE, WHO NEEDS A HERNIA

MORNING AT THE GLEN COVE ESTATE OF MOB LAWYER, CAESAR CICERO...
C'MON, YOU BUMS, YOU WANT YOUR OVER-TIME OR WHAT?
MR. MARKO, YOU CALLED US OUT IN THE MIDDLE OF THE NIGHT AND WE CAME-- WE'RE TIRED...
WHERE DID I LEAVE THAT LITTLE VIOLIN AGAIN?
MR. CICERO DON'T KNOW FROM TIRED!
I HAD IT IN MY HAND-- POWER-- SO MUCH POWER-- AND THAT SLAB-HEADED SLOB JUST TOOK IT AWAY!!
MONTHS OF PLANNING, WORKING THE TWO OF YOU THROUGH THE SYSTEM, FIGURING OUT THE PINCH AT THE MUSEUM...
...EVEN DEALIN' WITH SPIDER-MAN LOUSING UP THE HEIST BUT STILL MANAGING TO GET THE FRAGMENTS--
--ONLY TO HAVE HAMMERHEAD'S SHOESHINE BOY JUST BLAST HIS WAY RIGHT THROUGH MY STUDY WALLS --THROUGH MY WALLS!--
--AND TAKE THE TWO OF YOU INCOMPETENTS OUT PRETTY AS YOU PLEASE!
FREAKIN' BOOMERANG, FOR CRYING OUT LOUD!
WHY CAN'T I FIND BETTER MUSCLE THAN THE TWO OF YOUZE?
SOMETIMES, SKILL IS BETTER THAN MUSCLE.
MY LITTLE SLIPPERY EEL, YOU SAYING YOU THINK YOU CAN STEAL BACK THOSE FRAGMENTS?
I'M SAYING I WILL.
IT'S HEARTENING TO SEE PERPETUAL FIFTY-TIME LOSERS STILL ACT COCKY.
7

ONE OF MY HANDY-DANDY PATENTED SPIDER-TRACERS WILL KEEP TABS ON GREASY GUS--
--WHILE I WRAP UP MARKO AND LITTLE CAESAR...
...HMM, SUDDENLY, I'M IN THE MOOD FOR PIZZA, PIZZA...
HEY, MR. C, YOU WANT I SHOULD MOVE THIS BABY OUTTA THE ROOM?
YEAH, YEAH, SURE, MARKO-- JUST BE CAREFUL--IT'S BEEN IN THE FAMILY FOR FOUR GENERATIONS!
OH, C'MON, YOU JUST KNOW THE MINUTE YOU SAY THAT, IT'S GOING TO GET TRASHED!
SPIDER-MAN?!
AS IF I NEEDED TO BE ANNOUNCED...
DON'T WORRY, BOSS, I'LL SPLATTER THE BUG!
KRASH
THWIPP
PLEEEEASE, AS IF I COULD LET THAT HAPPEN!
THUK
THUK
I MEAN, I LET A TROUT LIKE YOU NAIL ME--
--THERE GOES THE MOVIE DEAL--
--THE TOY LINE--
--THE UNDEROOS CONTRACT...
NNNFF-- I'M STILL GONNA BUST EVERY BONE IN YOUR SCRAWNY BODY!
MARKO-- THAT CLOCK IS PRICE-LESS!
HEY! SO'S MY SCRAWNY BODY!

UGHH!
KRASH
AWW, NUTS, MARKO, YOU'RE FIRED!
WHAT A BIG MOUTH FOR SUCH A LITTLE GUY.
HEY, MANNY, GIMME A SEC TO PAY MY RESPECTS TO THE CLOCK YOU JUST KILLED WITH MY BACK.
HEY-- HE'S DOWN! FINISH HIM!
AM I REHIRED?
WE'LL NEGOTIATE AFTER YOU SQUASH HIM!
GRAAAA!
WHUPPA
MMMFF
UGH! SNORT! I ALWAYS LOSE INTEREST WHEN WE GET TO THE "MONOSYLLABIC GRUNTING" PORTION OF THE FIGHT...
GEEZ! DOES A GUY HAVE TO DO EVERYTHING HIMSELF?!
BLAM
BLAM
PINGGG
BLAM
OKAY, SEE, NOW THE RICOCHETS MADE ME LOSE COUNT--
PONGG
--WAS THAT FIVE OR SIX?

KLIK KLIK KLIK
THWIPP
BAGH!
THAT ANSWERS THAT!
THUK
EEEYAA!
STOP WHINING, CICCY, AND JUST BE THANKFUL I DON'T BUST UP THE CHANDELIER!
THIS IS TOTALLY UNFAIR!
LET ME DOWN!
AS SOON AS THE POLICE ARRIVE.
THE COPS? I'LL HAVE MYSELF OUTTA JAIL BEFORE YOU'RE OUT THE DOOR!
FINE THEN, I JUST WON'T LEAVE. EVER.
NOW AS FOR YOU, MANNY...
...SINCE HAMMERHEAD'S NOT A BIG "IMMORTALITY INFINITE POWER" KIND OF GUY--
--TELL ME WHY YOU THINK HE WANTED THE TABLET FRAGMENTS--?
WHAT DO I KNOW? BOOMERANG JUST TOOK THE FIVE PIECES OF ROCK I STOLE FROM WILSON AND LEFT!
SLABHEAD HAS SOME ONE-ARMED SCIENTIST WORKIN' FOR HIM!
YOU SHOULD BE GOING AFTER HIM, YOU CLOWN, 'STEAD OF BEATING ON INNOCENT LAWYERS!
AN OXYMORON AND A REGULAR MORON? THAT'S PRETTY FUNNY.
TIME TO EXIT STAGE LEFT. WE WON'T NEED YOU BOYS FOR THE REST OF THE SHOW, OKAY?
A ONE-ARMED SCIENTIST? IT HAS TO BE DR. CONNORS!
I HAVE TO FIND HIM BEFORE HE GETS HURT--OR THE LIZARD HURTS SOME-ONE! CONNORS IS A GOOD MAN, BUT A SERUM HE ONCE TOOK TO RESTORE HIS MISSING ARM TURNS HIM INTO A REPTILIAN BEAST NOW AND AGAIN.
10

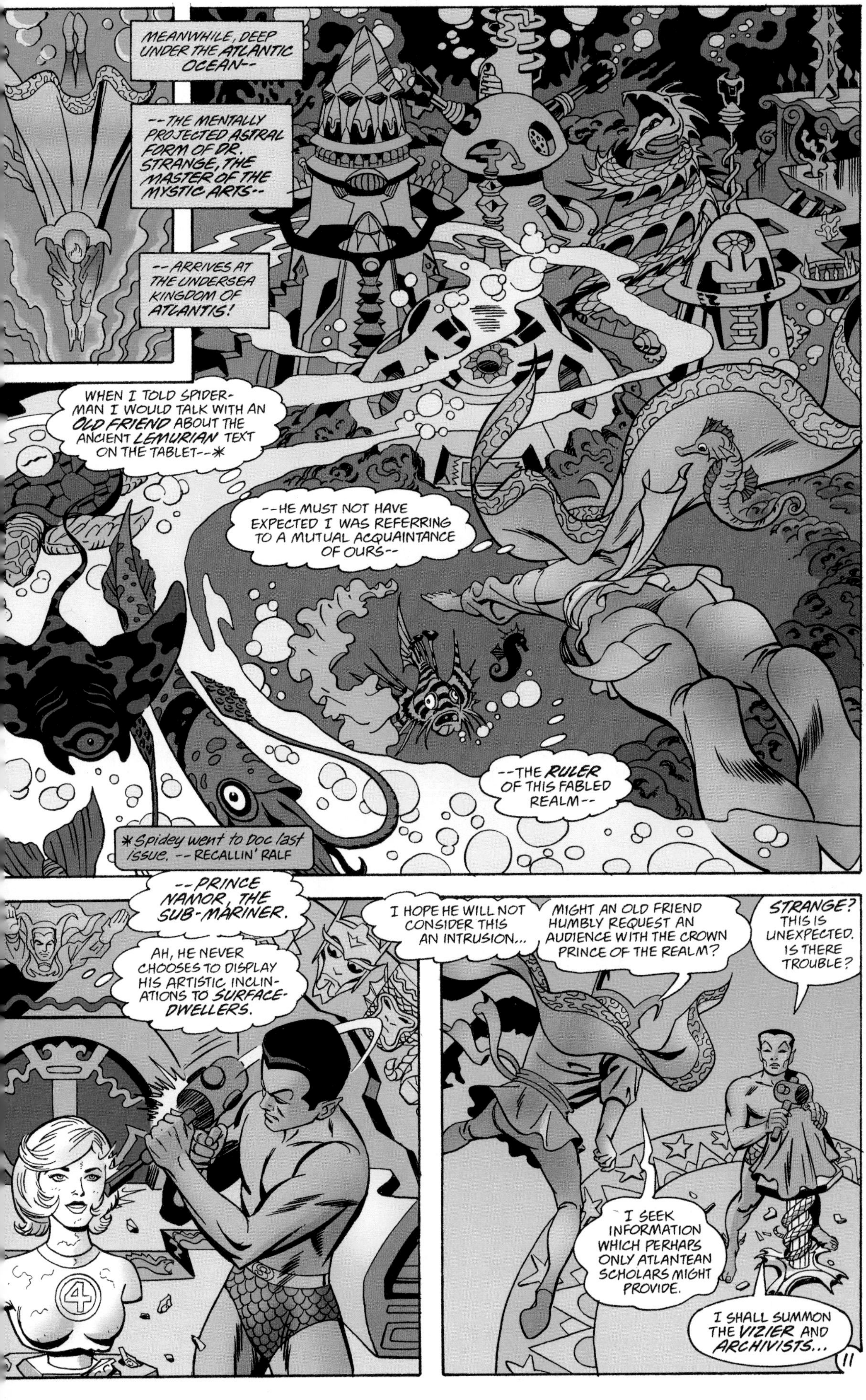

MEANWHILE, DEEP UNDER THE ATLANTIC OCEAN--
--THE MENTALLY PROJECTED ASTRAL FORM OF DR. STRANGE, THE MASTER OF THE MYSTIC ARTS--
--ARRIVES AT THE UNDERSEA KINGDOM OF ATLANTIS!
WHEN I TOLD SPIDER-MAN I WOULD TALK WITH AN OLD FRIEND ABOUT THE ANCIENT LEMURIAN TEXT ON THE TABLET--*
--HE MUST NOT HAVE EXPECTED I WAS REFERRING TO A MUTUAL ACQUAINTANCE OF OURS--
--THE RULER OF THIS FABLED REALM--
*Spidey went to Doc last issue. --RECALLIN' RALF
--PRINCE NAMOR, THE SUB-MARINER.
AH, HE NEVER CHOOSES TO DISPLAY HIS ARTISTIC INCLIN-ATIONS TO SURFACE-DWELLERS.
I HOPE HE WILL NOT CONSIDER THIS AN INTRUSION...
MIGHT AN OLD FRIEND HUMBLY REQUEST AN AUDIENCE WITH THE CROWN PRINCE OF THE REALM?
STRANGE? THIS IS UNEXPECTED. IS THERE TROUBLE?
I SEEK INFORMATION WHICH PERHAPS ONLY ATLANTEAN SCHOLARS MIGHT PROVIDE.
I SHALL SUMMON THE VIZIER AND ARCHIVISTS...

AN HOUR LATER IN THE SACRED HALL...
SILENCE TO ALL! VIZIER, YOU HAVE STUDIED THE TEXT-- BEGIN THE RITUAL OF REVELATION!
IN THE ANCIENT TONGUES OF OUR FOREBEARS-- ATLANTIS AND LEMURIA--
--SISTER CULTURES BORN TO PROSPERITY AND LOST TO TRAGEDY--
--THE ANCIENT TABLET IS THUS TRANSCRIBED...
EVEN WITH MY LINGUISTICS EXPERTISE--
--I CAN BARELY MAKE OUT MOST OF HIS WORDS!
FOR ALL THAT I KNOW, THERE IS STILL SO MUCH TO LEARN!
"THE TABLET PREDATES OUR SEASONS OF PROSPERITY-- THE AGE IN WHICH ATLANTIS AND LEMURIA WERE AT THE PINNACLE OF HUMAN CIVILIZATION!
"ITS HYBOREAN ORIGINS BESPEAK OF ULTIMATE POWER, ITS LEMURIAN TRANSLATION PROVIDES THE METHODS OF ACHIEVING SUCH A GOAL--!
"--MANI-FESTING ITSELF AS THE EVOLUTION-ARY PEAK THAT HUMANITY HAD TO OFFER!
"THE WRITINGS SPEAK: 'TO PARTAKE OF THE LEGACY IS TO DARE TOUCH THE OUT-STRETCHED HANDS OF TOMORROW!'"
AN EVOLUTIONARY ADVANCEMENT THROUGH BIO-CHEMICAL OR SORCEROUS MEANS
SURELY IT CANNOT BE THIS UTOPIAN PANACEA BEING PRESENTED?

VIZIER, A QUESTION, PLEASE...
...DO THE ANCIENT WRITINGS SAY IF THE ENLIGHTENMENT AND IMMORTALITY BEQUEATHED BY THE LIFELINE FORMULA--
--WOULD BE GRANTED EQUALLY TO ALL WHO PARTOOK OF IT?
NO, TO TASTE THE LIQUID WAS BUT "A PASSAGEWAY TO THE HALLS OF INFINITY.
"ONCE IN THE HALL OF FOREVER, AN INDIVIDUAL DID AS AN INDIVIDUAL COULD."
SO A FOOL WHO DRINKS OF THIS WELL IS STILL A FOOL?
F SPIDER-MAN IS CORRECT ABOUT THE MOTIVES AT PLAY HERE--
--THE PLAYERS IN THIS MAD GAME ARE NOT OF THE INCLINATION TO USE SUCH POWER WISELY!
AND IT APPEARS THAT THE POWER OF A GOD IS IN THE HANDS...
"...OF WHOEVER WIELDS THE TOTALITY OF THAT TABLET!"
HIDING SOMETHING?
AAH!
LOUIS WILSON, I PRESUME?
YOU KNEW MY BROTHER GEORGE.
YOU LOOK FAMILIAR.
A MUTUAL ACQUAINT-ANCE CALLED AND TOLD ME I HAD TO HAVE A LITTLE TALK WITH YOU.
HE SAID IF YOU DON'T COME CLEAN, WE'LL ALL BE PRESIDING OVER THE END OF THE WORLD!
13

MEANWHILE, AT HAMMERHEAD'S BROOKLYN BASE OF OPERATIONS...
"DOUBLE THE MEN ON THE ROOF," THE BOSS SAYS.
WHAT'S HE EXPECTIN'-- A FREAKIN' ARMY TO ATTACK?
WELL, WHOEVER'S COMIN'--
--BETTER HAVE PRETTY BIG STONES--
--T'TRY AN' BULLDOZE THEIR WAY--
--THROUGH THIS MUCH FIREPOWER!
HAM'S

THWUMPH
WHA--?
AAGH!
WHO THE--
SET UP THE CROSSFIRE, JOEY!
POWPOWPOW
SUCKER'S FAST!
POW
JOEY?!
POP POP POP
CROSSFIRE-- BRILLIANT IDEA, SAL!
GAAH!
THWIPP
?
THWIPP
15

SOME PRETTY SLICK MOVES, EEL...
BTOX
...BUT I BET YOU'D BE AGREEING RIGHT ABOUT NOW... THAT PLANTING A SPIDER-TRACER ON THE EEL-MOBILE WAS AN EVEN SLICKER ONE!
HMM... MAYBE I SHOULD'VE SAID THAT TO HIM WHILE HE WAS STILL CONSCIOUS.
NOW HE'S GOING TO WAKE UP WITH ALL KINDS OF ISSUES AND INSECURITIES ABOUT HIMSELF.
I FEEL BAD.
OKAY, I'M OVER IT NOW.
THERE'S BOOMERANG HOLDING CONNORS HOSTAGE!
HEAR THAT?
WHAT?
CLOCK TICKIN'.
TIME'S ALMOST UP, DOC.
I'M WELL AWARE OF HAMMERHEAD'S LUDICROUS DEADLINE.
AND IF IT WEREN'T FOR YOUR CONSTANT OBNOXIOUS CARPING, I MIGHT HAVE FINISHED MY WORK ALREADY!
THING OF IT IS, MATE... MAYBE I WANT YOU TO FAIL?
DON'T THINK I DON'T KNOW HOW YOU'RE PLAYIN' THIS GAME...
WH-WHAT DO YOU MEAN?
YOU'RE THINKIN' ANY "ULTIMATE POWER FORMULA" WILL ALSO GET RID OF THE LIZARD INSIDE OF YOU...
SO--?
SO YOU DOUBLE-CROSS HAMMY AN' I'M OUT OF SOME BIG BUCKS.

NOT T'MENTION YOU CURE YOURSELF, DOC, AN' YOU SPOIL MY CHANCE T'HUNT THE BIG CROC INSIDE YOU.
YOU--YOU ACTUALLY WANT THE LIZARD TO EMERGE?
FIGURE IT'S GOTTA BE BETTER SPORT THAN SLICIN' UP A ONE-ARMED SCIENTIST.
OH GOD--NO-- THE PRESSURE--FIRST HAMMERHEAD WITH THIS DEVIL'S OFFER.
A CHANCE TO CURE MYSELF-- ALTHOUGH IT MEANS HELPING HIM.
HIS LESS-THAN-SUBTLE THREATS AGAINST MY FAMILY.
AND NOW THIS--SAVAGE-- PUTTING A BLADE TO MY THROAT FOR WHAT?
DOES EVERY-ONE HAVE AN ANIMAL INSIDE THEM?
IT WOULD BE SO...EASY...TO LET MINE OUT...
I'VE SEEN THE DOC CHANGE TOO MANY TIMES NOT TO NOTICE THE SIGNS.
HE'S SO AGITATED--BOOMERANG IS PRACTICALLY INVITING THE LIZARD TO TAKE OVER DR. CONNERS' BODY!
TIME'S UP! DID YOU MAKE ME A "POWER DRINK"? HAW!
NOW THAT YOUR SADISTIC LAPDOG IS DONE INTERRUPTING, I CAN TELL YOU...
...THAT THE FORMULA HAS BEEN ENHANCED TO THE BEST OF MY ABILITY.
AND IT'S BASED ON THE INFORMATION PROVIDED AND THE LIMITED MEANS YOU HAVE MADE AVAILABLE TO ME.

BUT THERE ARE NO GUARANTEES IT WILL WORK ANY DIFFERENTLY ON YOU--
--THAN IT ORIGINALLY DID ON SILVERMANE!
ON THE OTHER HAND, DUE TO THE INFORMATION FROM THE ADDITIONAL FRAGMENTS--
--THIS FORMULA IS RADICALLY DIFFERENT THAN THE FIRST.
HOW YOU PLAN TO USE IT, HAMMERHEAD, MIGHT MAKE ALL THE DIFFERENCE IN HOW EFFECTIVE IT IS!
GEEZ, I'D CONSIDER LETTIN' YOU DRINK IT YOURSELF, CONNORS, IF IT WOULD JUST SHUT YOU UP!
OH, WOULD YOU?
HEY... CONNORS...
...DON'T YOU BE THINKIN'--
--HEY-- I NEED THAT FORMULA
PLAYERS ARE ALL IN PLACE. TIME FOR THE POOPY TO MEET THE FAN.
CONNORS!
MARTHA...
...BILLY...
...WISH ME LUCK...

I TOLD YOU NOT T'DOUBLECROSS TH' BOSS!
YA WANNA SEE HOW GOOD I AM, DOC--
--MY MINI-RANGS'LL SNAG THOSE FORMULA DROPS BEFORE THEY TOUCH YOUR LIPS!
KCHKSH
BUT THE FORMULA--!
HEY FOLKS, MIND IF I GET IN ON SOME OF THIS FUN?
AND SORRY ABOUT THE WINDOW, FLATHEAD.
BUT YOU REALLY COULD BE A MORE ACCOMMODATING SORT--
--AND JUST LEAVE THEM UNLOCKED, Y'KNOW...
BIO RESEARCH
BOOMERANG--AFTER RUININ' THE FORMULA--
YOU'D BETTER STOP THE WEB-SLINGER NOW!

MY NOTES!
ONE THING AT A TIME, DOC.
FIRST, LET'S TAKE CARE OF THE GUY WITH THE RAZOR-SHARP, EXPLODING BOOMERANGS--
--THEN WE'LL GATHER UP YOUR RESEARCH!
NO, YOU DON'T UNDERSTAND--THE REAL WORK WAS IN DECIPHERING THE TABLET'S EQUATION.
WITH MY FINISHED NOTES, ANY CHEMIST COULD RE-CREATE THE FORMULA!
OH. THAT'S NOT GOOD.
GEEZ, HAMMY! IT ALWAYS CREEPS ME OUT TO SEE YOU DO THAT!
DOESN'T IT HURT?
HEY--HEY--I NEED THAT SPLEEN!
HAMMY, ARE YOU SURE YOU DON'T NEED AN ASPIRIN?
THE NOTES...
VIRIDIUM
GOT 'EM!
THUP THUP THUP
HEY, YOU'RE NOT DONE!
YER RIGHT, WALL-CRAWLER... I AIN'T...

WAIT--THERE ON THE SHATTERED BEAKER!
REMNANTS OF THE FORMULA.
MUST REACH IT...
...BUT BOOMERANGS ARE RICOCHETING EVERYWHERE!
DID IT!
BUT IS THERE ENOUGH LEFT?
ONLY ONE WAY TO FIND OUT-- ONLY ONE CHANCE LEFT...
OKAY, BOOMY, ENOUGH'S ENOUGH!
THAT LAST ONE ALMOST NIPPED A PART OF ME I MOST CERTAINLY WOULD PREFER TO KEEP!
THAK
THIP
DO YOU KNOW THE TRADEMARK HASSLES I'D HAVE TO GO THROUGH TO CHANGE MY NAME TO "SPIDER-GIRL"?
WOK!
OH, YOU'D LIKE ME TO EXPLAIN THE NUANCES OF AMERICAN TRADE-MARK LAW?
SURE, LOVE TO, BUT FIRST-- HAVE A SEAT!

NOW TELL ME WHERE FLATTOP WENT!
UGHNN
HEY, ARE YOU UNCONSCIOUS?
MAN, I REALLY HAVE TO LEARN HOW TO KEEP YOU GUYS AWAKE...
RRRSSSSSSSS
UH-OH... THAT SOUNDS LIKE ONE GUY I WISH HAD STAYED ASLEEP...
I WOULD THANK YOU FOR LEAVING BOOMERANG SUCH EASY PREY FOR ME...
...BUT YOU WILL BE UNABLE TO ACCEPT SUCH GRATITUDE, SPIDER-MAN...
...SINCE YOU WILL BE QUITE BUSY DYING AT THE HANDS OF THE LIZARD!
BUT HE'S SO DIFFERENT THAN BEFORE!
IF THIS IS THE RESULT OF THE LIFELINE FORMULA--
--IS THERE ANYTHING OF CURT CONNORS LEFT INSIDE OF HIM?
WHAT HAPPENED TO THE LIZARD?
WHY DID ARTHUR STACY CONFRONT LOUIS WILSON?
HOW WILL HAMMERHEAD USE THE ULTIMATE SECRET OF THE LIFELINE LEGACY?
ALL THESE ANSWERS AND MORE IN... THE STUNNING CONCLUSION!

SPIDER-MAN: LIFELINE #3

Accidentally bitten by a Common Spider exposed to Radiation, **Peter Parker** soon discovered he had miraculously gained the arachnid's powers and had, in effect, become a Human Spider! But with Great Power... also comes **Great Responsibility!**
Stan Lee presents: THE AMAZING SPIDER-MAN!
A TASTE OF INFINITY
LIFELINE PART 3
HEY, LIZZIE-- WATCH IT!
THAT ONE ALMOST TOOK OFF A LAYER OF TUCHAS!
The Fateful Finale of our Titanic Trilogy! By the same gang who did the other two issues!
FABIAN NICIEZA - writer
STEVE RUDE - penciler
BOB WIACEK - inker
JOHN COSTANZA - letterer
GREGORY WRIGHT - colors
RALPH MACCHIO - editor
JOE QUESADA - editor in chief
WOW! OUR FRIENDLY NEIGHBORHOOD SPIDER-MAN ATTACKED BY THE NEFARIOUS LIZARD?! WHAT'S UP WITH THAT?!
WELL, IT BEGAN YEARS AGO WITH AN ANCIENT TABLET CONTAINING A SECRET EQUATION THAT CREATED A FAILED "FOUNTAIN OF YOUTH"!
NOW, ADDITIONAL FRAGMENTS OF THAT TABLET HAVE BEEN DISCOVERED, STARTING A RA RACE AMONG THE UNDERWORLD MAGGIA TO MODIFY THE FORMULA AND PROVIDE THE WINNER WITH ULTIMATE POWER!
BUT WHAT DOES ANY OF THAT HAVE TO DO WITH THE WORLD'S WACKIEST WEB-SPINNER GETTING SNAKE BIT BY HIS OLD FOE?
WELL, TURN THE PAGE ALREADY AND FIND OUT!

GRRMMFF!
HE SNAGGED ME IN MID-AIR?!
THAT DROP OF INFINITY FORMULA DR. CONNORS TASTED BEFORE TRANSFORMING INTO THE LIZARD HAS MADE HIM EVEN DEADLIER!
AH, YOUR UNUSUAL SILENCE SPEAKS VOLUMES OF YOUR SURPRISE!
INDEED, THE POTION WHICH THE INSIPID WARM-BLOODED CONNORS PREPARED FOR THE MOBSTER HAMMER-HEAD--
--HAS RESULTED IN UNEX-PECTED IMPROVE-MENTS TO MY FORM!
K-TOW!!
OOMPH!
BUT IT HASN'T DONE A THING FOR YOUR BREATH!
I'VE GOT TO ASSUME THE ONLY REASON A GOOD GUY LIKE CURT CONNORS IS WORKING FOR HAMMERHEAD IS BECAUSE HIS LIFE--OR HIS FAMILY'S--HAS BEEN THREATENED.
OKAY, I'M THE ONE WHO GOADED CONNORS INTO CHANGING.
SO, TIME FOR OL' BOOMERANG T'PUT HIS MONEY WHERE HIS MOUTH IS AN' GET HIM A NEW PAIR OF ALLIGATOR SHOES!
'SIDES, EVEN THOUGH THE FORMULA IS SPILLED EVERYWHERE, THIS GAME AIN'T OVER YET.
MY BOSS HAMMERHEAD ESCAPED WITH CONNORS' NOTES ON THE FORMULA AN' HE NEEDS ME T'BUY HIM SOME TIME!
WHOA--MATE, THOSE RIBS DO TEND T'BREAK Y'KNOW!
I AM WELL AWARE OF HOW FRAGILE YOU HUMANS ARE!
INDEED, IT IS A SHORTCOMING OF YOUR SPECIES ON WHICH I INTEND TO CAPITALIZE!
THE LIFELINE FORMULA HAS GIVEN ME A BETTER UNDER-STANDING OF MY VERY REASON FOR BEING!
THE TIME HAS COME FOR THE REPTILIAN RACE TO RECLAIM THAT WHICH THE MAMMALS TOOK AWAY WITH THEIR ASCENDANCE.

C'MON, LIZZIE, "JURASSIC PARK" DID A BOX OFFICE BEATING ON "KING KONG," SO WHAT'RE YOU COMPLAINING ABOUT?
SQUASH
FLIK
THOUGH IF THEY MAKE A MOVIE ABOUT ME, I'LL X-TINGUISH THE COMPETITION!
GRRMMMPH
I DO NOT NEED TO SEE YOU, ARACHNID--
--IN ORDER TO KILL YOU!
WHOA!
CATCH/DON'T CATCH? OOOH... I'M SUCH A STINKER...
DON'T CATCH!
I CAN'T TELL YOU HOW SORRY I AM, BOOMY--
BBASH
--BUT MY SPECIALTY IS DODGING, IPSO FACTO.
HEY, BONUS, I GET TO PLANT A SPIDER-TRACER ON HIM AT THE SAME TIME,
SO IF HE DOES GET AWAY, I'LL TRACK HIM DOWN LATER...
...AND THAT WAY, I CAN CONTINUE DANCING WITH LIZZIE.
WAIT A MINUTE, WHERE YOU GOING?
3

GONE? WOW, HE IS FASTER THAN HE USED TO BE.
NO PARKING 8AM—6PM
HE REMINDS ME MORE NOW OF THE LIZARDS I USED TO WATCH AT THE BRONX ZOO.
THEY MOVED IN SHORT JUMPS FASTER THAN THE EYE COULD FOLLOW--
--AND THEY COULD CRAWL UP THOSE SLIPPERY TANK WALLS.
I JUST HOPE HE DOESN'T HAVE ANY OTHER TRICKS UP HIS SLEEVE.
HE MUST'VE HEADED INTO THE SEWER SYSTEM. I'LL NEVER FIND HIM NOW.
BUT HE'S GOING TO WANT HIS NOTES BACK ON THE TABLET'S FORMULA, WHICH MEANS HE'LL BE LOOKING FOR HAMMERHEAD...
...WHO I CAN FIND BY ASKING MY--
--BUDDY WITH THE SPIDER TRACER SLAPPED ON HIS BACK.
WELL, I KNOW WHAT'S AUSTRALIAN FOR BEER, BUT WHAT'S AUSTRALIAN FOR "WALKING AROUND WITH A SET OF CRACKED RIBS"?
HMM... NOTHING LEFT BUT THE CLEANUP--
"--ON THE ROOF."
SOME TOUGH GUY DIS EEL IS, HUH, VITO?
THEY'RE ALL PANSIES, YOU AXE ME, CARMELO.
SURE, WEARIN' LIKE SKINTIGHT SPANDEX IN ALL KINDSA SISSY COLORS.
LIKE PURPLE AND BLUE HERE, WHAT'S DAT ABOUT?
OR DAT SPIDER-MAN IN RED AN--
--OOMF!
PARDON ME, BUT THEY WERE THE ONLY COLORS MY DEAR OLD AUNT HAD AVAILABLE AT THE TIME.
WELL, A PLAID PATTERN TOO, BUT CAN YOU PICTURE THAT WITH WEBS?
4

HEY, BRING THAT SLIMY EEL GUY BACK!
THWIP
ZZING
ZING
VNG
OUR BOSS HAS A SCORE T'SETTLE WITH HIS BOSS!
OR MAYBE I'LL JUST TURN HIM OVER TO THE POLICE, TRY DISPENSING JUSTICE THE OLD-FASHIONED WAY.
YOU KNOW, ONE THAT DOESN'T INVOLVE PER-FORATION?
IN AN ABANDONED WAREHOUSE ON THE LOWER EAST SIDE OF MANHATTAN...
OUCH
OUCH
OUCH
RIBS'RE KILLIN' ME!
BLOODY SIMP! JET-BOOTS NEARLY GAVE OUT HALFWAY OVER THE EAST RIVER!
HAVE THE TINKERER CHECK 'EM OUT LATER!
AN' T'MAKE MATTERS WORSE, NOT ONE BLINKIN' ICE PACK LEFT IN THE LOFT!
IF THE MONEY WEREN'T SO GOOD, I'D GO BACK T'BEING A TRAIL GUIDE!
BETTER DIAL UP THE BOSS AN' SEE WHERE HE IS NOW.
BA-DEEP
-BEEP
BA-DEEP
IN MIDTOWN MANHATTAN...
BREEP
MR. H? IT'S ME. I GOT AWAY.
CALLER I.D.? STUPID AUSSIE...
YEAH?
WHERE'S CONNORS?
YOU KIDDIN' ME? BLOODY GEEK TURNED INTO THE LIZARD!
WHAT IF I CAN'T RECREATE THE FORMULA WITH HIS NOTES?
THEN WE WAIT 'TIL HE CALMS DOWN AN' CHANGES BACK TO CONNORS--AN' FIND HIM USIN' THE BOOMERANG TRACER I PLANTED ON HIM!
HEY, NOT BAD, FREDDIE. NOW HEAR THIS...

...I WANT YOU TO FIND HIM NOW BECAUSE I NEED THE FORMULA NOW!
NOT LATER, NOT TOMORROW-- NOW!
YOU UNDERSTAND? GOOD! SO DO IT!
CLIK
CLANK
ONLY THING FLAT-TOP'S GOOD FOR 'SIDES THE PAY IS RESTING A FOSTERS ON HIS NOGGIN.
WAS HOPIN' T'GET SOME SHUT-EYE, MAYBE POP A DOZEN MOTRIN...
WHOOSH
...BUT I BETTER AT LEAST USE MY TRACERANG--
ACME
--T'FIND OUT WHERE LIZZIE IS RIGHT NOW.
WHILE IN THE MAZE OF SEWER CONDUITS BETWEEN MANHATTAN AND BROOKLYN...
SSSSULLSS
I CAN DELAY NO LONGER--I MUST ACT NOW!
THE POWER-- THE BIRTHRIGHT-- INHERENT IN THE LIFELINE FORMULA FOR THE REBIRTH OF THE REPTILIAN RACE IS UNPRECEDENTED!
I HAVE WAITED MY ENTIRE EXISTENCE TO HAVE SUCH A STRENGTH OF PURPOSE!

BEFORE, WHEN I WOULD EMERGE FROM MY FORCED INCARCERATION WITHIN CONNORS--
-- I WOULD MERELY SERVE AS A CONDUIT FOR HIS RAGE, HIS FAILINGS!
BUT NOW I SERVE MY OWN GREATER DESTINY!
AND YET... I NEED CONNORS TO FULFILL THIS GRAND SCHEME!
HSSSTT HOW AM I TO RECREATE THE FORMULA WITHOUT HIM?!
GRAB
HMM. HE MADE HIS WAY CROSS-RIVER, UNDER CANAL STREET-- NOW HE'S HEADING UP HUDSON... THAT'S NOT A GOOD SIGN.
BETTER ALERT THE BOSS...
TOOK YOU LONG ENOUGH, BABY.
MARY'S
OSPITAL
YEAH, I'M AT THE HOSPITAL NOW. YOU SURE ABOUT THAT?
HEY, THIS COULD WORK OUT. MEET ME HERE--HUDSON AN' EIGHTH.
AN' YA BETTER COME PACKIN' SOME HEAVY AMMO!
ENTRANCE
UPTOWN...
ARTHUR STACY WAS DOING SOME LEGWORK ON THE TABLET FRAGMENTS--
THERE HE IS NOW, WITH LOUIS WILSON, THE ARCHAEOLOGIST WHO FOUND THEM.
--AND HE TOLD ME TO MEET HIM HERE AT THE MUSEUM WHERE THEY WERE TAKEN. EVEN THOUGH HE'S A RETIRED INVESTIGATOR, THERE'S NO ONE I'D SOONER TRUST ON A CASE OF THIS IMPORTANCE.
HEY, BOYS. YOU TWO LOOK LIKE THREE BLOCKS OF OLD ROAD!
LUCKY FOR ME, I GET TO HIDE MY LACK OF SLEEP BEHIND A MASK!
WELL, WE SHOULD ALL GET A GOOD NIGHT'S SLEEP TONIGHT--IF YOU USE WHAT WE'RE ABOUT TO GIVE YOU WISELY.
GO AHEAD, WILSON.
I-I HAVEN'T BEEN AS FORTHCOMING WITH YOU, OR THE POLICE--EVEN THE MUSEUM CURATORS--AS I MIGHT HAVE BEEN.
BUT MY REASONS WERE NOT SELFISH IN MOTIVE.
FOR THE BENEFIT AND SAFETY OF MANKIND, I HAD TO WITHHOLD CERTAIN THINGS...

THIS IS THE KEY TO--
EVERYTHING?
ACTUALLY, YES, IT IS.
BUT IT WON'T DO YOU MUCH GOOD UNLESS YOU STOP THAT THUG HAMMERHEAD FROM USING THE FORMULA!
FIRST I TRACK DOWN BOOMERANG, AND HE'LL TAKE ME TO FLAT-TOP!
SEVEN MINUTES LATER...
PUT ANOTHER SHRIMP ON THE BARBIE, BOOMY!
COMPANY'S HERE!
GREAT, HE'S GONE!
BUT MY SPIDER-SENSE IS ATTUNED TO MY TRACER--
--AND IT'S STILL BUZZING LIKE AN AMPHETAMINE FIEND ON JEOPARDY!
FRAGILE
AAAH, THERE'S THE LITTLE BUG.
THE OLD PARKER LUCK STRIKES AGAIN!
I HAVE TO FIND THE ONE SUPER-VILLAIN WHO ACTUALLY CHANGES HIS SWEATY COSTUMES!
SPIDER-MAN!
DR. STRANGE?! GRAND POO-BAH OF ALL THINGS MAGICAL.
THAT ASTRAL FORM OF YOURS ALWAYS CINCHES MY TIGHTS IN ALL THE WRONG PLACES!
MY APOLOGIES FOR THIS RATHER ABRUPT ENTRANCE, BUT TIME IS OF THE ESSENCE!
AS YOU HAD REQUESTED, I HAVE USED MY MYSTICAL CONNECTIONS TO OBTAIN ADDITIONAL INFORMATION ON THE LIFELINE TABLET!
THESE REVELATIONS WERE MOST PROFOUND AND REQUIRE I CONVEY THEM TO YOU WITH THE UTMOST URGENCY!
WELL THE METER'S TICKING ON MY END, TOO, DOC!
8

THEN I SHALL DELAY NO FURTHER! THE TABLET SPEAKS OF AN ANCIENT, ALMOST PREHISTORIC LEGACY.
IT IS A LIFELINE-- A LINK TO PRIMORDIAL TIMES WHEN SENTIENT REPTILLIAN AND AMPHIBIAN LIFE WAS DOMINANT.
BUT THE INFORMATION CONTAINED IN THE TABLETS CAN BE USED BY ANY LIVING BEING--
--TO DRAMATICALLY INCREASE THE EVOLUTIONARY POTENTIAL WITHIN THEM!
WHICH I GUESS EXPLAINS WHY THE LIZARD HAS SUCH AN AFFINITY FOR IT.
LIZARD? THE ALTER EGO OF DR. CURT CONNORS? SURELY THE SITUATION HERE HAS BECOME COMPLICATED!
UNFORTUNATELY, THE LIFELINE FORMULA AND ITS EFFECTS ARE MORE THE PROVINCE OF SCIENCE THAN MAGIC, MY YOUNG FRIEND!
AND THAT MEANS IT'S UP TO ME TO STOP ITS USE.
EVEN WERE I TO SUMMON MY FELLOW DEFENDERS, I FEAR THEY WOULD NOT GATHER IN TIME!
NO PROBLEM, DOC-- SAVING HUMAN CIVILIZATION AS WE KNOW IT IS ALL PART OF THE FRIENDLY NEIGHBORHOOD SPIDER-MAN'S WARRANTY PLAN!
HE MAKES LIGHT OF THE IMMENSE RESPONSIBILITY HE BEARS.
I WONDER IF HE REALIZES JUST HOW COURAGEOUS HE TRULY IS?
AT ST. MARY'S HOSPITAL...
HERE... I CAN SMELL HAMMERHEAD-- THE SCENT OF CONNORS ON THE NOTES HE WROTE--
--AND THE PULSING ENERGY INHERENT IN THE VERY THOUGHT OF RECREATING THE LIFELINE FORMULA!
ENTRANCE

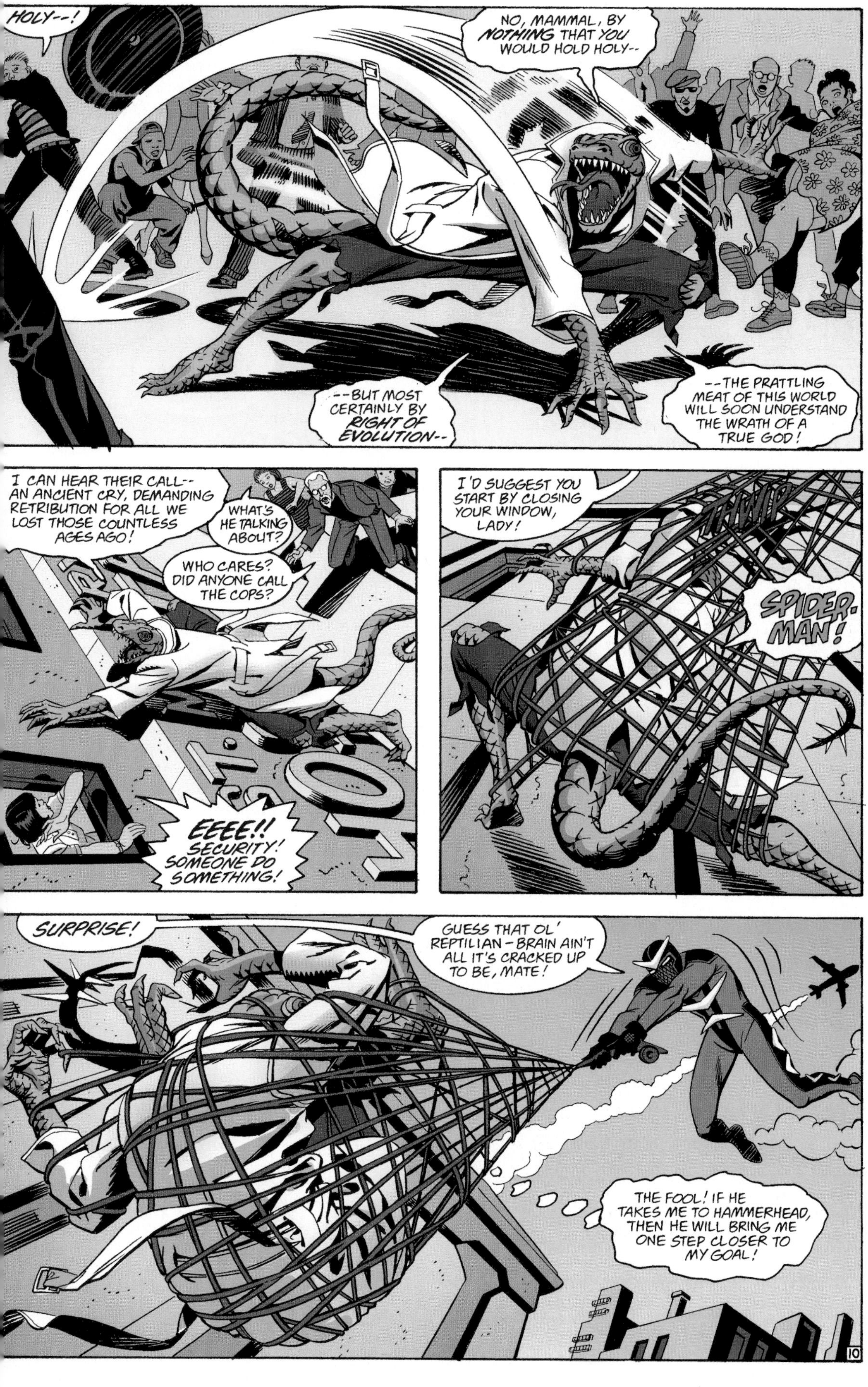
HOLY--!
NO, MAMMAL, BY NOTHING THAT YOU WOULD HOLD HOLY--
--BUT MOST CERTAINLY BY RIGHT OF EVOLUTION--
--THE PRATTLING MEAT OF THIS WORLD WILL SOON UNDERSTAND THE WRATH OF A TRUE GOD!
I CAN HEAR THEIR CALL--AN ANCIENT CRY, DEMANDING RETRIBUTION FOR ALL WE LOST THOSE COUNTLESS AGES AGO!
WHAT'S HE TALKING ABOUT?
WHO CARES? DID ANYONE CALL THE COPS?
EEEE!! SECURITY! SOMEONE DO SOMETHING!
I'D SUGGEST YOU START BY CLOSING YOUR WINDOW, LADY!
THWIP
SPIDER-MAN!
SURPRISE!
GUESS THAT OL' REPTILIAN-BRAIN AIN'T ALL IT'S CRACKED UP TO BE, MATE!
THE FOOL! IF HE TAKES ME TO HAMMERHEAD, THEN HE WILL BRING ME ONE STEP CLOSER TO MY GOAL!

AT THE STACY HOME IN QUEENS...
THOSE BRIEF MINUTES OF SLEEP I CAUGHT WERE REFRESHING.
ARTHUR, WITH COFFEE THIS STRONG, IT'S AMAZING YOU EVER GET TO SLEEP AT ALL!
OR "THANKS FOR THE JAVA AND MY LAST BAGEL" WOULD WORK, TOO.
PROBABLY, BUT THEN YOU WOULDN'T TRY AS HARD TO GET RID OF ME!
SPEAKING OF WHICH, YOUR HUNCH WAS CORRECT.
WE'D SPENT SO MUCH TIME FIGURING OUT WHO AND HOW IN ALL THIS--
THAT WE NEVER REALLY FOCUSED ON WHY!
AND--?
I DID A REFERENCE CHECK ON EVERYTHING THE NYPD AND EVEN THE JUSTICE DEPARTMENT HAVE ON HAMMERHEAD--
--AGAINST A SPOT CHECK OF HIS USUAL HAUNTS FOR CREDIT CARD SWIPES, EZ PASS TOLLS.
I GOT A CAR REGISTERED TO HIS DRIVER COMING INTO MANHATTAN RIGHT AFTER YOUR BLOW-UP IN BROOKLYN.
I COMBINED THAT WITH A REFERENCE LIST OVER THE LAST MONTH--RESTAURANTS, GAS CHARGES, PARKING PAYMENTS--
--ALL OF WHICH SHOW THAT HE'S BEEN SPENDING A LOT OF TIME AROUND HUDSON AND EIGHTH.
BECAUSE HE'S BEEN GOING HERE.
ST. MARY'S HOSPITAL? IS HAMMERHEAD AN OUTPATIENT?
IT WOULD EXPLAIN WHY HE WANTED AN IMMORTALITY FORMULA!
SO WOULD THE FACT THAT HIS SISTER HAS BEEN THERE FOR SIX WEEKS!

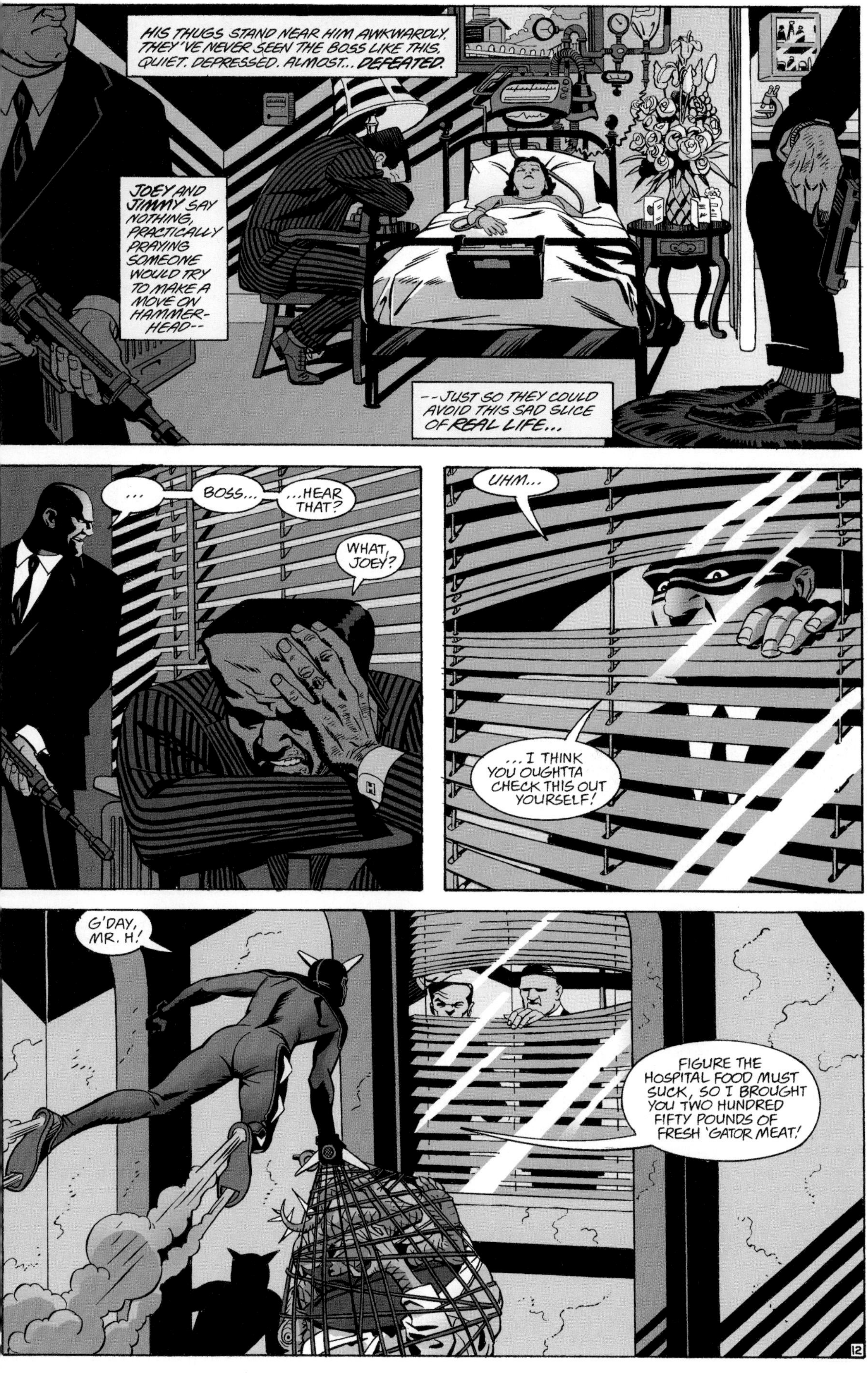
HIS THUGS STAND NEAR HIM AWKWARDLY. THEY'VE NEVER SEEN THE BOSS LIKE THIS. QUIET. DEPRESSED. ALMOST... DEFEATED.
JOEY AND JIMMY SAY NOTHING, PRACTICALLY PRAYING SOMEONE WOULD TRY TO MAKE A MOVE ON HAMMER-HEAD--
--JUST SO THEY COULD AVOID THIS SAD SLICE OF REAL LIFE...
...
BOSS...
...HEAR THAT?
WHAT, JOEY?
UHM...
...I THINK YOU OUGHTTA CHECK THIS OUT YOURSELF!
G'DAY, MR. H!
FIGURE THE HOSPITAL FOOD MUST SUCK, SO I BROUGHT YOU TWO HUNDRED FIFTY POUNDS OF FRESH 'GATOR MEAT!
12

HERE HE IS, JUST LIKE YOU WANTED!
YOU IDIOT!
I WANTED CONNORS, NOT THIS--THIS ANIMAL!
DON'T BE AFRAID, THE NET IS ELECTRICALLY CHARGED--HE'LL CALM DOWN AN' CHANGE BACK!
AND WHAT IF HE DOESN'T? MORON--MY SISTER IS LYIN' HERE DYIN'--
--YOU THINK THE LIZARD RUNNIN' AROUND IS GONNA BE GOOD FOR HER HEALTH?
MOSSST CERTAINLY, HAMMERHEAD--SHE ISSS NOT THE ONE WHO SHOULD WORRY...
ZZT
ZZTT
ZZTT
THE CHARGE AIN'T STRONG ENOUGH? BUT--
...YOU ON THE OTHER HAND...
ZZZZZ
KEEP 'IM AWAY FROM ANTONIA!
BRAPAPAPA
BRAP
POW
POW
POW
GUNFIRE? DRAT AND DARN IT ALL TO HECK!
THE STOP I MADE ON MY WAY HERE* COST ME TOO MUCH TIME!
BUT I HAD NO CHOICE!
* Don't worry, True Believers, you won't be in the dark for long! --REASSURING RALF
13

GREETINGS, AVERAGE CITIZENS! ANYONE SEE A BIG TALL LIZARD AROUND?
SPIDER-MAN?
BONUS POINTS TO MY PUBLICIST!
THE LIZARD WENT CRAWLING UP THE BUILDING, THEN SOME FLYING GUY SNAGGED HIM IN A NET!
LIZZIE, HAMMY AND BOOMY-- A NICKNAME TRIFECTA!
THANKS, GOOD CITIZENS.
FROM THOSE TELLTALE SIRENS, NEW YORK'S FINEST ARE ON THEIR WAY. TELL THEM I'M ON THE JOB! AND THEN TELL THEM NOT TO SHOOT AT ME!
HAMMERHEAD...
...YOU HAVE SOMETHING OF MINE...
I--DON'T KNOW--ACK--WHAT YOU'RE--TALKIN' ABOUT!
I SSSMELL YOUR FEAR AS YOU LIE TO ME!
CONNORSSS' NOTEBOOK! GIVE IT TO ME!
YOU THINK I DON'T STILL HOLD THE CARDS, YOU FREAK? I STILL GOT CONNORS' WIFE AN' BRAT!
IF YOU DON'T REMAKE THE FORMULA FOR ME--SAVE MY SISTER'S LIFE--THEY'RE DEAD!
DO YOU HONESSTLY THINK I CARE ABOUT TWO PALTRY HUMAN LIVESSS?
THE LIFELINE FORMULA WILL ENABLE ME TO RECREATE A DOMINANT REPTILIAN SSPECIES--
--AND REPLACE THE HUMAN RACE AS YOUR ANCESTORSS ONCE DID TO MINE!
HMM... I MIGHT NEED TO POLL THE AUDIENCE, BUT MY GUT TELLS ME THAT'S THE ROOM.
AT LEAST THAT'S ONE LESS HEMORRHOID I HAVE TO WORRY ABOUT!

EVEN IF YOU--DON'T--CARE--MMFF--ABOUT THEM--
--YOU STILL NEED MY HELP--TO PULL OFF YOUR CRAZY PLAN--
--AN' I STILL NEED--MMFF--YOUR HELP--
--TO SAVE ANTONIA! SHE'S BEEN SICK FER SO LONG--
--YOU DON'T CARE ABOUT HUMAN MEAT--NEITHER DO I--
--BUT... I DO CARE... ABOUT HER!
RRRSST?
THE DANGLING FLESH HASS FALLEN UNCONSCIOUSS!
HISS COMPASSION FOR HISS SSIBLING... SSO TYPICALLY... HUMAN...
...BUT FROM SSUCH A COLD-HEARTED MAN?
HEY, LIZZIE, DON'T THINK TOO HARD, YOU'LL GET A HEADACHE!
HSST!
SSSPIDER-MAN--AGAIN AND AGAIN!
GOOD GUESSS.
DON'T BOTHER SMACKING HAMMY AROUND--
--I'M THE ONE WHO'S GOT WHAT YOU'RE LOOKING FOR!
WHAT ARE YOU TALKING ABOUT?
ZIP IT AND LISTEN--
WHO DO YOU THINK IS HOLDING THE MISSING PIECE OF THE LIFELINE TABLET?
AND WHO WON'T POSSESS THE FULL POWER OF THE FORMULA WITH-OUT IT?
JEOPARDY THEME SONG IS PLAYING, TIME WINDING DOWN...
CICERO WANTED CLOUT, HAMMERHEAD WANTED TO SAVE HIS SISTER--
EMERGENCY
--YOU WANT TO RECREATE ALL LIFE ON EARTH...
...BUT YOU CAN'T DO IT WITHOUT ME!
15

MINUTES LATER, IN AN ADJOINING LAB...
WELL, PUT ME IN A TUTU AND COLOR ME PERPLEXED!
WHO'DA THUNK YOUR FRIENDLY NEIGHBOR-HOOD SPIDER-MAN WOULD EVER BE BREAKING BEAKERS WITH THE LIZARD? BUT I'VE GOT TO REMEMBER THAT IS CURT CONNORS UNDER THAT SCALY HIDE.
GEEZ, PUT UN-LIMITED POWER IN FRONT OF SOME-ONE AND IT SURE MAKES FOR STRANGE BEDFELLOWS!
A HEEL LIKE HAMMERHEAD ACTUALLY HAD GOOD INTENTIONS FOR IT.
SURE, HE DIDN'T APPROACH IT IN A MR. ROGERS-APPROVED FASHION--
--BUT CAN I REALLY HOLD IT AGAINST HIM THAT HE WANTED TO SAVE HIS KID SISTER?
AND WARPED THOUGH THEY MAY BE, THE LIZARD EVEN HAS HIS OWN REASONS--SAME AS I DO...
...BECAUSE PLAYING THIS OUT NOW IS THE ONLY WAY TO USE THE FORMULA THE WAY I HOPE TO--
--TO CURE DOC CONNORS OF THE CURSE OF THE LIZARD FOREVER!
BUT IT'S MORE THAN THAT, PARKER, AND YOU KNOW IT...
...IN THE BACK OF YOUR MIND, YOU KEEP THINKING--WHAT COULD I DO WITH THAT KIND OF POWER?
COULD I BRING BACK UNCLE BEN TO LIFE? GEORGE OR GWEN STACY?
I'VE DONE THE COSMIC BIT BEFORE AND HAD TROUBLE HANDLING IT--
--BUT WOULD THINGS BE DIFFERENT NOW? THINK OF ALL THE PEOPLE I COULD HELP...
HMM... LIZZIE SURE IS QUIET OVER THERE.
NEED SOME HUMAN HELP YET, HANDBAG?
SSSILENCE!
I HAVE ISSOLATED THE ELEMENTSS--WITHIN MOMENTSS I SHALL KNOW IF IT HASS WORKED!
IRONIC, SINCE YOU NEEDED THE MEMORIES OF CURT CONNORS TO DO IT!
OH, REALLY, MAMMAL?
16

AND WHERE DO YOU THINK HE GETSS HIS AMBITION? HIS PERSEVERANCE?
HIS RESSOLVE TO CONTINUE LIVING IN THE FACE OF CONSSTANT ADVERSSSITY?
IT ISS FOR ALL THAT I BRING TO CONNORSS THAT MY SPECIESS SHOULD BRING TO ALL OF CIVILIZATION!
NO, YOU SNAKE--YOU THINK YER THE ONLY ONE WHO'S CORNERED THE MARKET ON TOUGH?
I WAS STEPPIN' ON SQUEALS BEFORE YOU WERE EVEN A DROP IN ONE OF CONNORS' TEST TUBES!
THE POWER--THE DECISION ABOUT WHAT SHOULD BE DONE WITH THE TABLET'S FORMULA--BELONGS TO PEOPLE LIKE ME!
PEOPLE WHO'VE LIVED HARD LIVES AN' MADE HARD CHOICES!
PERHAPSS THERE ARE TRAITSS I COULD ADMIRE IN MEAT SUCH AS YOURSELF, HAMMERHEAD.
BUT, ULTIMATELY, MY CALL IS NOT ABOUT INDIVIDUAL LIVESS--
--OR EGO, OR COM-PASSION...
...IT IS TO RESSTORE A PRIMAL ORDER TO THE WAY OF THISS WORLD!
AND AS I AM THE ONE WHO HOLDSS THE FORMULA, I AM THE ONE TO DECIDE!
GUARDS'RE WAITIN' ON HAMMY'S ORDER...
...LUCKY FOR ME, I DON'T WORK THAT WAY--USE 'EM TO COVER ME AS I GET READY TO--
--LOOK ALIVE, BOYS!
TIME FOR THE BONUS BUCKS I WAS PROMISED!
SLISS
NO--NOOOO!
THUK
SPLIT SECOND TIMING, PETEY--
THWIPP
IT'S MINE!
MY MONEY--MY PLAN--MY SISTER!
THWUPP
17

HEY, DON'T MESS WITH MY PAY-CHECK!
AND WHAT WOULD YOU DO WITH THAT MONEY--
--IF HAMMER-HEAD OR LIZARD DRINK THE FORMULA AND WIPE YOU FROM EXISTENCE?!
NEVER THOUGHT OF THAT.
DOPE.
MY KIND HAVE WAITED TOO LONG! WE WILL NOT BE DENIED!
OH YEAH, YOU WILL!
I'M GONNA SAVE YOU, ANTONIA!
UNMITIGATED FOOLS!
ALL THAT POWER IN THE HANDS OF SUCH A FEEBLE MIND!
ISN'T THAT THE POT CALLING THE KETTLE BLACK!
WHERE'D HAMMER-HEAD GO?
UHM... LOOK UP...

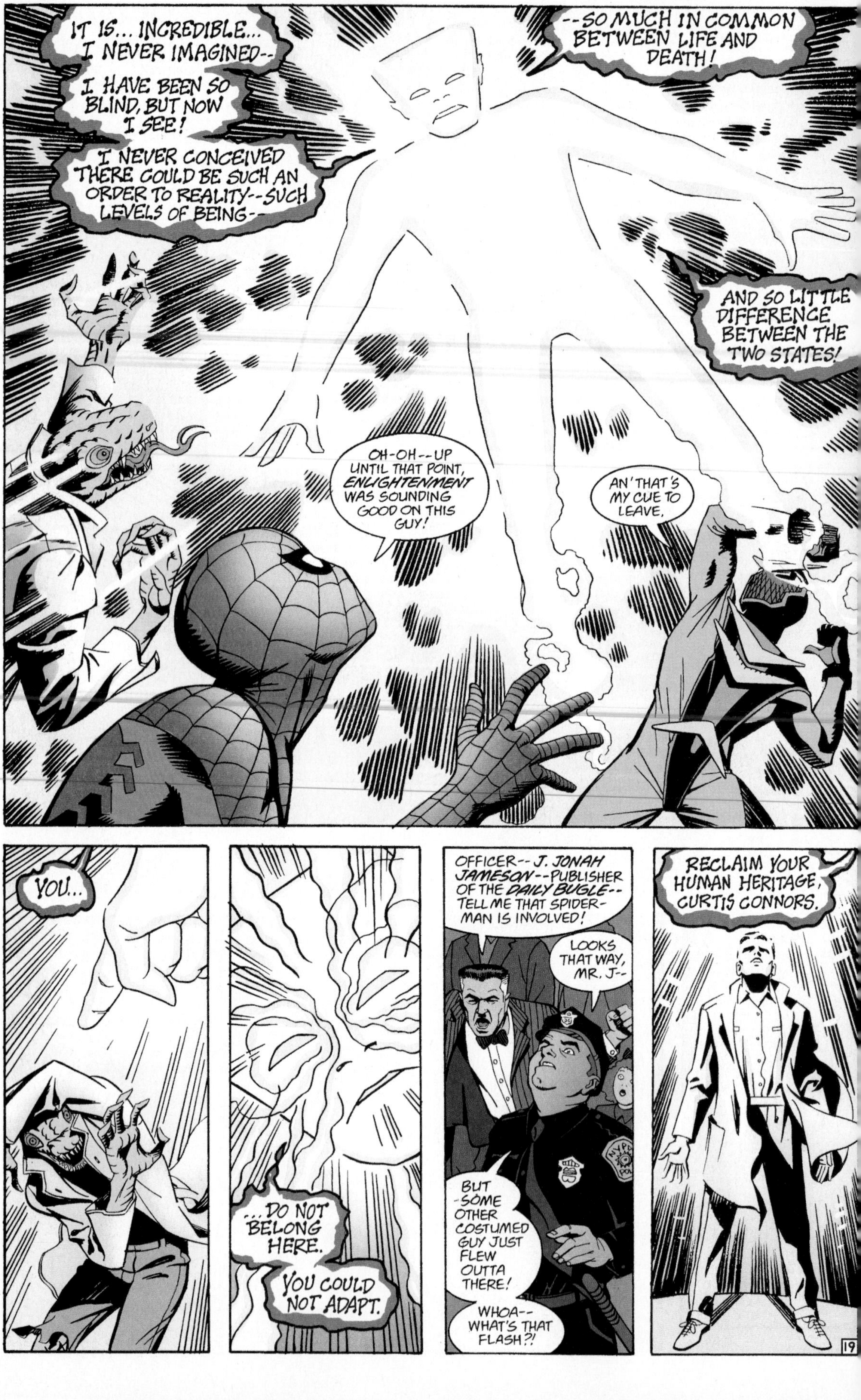
IT IS... INCREDIBLE... I NEVER IMAGINED--
I HAVE BEEN SO BLIND, BUT NOW I SEE!
I NEVER CONCEIVED THERE COULD BE SUCH AN ORDER TO REALITY--SUCH LEVELS OF BEING--
--SO MUCH IN COMMON BETWEEN LIFE AND DEATH!
AND SO LITTLE DIFFERENCE BETWEEN THE TWO STATES!
OH-OH--UP UNTIL THAT POINT, ENLIGHTENMENT WAS SOUNDING GOOD ON THIS GUY!
AN' THAT'S MY CUE TO LEAVE.
YOU...
...DO NOT BELONG HERE.
YOU COULD NOT ADAPT.
OFFICER-- J. JONAH JAMESON--PUBLISHER OF THE DAILY BUGLE--TELL ME THAT SPIDER-MAN IS INVOLVED!
LOOKS THAT WAY, MR. J--
BUT--SOME OTHER COSTUMED GUY JUST FLEW OUTTA THERE!
WHOA--WHAT'S THAT FLASH?!
RECLAIM YOUR HUMAN HERITAGE, CURTIS CONNORS.

BE FREE TO LIVE YOUR MEAGER LIFESPAN KNOWING THAT THE SHADOW OF THE LIZARD--
--WILL NEVER DARKEN YOUR DAYS AGAIN!
I UNDERSTAND THE COMPLEXITY OF THE UNIVERSE NOW, AS IF IT WERE A CHILD'S PLAYTOY!
I SEE HOW PULLING THE STRING OF ETERNITY THERE...
...COULD TUG AT THE CLOAK OF INFINITY HERE!
I REALIZE HOW CHAOS AND ORDER DANCE THEIR DANCE OF LIFE AND DEATH.
AND I UNDERSTAND THAT THEY CARE NOT A WHIT ABOUT THE INDIVIDUAL PIECES PLACED ON THE SCALES--
--SO LONG AS THE UNIVERSAL CONCEPTS REMAIN BALANCED!
YOU, PETER, HAVE LOST SO MUCH TRYING TO BALANCE THOSE SCALES...
...I CAN RESTORE THE BALANCE FOR YOU.
I LIKED YOU BETTER WHEN YOU TALKED LIKE MARLON BRANDO...
FROM A COSMIC PERSPECTIVE, IT IS NOT SUCH A DIFFICULT THING--
--RESTORE A LIFE HERE... TAKE A LIFE THERE...
THIS GUY IS SERIOUS!
TO HAVE UNCLE BEN BACK--OR GWEN--HOW DIFFERENT COULD MY LIFE BE--OR AUNT MAY'S--?
WHY SHOULDN'T I JUST ASK FOR THEM TO BE BROUGHT BACK?
HE'S IN THE THROES OF SOME DEEP, PERSONAL PAIN--I CAN FEEL IT.
SPIDER-MAN--THERE IS NO EASY ANSWER.
I KNOW--LOOK AT WHAT A PRICE I PAID FOR TRYING TO RESTORE MY MISSING ARM.
I KNOW, DOC--BUT THIS ISN'T JUST ME--IT'S FOR PEOPLE WHO DIDN'T DESERVE TO DIE--WHO DIED BECAUSE OF ME!
BUT BEFORE THE TORTURED SPIDER-MAN CAN MAKE A DECISION...
SOMETHING IS WRONG...
...WHAT...
...IS...
...HAPPENING?
THE POWER--IT'S--
--LEAVING ME--
--DISSIPATING...
20

...NO--NO!!
ZZZTTT
ANTONIA!
IT'S TOO LATE...
TTT
...I WAS SO BUSY LOOKIN' AT THE FOREST... I FORGOT ABOUT THE TREES!
WHAT DID THE TWO OF YOU DO?
DON'T YOU SEE WHAT YOU'VE DONE?
THE LAST HOPE MY SISTER HAD FOR SURVIVIN' THIS DAMNED CANCER WAS FOR ME TO USE THE LIFELINE FORMULA!
EVER SINCE I HEARD ABOUT WILSON FINDIN' THOSE MISSIN' PIECES... I THOUGHT THIS WOULD BE HER LAST CHANCE...
...AND NOW, AFTER ALL THAT PLANNIN', SHE'S GONNA DIE...
...BECAUSE I DIDN'T ACT FAST ENOUGH!
MAYBE NOT.
DO YOU THINK THE LIZARD WAS THE ONLY ONE SWEATING IT OUT IN THAT LAB?
IF LIZARDS EVEN SWEAT, THAT IS.
THIS DOSAGE SHOULD HELP YOUR SISTER, HAMMERHEAD.

YOU'RE OUTTA TIME UP THERE AN' WE'RE OUTTA DONUTS!
YOU KNOW WHAT THAT MEANS? WE'RE COMIN' IN!
WHY DON'T YOU JUST MAIL THEM INVITATIONS TO ESCAPE?!
LOOK UP THERE! IT'S SPIDER-MAN --AND HE'S GOT A BOMB!
OH, STUFF A SOCK IN IT, JONAH, CAN'T YOU SEE IT'S A CUTE LITTLE WHITE FLAG?!
PLAYTIME'S OVER, BOYS IN BLUE. ALL THAT'S LEFT IS THE CLEANUP!
YOU--YOU SAVED ME?
TONI--NO... NO... KID... I'M THE ONE WHO ALMOST KILLED YA...
SPIDER-MAN, APPARENTLY THERE'S SOMETHING ELSE YOU SHOULD BE THANKED FOR!
WHO, ME? I'VE BEEN SO BUSY BABYSITTING LIQUID COSMIC CUBES OVER HERE...
IT WAS TOTALLY COOL! ME AN' MOM WERE TIED UP A FEW DOORS DOWN--ON ACCOUNTA THAT ALWAYS HAPPENS TO US CAUSE A' DAD AN' ALL.
THEN, ALLOFA SUDDEN, POW! TWO GUYS BUST IN--ONE OF 'EM BIG AS A MOUNTAIN, THE OTHER ALL SLIPPERY-- TAKE THE GUARDS OUT! BAM!
AND WITH THAT, CAESAR CICERO, MAN-MOUNTAIN MARKO AND THE EEL CAN FILE FOR A SENTENCE REDUCTION...
22

I DO HAVE TO ASK--EVERYTHING THAT HAPPENED WHILE HAMMERHEAD ASCENDED IS ALL A FOGGY BLUR NOW--
--BUT WHY DID HE FAIL TO MAINTAIN HIS ALL-POWERFUL STATE?
WAS IT A SHORTCOMING IN THE LIZARD'S APPLICATION OF MY NOTES?
NOPE, THE LIZARD FOLLOWED YOUR NOTES TO THE LETTER, DOC--IT'S WHAT I WAS COUNTING ON!
BUT--?
SORRY, DOC.
MY LITTLE SECRET.
THE MAIN THING IS YOU GOT YOUR FAMILY BACK AND THE CURSE OF THE LIZARD HAS BEEN LIFTED FROM YOU FOREVER!
HE IS SO COOL!
THAT HE IS, SON.
CIAO FOR NOW, SUNSHINE--DON'T FORGET TO PUT THE HYPHEN BETWEEN SPIDER AND MAN!
@#!%
I KNOW HOW HARD IT IS FOR YOU JOURNALISTS TO GET STUFF LIKE THAT RIGHT.
HAMMERHEAD'S IN CUSTODY NOW!
EVERYTHING BY THE BOOK!
CAN'T WAIT TO SEE HOW YOUR SHYSTERS TRY TO WORM YOU OUT OF THIS ONE, FLAT-TOP!
I DON'T CARE--ALL THAT MATTERS IS MY SISTER'S OKAY...
...I'LL WORRY ABOUT WIPIN' THAT SMILE OFF YER FACE TOMORROW!
AND SO, SPIDEY SAVES THE UNIVERSE AGAIN! BORING!
OH, WHO AM I KIDDING? I CAN RATIONALIZE AND OBFUSCATE WITH THE BEST OF THEM--
--BUT KNOWING I COULD HAVE SAVED MY LOVED ONES IS GOING TO HAUNT ME FOREVER!
ONE MORE STOP AND WE'LL WRAP THIS WHOLE MESSY NIGHT UP IN A PRETTY PINK BOW...
MINUTES LATER IN GREENWICH VILLAGE...
ALLOW ME TO BE A CORDIAL HOST, SPIDER-MAN ...YOU MUST BE FAMISHED AFTER RUNNING AROUND SINCE LAST NIGHT!
GEEZ, DOC, YOU SHOULDN'T HAVE--BUT AS LONG AS YOU'RE OFFERING!
WELL, I COPPED A BAGEL EARLIER... THANKS, DOC--JUST WARN ME WHEN I'M ABOUT TO MUNCH ON "EYE OF NEWT!"
2

OR, APPARENTLY, THROAT, TONGUE AND ESOPHAGUS OF NEWT, TOO!
UHM... SO, DOC, WHO DOES YOUR CATERING?
AH, THEY WERE GIFTS FROM MY FRIENDS IN ATLANTIS!
THEIR FINEST DELICACIES, I HAVE BEEN ASSURED.
YEAH, BUT HAVE YOU BEEN INSURED?
I GOTTA TELL YOU, DOC, FIGURING OUT THE REAL SCOOP ON THAT LAST TABLET FRAGMENT TURNED THE TRICK!
THANK YOURSELF THEN, MY FRIEND.
THOUGH MY ATLANTEAN COUNSEL MADE NO MENTION OF ITS TRUE PURPOSE--
--AND I ASCERTAINED ITS MEANING WOULD PROVE OF VITAL IMPORTANCE...
...YOU ARE THE ONE WHO CORRECTLY DEDUCED THE WATCHING EYE AT THE APEX OF THE RECONFIGURED TABLET--
--WOULD PROVIDE A PROTECTIVE ELEMENT AGAINST THOSE WHO ARE UNPREPARED FOR THE ENORMITY OF ITS EFFECTS.
AND NOW, ALLOW ME TO REMOVE THE TABLET FROM THIS PLANE OF REALITY--
--UNTIL SUCH A TIME AS MANKIND CAN BETTER ACCEPT ITS DESTINY!
ZOOF
COMING FROM THE CIVILIZATION THAT BROUGHT US "BIG BROTHER," I WON'T HOLD MY BREATH WAITING!
THANKS FOR ALL YOUR HELP, DOC--AND COOK THE SQUID BEFORE YOU FEED IT TO ANY MORE GUESTS!
AS ALWAYS, NO MATTER THE DEPTH OF THE PAIN FROM HIS ACTIONS AND DECISIONS--
--HE CONCEALS IT ALL BENEATH A QUIP AND A QUEST!
HOW FEW UNDERSTAND THE MEANING OF THE WORDS HE LIVES BY, "WITH GREAT POWER THERE MUST ALSO COME GREAT RESPONSIBILITY"--?
AND HOW FEW WILL EVER KNOW THE PRICE HE HAS PAID FOR THE GOOD OF THE MANY...
...NO MATTER HOW MUCH IT HURT THE ONE.
The End

SPIDER-MAN: LIFELINE #1 PINUP BY **STEVE RUDE**

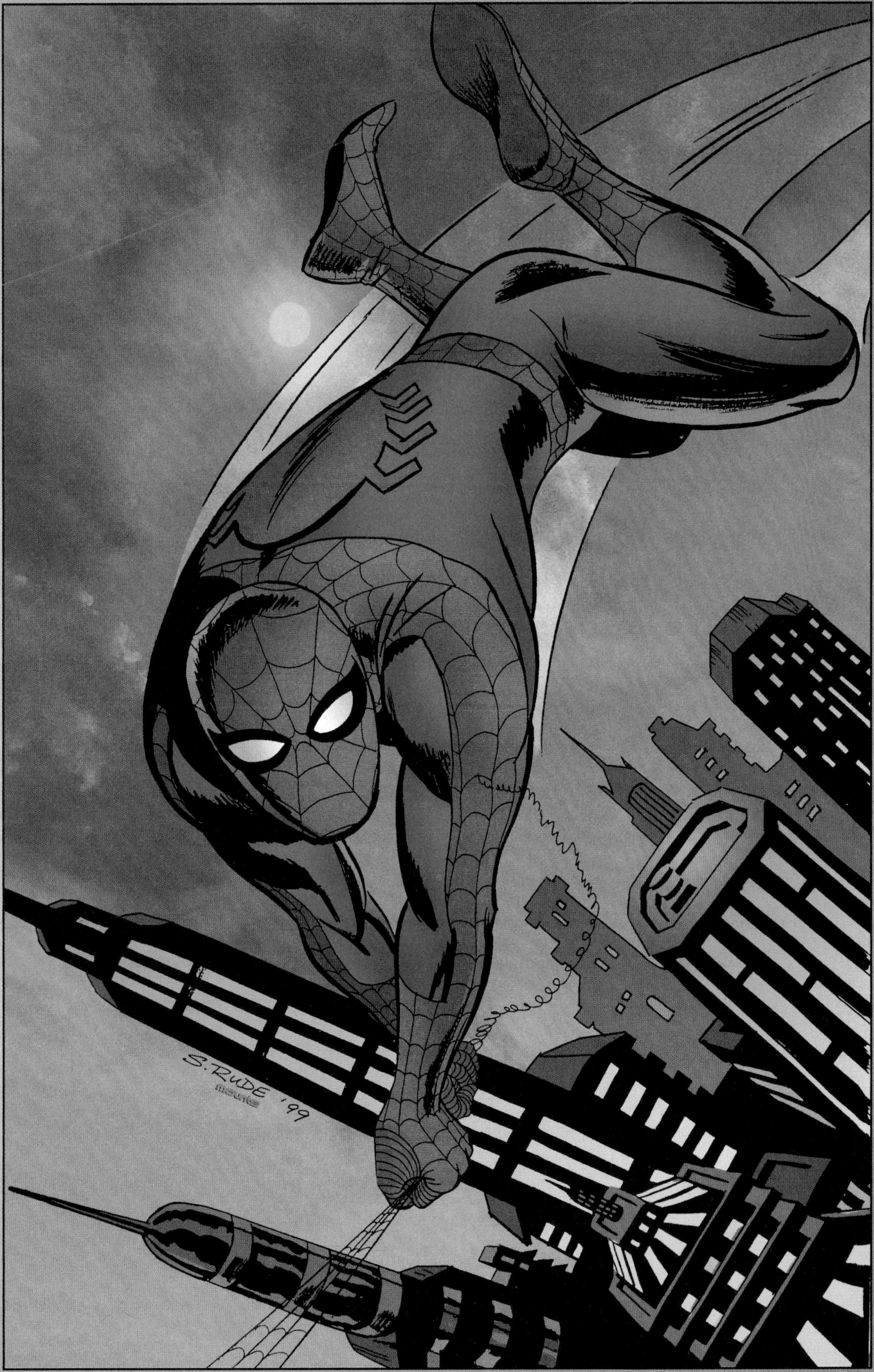

SPIDER-MAN: *LIFELINE* #2 PINUP BY **STEVE RUDE** & **PAUL MOUNTS**

SPIDER-MAN: *LIFELINE* #2 PINUP BY **STEVE RUDE**

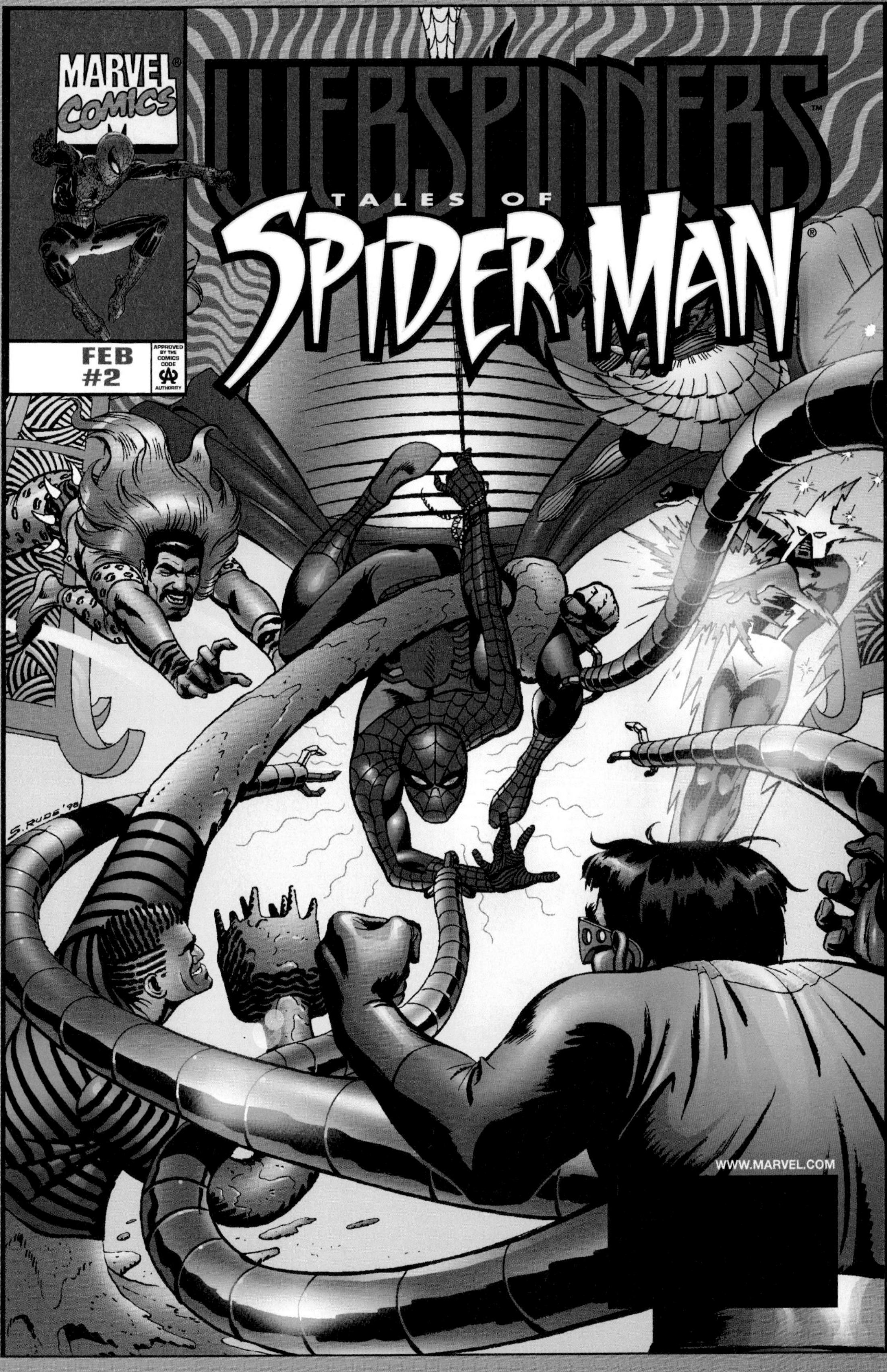

***WEBSPINNERS: TALES OF SPIDER-MAN* #2** VARIANT COVER BY **STEVE RUDE**

SPIDER-MAN: *LIFELINE* #2, PAGES 5 & 14-15 ART BY **STEVE RUDE** & **BOB WIACEK**

COURTESY OF HERITAGEAUCTIONS.COM

MARVEL MASTERWORKS: THE AMAZING SPIDER-MAN VOL. 8, COVER BY **JOHN ROMITA** & **RICHARD ISANOVE**